About the Author:

Barbara Mandell spent several years in Africa, where she became an announcer/producer with the South African Broadcasting Corporation. Back in England she worked for the BBC in both radio and television, mainly writing and voicing with the 'TV Newsreel'. When Independent Television News went on air she became the first woman newscaster in Britain. She has travelled widely in Europe, Africa and America and now combines this with travel writing.

Barbara Mandell has written several other MPC Visitor's Guides: *The Dordogne, Massif Central, Southern Spain & Costa del Sol, Costa Brava to Costa Blanca,* Visitor's Guide: *Portugal* (World Traveller Series) as well as contributing to MPC's *Off the Beaten Track: France* and *Off the Beaten Track: Spain*.

Northern and Central Spain

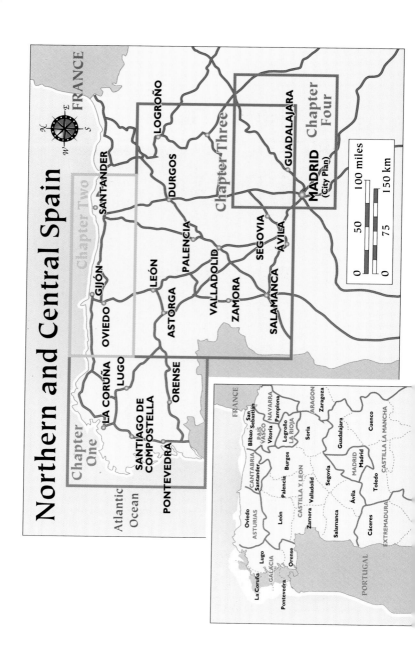

Visitor's Guide
NORTHERN & CENTRAL
SPAIN

Barbara Mandell

MPC
HUNTER

Published by:
Moorland Publishing Co Ltd,
Moor Farm Road West, Ashbourne, Derbyshire DE6 1HD England

ISBN 0 86190 635 7

Published in the USA by:
Hunter Publishing Inc, 300 Raritan Center Parkway,
CN 94, Edison, NJ 08818

British Library Cataloguing in Publication Data:
A catalogue record for this book is available from the British Library.

Colour origination by:
P. & W. Graphics Pte Ltd, Singapore

Printed in Spain by:
GraphyCems

Picture credits

Front cover: Segovia Cathedral. Back cover: Collecting grass for cattle which are kept in byres (large pic); The marina at Santander was designed entirely for pleasure craft (top left) ; The twelfth-century San Marcos Monastery is León's third great architectural masterpiece (middle); The Episcopal Palace at Astorga was designed by Antonio Gaudi (botton left).

Illustrations have been supplied as follows: Martin Gray: pp 15, 50 (top), 58 (both), 66 (top), 83 (top), 90, 94, 107 (bottom), 114 (bottom), 123 (both), 127, 159 (both). All other illustrations supplied by the Spanish National Tourist Office.

MPC Production Team:
Editorial: Tonya Monk
Design: Dick Richardson
Cartography: Mick Usher

Contents

Symbols Used In Margins And On Maps

Castle / Fortification   **Other Places of Interest**

Mountain   **Birdlife**

Museum/Art Gallery   **Caves**

Church   **Building of Interest**

Watersports   **Archaeological Site**

Topography

River/Lake   Motorway
Town/Village   Main Road
City   Secondary Road

How To Use Your Guide

Your Travel Guide has been designed in an easy to use format. Each chapter covers a region or itinerary in a natural progression which gives you all the background information to help you enjoy your visit. Distinctive margin symbols, the important places printed in bold type and a comprehensive index enables you to find the most interesting places to visit with ease.

At the end of each chapter, an **Additional Information** section gives you specific details such as addresses and opening times, making your guide a complete sightseeing companion.

The **Facts for Visitors** at the end of this guide lists practical information, including a comprehensive accommodation and eating out section, and useful tips to help you before you go and during your stay.

Introduction

Northern and Central Spain, like any other large section of the Iberian Peninsula, is an area rich in contrasts almost amounting in some cases to contradictions. It is bounded in the north by both the Pyrénées and the Bay of Biscay and extends southwards as far as an arbitrary line drawn through Madrid, in the centre of the country. To the west, Portugal takes up all but a small portion of the Atlantic seaboard but this still leaves an area roughly half the size of France into which the United Kingdom would fit quite comfortably.

Mountain ranges, such as the Cantabrian Cordillera, which is virtually an extension of the Pyrénées, the Iberian Cordillera, branching off south-eastwards along the Ebro Depression, and the Central Cordillera above Madrid, were thrown up in a haphazard fashion millions of years ago when the earth was shrugging itself into something like its present contours. The interior consists mainly of an enormous plateau known as the Meseta, an arid and sometimes monotonous expanse of limestone ridges interspersed with seemingly endless plains speckled with historic towns and lonely villages. The two most important rivers are the Ebro, rising in the far north and flowing into the Mediterranean south of Tarragona, and the Duero wending its way across the Meseta and into Portugal. Other smaller rivers like the Miño, the Sil and the Navia help to make the far north-western corner of the country remarkably green and fertile, reminiscent in many ways of Ireland or Brittany.

The Pyrénées, stretching right across the 500km (310 miles) isthmus connecting France and Spain, are an entity on their own while Catalunya, because of its long Mediterranean coastline, has more in common with the other eastern costas than the interminable plains and stunted natural vegetation of the Meseta. As a result this definition of Northern and Central Spain concerns itself exclusively with Madrid and its environs, the large autonomous region of Castilla y León, divided up into nine different provinces each with their own outstanding attractions, the wine producing area of La Rioja, sandwiched between the Ebro and the Basque country, and the northern coastal provinces of Galicia, Asturias and Cantabria.

There is nothing particularly memorable about the countryside around Madrid, where the winters are usually bitterly cold and the summers unpleasantly hot and enervating. Fortunately for the inhabitants the Sierra Guadarrama is close at hand. It is a mountainous area with peaks blanketed in snow well into the spring, lakes inherited from ancient glaciers augmented by modern reservoirs, streams and woodlands, winter resorts and an ever increasing number of holiday villas. This chain is part of the Central Cordillera, the natural as well as the historical dividing line between Old and New Castile. Beyond it is the vast northern basin of the Meseta, dressed overall with grain and cereals that change gradually from spring green to harvest gold, flocks of sheep and goats grazing over the barren scrubland and pastures used almost exclusively for raising fighting bulls.

North of the Cantabrian Cordillera the coastline facing the Bay of Biscay is rough and rugged with high cliffs, rocky inlets, creeks and pleasant sandy beaches. Further west it begins to level out, the fishing ports become larger and more numerous and many of the most attractive beaches are rapidly becoming popular holiday resorts. Slightly inland there are wooded hillsides, orchards, meadows and moorland as well as literally hundreds of smallholdings producing everything from maize to beef cattle and pigs to potatoes. Fishing and mining have always played an important role in the scheme of things but now heavy industry, which originated in the Basque country, has gained a number of toeholds, especially in Astu-

rias. Other innovations are food processing factories, textile plants and various light manufacturing interests while at the same time there has been a revival of traditional crafts such as lace-making, inlaid jewellery and wickerwork.

At one time the whole of Spain was covered with forests but constant warfare down the ages, coupled with erosion, the shortage of water and poor farming practices have made large areas almost uninhabitable. Small communities still scrape a living from the land, especially along the shallow valleys, but despite new irrigation schemes and afforestation programmes the younger people tend to leave home to find an easier life elsewhere. Some of them emigrate while others head for the larger towns and industrial centres where national training schemes are available and an increasing growth of tourism is providing a variety of new openings.

So far the northwestern corner of the country barely figures in the glossy brochures put out by coach-tour companies but, with an ever-increasing number of people organising their own holidays, the ground swell of visitors in search of something different is growing steadily. Campsites have been established all along the coast and within easy reach of most of the larger towns like Avila, Segovia and Burgos, which are scattered across the region, seldom more than two or three hours' drive apart. There is a comprehensive network of state paradores, some custom-built while others are sited in ancient mansions or refurbished palaces, a wealth of historic castles, monasteries and decorative churches as well as museums of all descriptions. Open-air enthusiasts will find mountains to climb, plenty of opportunities for trout and salmon fishing, hunting reserves and wild life parks in addition to all the usual sporting facilities in the various holiday resorts.

The famous caves of Altamira, and others whose rock paintings are rather less spectacular, prove beyond doubt that the country was occupied in prehistoric times. The Celts who moved down from the north in the fifth or sixth centuries BC settled mainly in Galicia and Portugal and stubbornly resisted the Romans under Augustus until they were finally brought to heel in about 19BC. The Visigoths were the next on the scene, followed swiftly by the Moors who suffered an early defeat at Covadonga, in the Picos de Europa, after which they left the far north-west very much to its own devices. Galicia promptly joined forces with the Christian kingdom of Asturias and when, in AD830, it was claimed that the tomb of St James had been discovered at Compostela the site became an important place of pilgrimage and a symbol of national unity.

Such an apparently satisfactory state of affairs could not be expected to last indefinitely, especially during the Middle Ages. León was recaptured from the Moors and became the official capital until Castile broke away, only to fall into the hands of

the kings of Navarre. It was 1230 before the area was reunited under Ferdinand III but its troubles were by no means over. Rivalry between Pedro the Cruel and his brother Enrique de Trastamara led to civil war which was further complicated when John of Gaunt, who had married Pedro's daughter, landed with a large army in Galicia in 1386 and had himself crowned King of Castile and León in the cathedral at Compostela.

The struggle for power between Isabel of Castile, who had married Ferdinand of Aragon, and her niece Juana ended with the latter's defeat at the Battle of Toro in 1476, thereby uniting the two kingdoms and paving the way for the most glorious, although undeniably grisly, period in the history of the country. The Moors were thrown out, the Jews were expelled and the Inquisition flourished but at the same time Columbus discovered the New World, the Conquistadores overran and exploited vast areas of it and Spain grew rich on the proceeds. The north-western provinces played a very minor role while all this was going on although they certainly had their moments in the years that followed. Emperor Charles V landed in Asturias in 1517 to claim his Spanish inheritance, some 70 years later the Armada sailed from La Coruña on Philip IIs ill-fated attempt to invade England while Galicia took a pounding during the War of Succession in the early eighteenth century. During the Peninsular War the British forces under Sir John Moore were soundly beated by the French at the Battle of

Elviña but, although their commander was killed, most of the troops were evacuated from La Coruña and returned to fight again under Wellington.

Although Madrid had existed first as an ancient settlement and later as an Arab fortress, it was far less important than any of the established cities of Castile until, in 1561, Philip II decided to make it the official capital of Spain. He and his successors built palaces there but nothing was done to beautify or modernise the rather parochial town that grew up round them, although it managed to attract men of letters, like Calderón, and artists of the calibre of Goya and Velázquez. It was not until the early nineteenth century that the citizens took matters into their own hands. They objected to Napoleon's armies traipsing backwards and forwards across the country following their invasion of Portugal and resented the presence of a French garrison in the city. Matters came to a head when Bonaparte summoned the royal family to Bayonne before forcing them to abdicate. Crowds gathered outside the palace to prevent them leaving, the

Colourful regional costumes are worn at fiestas and religious festivals

French opened fire and although the revolt was quashed it was followed by uprisings all over the country that led eventually to the Peninsular War.

For the next 100 years or so Spain was racked by uprisings, power struggles and general discontent but despite all this Madrid developed into a sophisticated and thoroughly cosmopolitan metropolis, full of writers and artists, politicians and socialites. When the Civil War broke out in 1936 it sided firmly with the Republicans and even after the government fled to Valencia the city held out against Franco until the new regime had been officially recognised by everybody.

Instead of making the capital pay for its years of opposition the Franco government set about enlarging and restoring it, introducing fresh industries, bulldozing old quarters to make way for new thoroughfares and surrounding it with shabby suburbs, factories and industrial estates. With the return of the monarchy in 1975 Madrid regained its pleasant, cosmopolitan atmosphere, undisturbed by an occasional hiccup such as the attempted coup by a section of the army 6 years later that was dealt with promptly and efficiently by King Juan Carlos. Today Spain is a federal state, a member of both NATO and the EU, with a government that is determined to sort out its problems without resorting to the kind of drastic measures so often adopted in the past.

Madrid is unexpectedly short of ancient buildings, having a few of any real interest that are more than 400 years old, but its many other attractions amply compensate for this. Foremost among them is the Museo del Prado, generally acknowledged to be one of the really great art galleries of the world. Then there is the Thyssen-Bornemisza Museum, coveted by so many different countries before Baron Thyssen decided to house his famous collection in Madrid. These are augmented by about twenty other assorted museums, each specialising in a different subject, as well as theatres, an opera house and a casino, a racetrack, a busy bullring and the Bernabeú Football Stadium, home to Real Madrid. Visitors in search of famous cathedrals, ancient walled cities and medieval fortresses can take their pick of a dozen different provincial capitals. Some, like Toledo, Avila and Segovia, are near enough to be visited in a day while other rather more distant but equally inviting centres, including Burgos, Salamanca, Soria and Santiago de Compostela, really need a bit more travelling time. Meanwhile anyone on the lookout for sea and sand can head for well-established resorts like Santander on the Cantabrian coast about 400km (248 miles) away.

Like the rest of their countrymen the majority of people in Northern and Central Spain are Catholics and celebrate the many religious festivals, such as Holy Week and Corpus Christi, with as much fervour but usually fewer additional trappings than, for example, the cities of Andalucia. Local saints' days are observed in the traditional manner with solemn processions, rituals handed down for generations, music and dancing, colourful regional costumes, bullfights and general jollification. In addition there are seasonal pilgrimages and a whole range of agricultural events including wine and harvest festivals. These sometimes call for special dishes associated with the particular occasion, partly dictated by custom but just as frequently included because they are easy to carry on a picnic or a pilgrimage. A case in point is octopus cooked *a feira* in Galicia. It is prepared whole and cut up later, after a good pounding to soften it, and then dressed with a mixture of oil, salt and paprika.

Galicia is famous for seafood of every description but several of its meat dishes are also well worth trying. Among the most traditional are *lacon con grelos*, made from salt pork and the top leaves from young turnips served with a piquant sauce, and chickens that have been fattened on wheat, wine and chestnuts. The most popular drink is *queimada*, prepared in situ from a local brandy called Orujo with the addition of lemon and sugar and set alight at the last moment. Asturias goes in for a lot of stews containing soft white beans, or *fabes*, which give them a distinctive flavour, or else hake cooked in cider or salmon preferably soaked in milk, salt and lemon before grilling.

Castile takes great pride in its roast meat, especially suckling pig, or *tostón*, which must be between 15 and 20 days old and cooked in the oven with thyme until it is tender enough to be divided into portions by simply knocking it with the edge of a plate. Each of the provincial capitals has its own specialities whereas Madrid covers the whole spectrum from the simple to the sophisticated with as many different types of restaurants as any other European capital and *tapas* bars to bridge the gap between lunch at midday and dinner in the late evening.

1
Galicia

Galicia, as most people would undoubtedly agree, bears very little resemblance to the rest of Spain. If anything it is more akin to Ireland, Cornwall or Brittany with a touch of Norway about its fjord-like indentations — known as *rias* — particularly when they eat into the coastline between high granite cliffs. There are also innumerable little coves, beautiful sandy beaches, isolated creeks, fishing ports and sheltered harbours that are among the finest in the country. Inland the region is green and wooded, especially along the valleys where trees blanket the lower slopes, overlooking lush meadows, orchards and small cultivated plots, each with its own sturdy dry-stone walls. Some rivers wander about rather aimlessly on their way down to the sea while others have well-defined courses. For example, the Río Sil made life much easier for armies on the march and for the planners of a stretch of railway from León to Orense which makes contact with the coast at La Coruña.

The Celts established themselves in Galicia about 3,000 years ago and moved on southwards beyond the Río Miño into what is now Portugal. They were followed in rapid succession by the Romans, the Visigoths and briefly by the Moors before the region was incorporated into the kingdom of Asturias and, eventually, into a united Spain. In many ways the Galicians paid scant attention to any of the more recent changes of management, preserving their own language, which has a certain amount in common with Portuguese, and escaping from the rigours of life in this remote north-western corner of the country by emigrating in droves to the New World at the earliest possible moment.

Legend has it that St James the Elder travelled to the Iberian peninsula after the Resurrection and spent the next years spreading the gospel before returning to Palestine where Herod ordered him to be beheaded in AD44. His remains were then smuggled back by some of his followers and buried at *Campus Stellae* where they were discovered with the aid of divine intervention in AD813. Some 30 years later, when Ramiro I was leading an attack against the Moors at Clavijo, near Logroño, a knight on horseback, wearing armour and carrying a standard distinguished by a red cross, helped him to rout the infidels. This champion was St James and given the title of Mat-amore, Slayer of the Moors. Although there is no historic

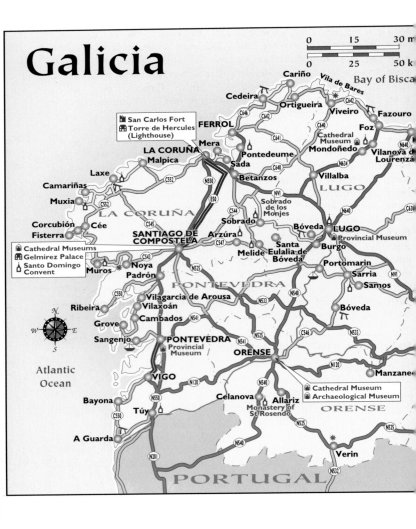

Galicia

San Carlos Fort
Torre de Hercules
(Lighthouse)

Cathedral Museums
Gelmirez Palace
Santo Domingo
Convent

Cathedral Museum
Archaeological Museum

Bay of Biscay

Cariño
Vila de Bares
Cedeira
Ortigueira
Vila de Bares
Viveiro
Fazouro
Foz
Cathedral
Museum
Mondoñedo
Vilanova de
Lourenzá

FERROL
Mera
LA CORUÑA
Malpica
Pontedeume
Sada
Betanzos
Villalba
LUGO

Laxe
Camariñas
Muxia
LA CORUÑA
Sobrado
de los
Monjes
Sobrado
Bóveda
LUGO
Provincial Museum

Corcubión   Cée
Fisterra
SANTIAGO DE
COMPOSTELA
Arzúra
Melide
Santa
Eulalia de
Bóveda
Burgo
Portomarin
Sarria
Samos

Muros
Noya
Padrón
PONTEVEDRA
Bóveda

Ribeira
Vilagarcia de Arousa
Vilaxoán
Grove
Cambados
Sangenjo
PONTEVEDRA
Provincial
Museum
ORENSE
Manzane

Atlantic
Ocean
VIGO
Celanova
Allariz
Monastery of
St Rosendo
ORENSE

Bayona
Túy
A Guarda
PORTUGAL
Verin

0   15   30 m
0   25   50 k

evidence to substantiate these stories
Santiago de Compostela became not
only a place of pilgrimage but also a
symbol of Christian unity.

Apart from Santiago de Com-

postela and the four provincial capitals there are hardly any towns of
substance in Galicia, most of the
population showing a marked preference for village life. There are said

14

to be in the region of 30,000 communities of various sizes some still adopting the attitude that what was good enough for their ancestors is quite good enough for them. However, mechanised equipment is beginning to replace traditional farming methods and the influx of holidaymakers from the interior is turning quite a few out-of-the-way beaches into potential seaside resorts. The climate is in their favour, being generally mild if sometimes rather wet and windy.

Galicia is divided into four distinct provinces. Lugo borders on Asturias and León with about 80km (50 miles) of low coastline overlooking the Bay of Biscay. La Coruña is more rugged with huge cliffs and deserted moorlands in the Sierra de Capelada, separated by the enormous Ría de Santa Marta de Ortigueira from the slender thrusting Punta de la Estaca de Bares, the most northerly headland in Spain. Pontevedra joins La Coruña on the Atlantic seaboard to the south of Santiago de Compostela and occupies the entire south-western corner down to the frontier with Portugal while landlocked Orense takes care of all the rest.

A network of major roads links all the provincial capitals as well as the seaports of El Ferrol and Vigo, interlocked by secondary routes and byways that keep most of the little villages in touch with one another. There is also an *autopista* with its head in La Coruña and its feet in Vigo and a scenic coastal road that calls in at towns like Foz,

Many farmers in Galicia still use traditional equipment and methods

Viveiro and Ortigueira which otherwise might be rather isolated. Most places of interest can be visited by train or bus, although this may involve a few changes, while for people in a hurry there is an airport at Labacolla, on the outskirts of Santiago de Compostela, with direct flights to London, Paris and Amsterdam and regular services to Madrid and other Spanish cities including Barcelona, Sevilla, Santander and San Sebastián.

Although Galicia is sometimes described as being well off the beaten track it is certainly not backward where accommodation is concerned. There are paradores, comfortable hotels, a full compliment of perfectly acceptable smaller establishments and hostales and even one or two monasteries which provide accommodation for paying guests. It is easy to find a suitable campsite and there are no problems about eating out. Apart from first class restaurants, mainly in the larger centres, the whole region bristles with inns and taverns specialising in traditional dishes.

The seafood on offer in Galicia is among the best in Europe, particularly octopus and oysters, clams, sardines and lobsters, not to mention the less familiar sea-spiders and goose barnacles. However the most famous local recipe is *Coquilles Saint Jacques* — scallops chopped up with shallots and perhaps mushrooms, folded into a cream sauce, replaced in the shell and topped with breadcrumbs before being browned in the oven.

Caldo Gallego is excellent for keeping out the cold, made from a variety of different meats cooked with cabbage, beans and potatoes. *Empanada* may include either fish or meat seasoned with onions and encased in thin saffron coloured pastry to hold in both the moisture and the flavour, whereas *lacon con grelos* is pork served with young turnip tops, potatoes and a special kind of sausage. Chicken fed on wheat, wine and chestnuts is particularly tasty and so are almond tarts, smoked *perilla* cheese and the milder *tetilla*. The most popular wines of the region are Ribeiro and Albariño which is produced from vines originally grown along the Rhine and the Moselle and subsequently introduced into the area by the monks. Finally, anyone with a strong head might care to try the *eau-de-vie*, or even Queimada, a rough Galician brandy called *orujo* mixed with lemon and sugar and set on fire at the last moment.

Galicia is not nearly so imaginative when it comes to souvenirs. However, it is worth looking for handmade lace along the coast, and especially at Camariñas, a large fishing village somewhat isolated on its own ria north of Cape Finisterre. Pontevedra concentrates more on basketwork and, as one would expect, Santiago de Compostela is awash with reminders of St James and his cockle shells. Anyone who can play the Irish bagpipes would undoubtedly be interested in the local version, known as the *gaita*, which appear almost without fail at literally hundreds of folk festivals which take place every year.

Many of these celebrations are rooted in pagan times, such as Carnival which is thought by some people to have developed from the Roman Feast of Isis, but the majority now have very definite Christian overtones. Pontevedra starts the year with a get-together on the wasteland of Budino which is designed mainly for people who want to thank St Blaise for curing their sore throats. The province lays down carpets of flowers for Corpus Christi and stages a bizarre pilgrimage at Las Nieves on 29 July in honour of Santa Marta, the sister of Mary Magdalene. The procession consists almost entirely of coffins, some of them occupied by people who expected to die during the year and attribute their miraculous recovery to the saint's good offices.

On a less gloomy note, Los Curros (Horse Corrals) are held in several places from early May to the beginning of July. For centuries they were simply the occasions on which wild horses were driven down from the mountains to be branded by their owners and have their manes and tails trimmed. This was too good an opportunity to miss and gradually they developed into a series of fiestas. The Feast of Santiago, the patron saint of Spain, is celebrated everywhere on 25 July and nowhere more devoutly than in Compostela with processions, special church services and fireworks outside the cathedral. Betanzos, also in La Coruña, pays its summer tribute to San Roque on the Río Mendo with a procession of decorated boats illuminated with lanterns but the pilgrimage to the shrine of San Andrés de Teixido on 30 November is even better attended because it is believed that 'those will go in death who do not visit it alive'.

LA CORUÑA

La Coruña is the most remote of Galicia's four provinces, but it is also the most beautiful and in many ways the most historic, due in no small measure to both its provincial capital and to Santiago de Compostela. It stretches from the Ría del Barqueiro, tucked in behind the Punta de la Estaca de Bares, the most northerly headland in Spain, round and down along the Atlantic past Cape Finisterre to the Ría de Arousa. The coast is a magnificent succession of jagged cliffs and long sandy beaches, rias of all shapes and sizes, busy ports, small fishing villages and seaside resorts in various stages of development. Much of the interior is pleasantly wooded and, generally speaking, less dramatic, although it certainly has its highlights. Quite a few of the little hamlets are totally forgettable while others hark back to the distant past with dolmens, prehistoric burial grounds, miniscule churches and an occasional medieval monastery. It would take quite a

Strolling around the
gardens of La Coruña

The remarkably long
bridge at Pontedeume
over the Río Eume

while to explore the province thoroughly but, with a certain amount of forethought, even a short visit can be very rewarding.

Nearly all the major roads radiate from the provincial capital. The NV1 provides a direct link with the A6 *autopista* into Madrid, 603km (374 miles) to the south-east, the C642 follows the northern coast, changing its number but not its direction on the way to Bilbao, a total distance of 622km (386 miles), whereas the A9 *autopista* and the N550 make short work of the 72km (45 miles) separating La Coruña from Santiago de Compostela and then press on towards Portugal. There are airports at both La Coruña and Compostela, train services operate to and from Madrid, Barcelona and Irún as well as several large towns in the north of the country leaving most other places in Galicia to the tender mercies of the local buses.

The port of **La Coruña** was well established on its rock-strewn promontory before the Romans arrived and built the famous Torre de Hercules in the second century AD, said to be the only Roman lighthouse still in working order. Charles III saw fit to alter it considerably in the late eighteenth century, adding the square base and replacing the ramp with a stairway, but it is still a most impressive sight. From its superb vantage point the lighthouse has seen many historic events and famous people in its time. Among them were Charles V, Philip II, the departure of the ill-fated Armada in 1588 and the damage caused by Sir Francis Drake when he attacked the town soon afterwards. In 1809 the remnants of a British force were evacuated from the port under the noses of the French after the battle of Elviña. Their general, Sir John Moore, was fatally wounded by a cannon ball and buried 'darkly, at dead of night' in the precincts of the San Carlos Fort, now transformed into a pleasant garden.

Despite its long history La Coruña has very little in the way of ancient buildings. One of its most distinctive features is the sweep of tall, nineteenth-century houses along the Avenida de la Marina overlooking the harbour, each one faced from top to bottom with glassed-in galleries and known collectively as the Cristales. Behind them the business quarter with its wide avenues, shops, hotels and restaurants blends into the older section of narrow streets and quiet little squares. At the far end, the twelfth-century church of Santiago on the Plaza de Azcárraga is only a short stroll from the Santa Bárbara convent which gives its name to a delightful little square hemmed in by antiquated houses. Its most historic neighbours are the Santa Maria del Campo church and the house in the Calle de Herrerias associated with Maria Pita who gave the alarm when Drake staged his attack in 1589. The old sea gates, namely the Puerta San Miguel, the Puerta del Clavo and the Puerta de la Cruz, on the Paseo del Parrote are all that is left of the original city walls.

La Coruña has two popular beaches on the opposite side of the isthmus from the port. Other attributes are the colourful Jardines de Méndez Núñez near the casino, an 18-hole golf course within easy reach and the excellently sited Hotel Finisterre on the Paseo del Parrote, with its own tennis courts and heated swimming pool. There are two or three other up-market hotels and a plentiful supply of small establishments, most of them filled to capacity during the summer when it is as well to book in advance.

Motorists approaching La Coruña along the coast road from the north will find any number of reasons for pausing on the way and even diverting briefly from the main route. One such distraction is the LC 100 from Porto do Barqueiro, just inside the border with Lugo. This leads to Vila de Bares whose minute port has a prehistoric breakwater and a lighthouse nearby. Back on the C642, the first place of any size is **Ortigueira**, set against green hills and flanked by sandy beaches with a fourteenth-century convent that was enthusiastically renovated about 200 years ago. Some 9km (6 miles) further on, at the head of the sinuous Ría de Santa Marta de Ortigueira, **Mera** is the jumping off point for a short excursion through woods to the port of **Cariño** and the lonely moorlands of the Sierra de la Capelada, inhabited by cattle and wild horses. There are some paths for people who want to explore on foot but only a single road round the area with a turning off to the sanctuary of San Andrés de Teixido, well-known throughout Galicia for its September pilgrimage. This is the time when, for some obscure reason, pilgrims build little mounds of stones by the wayside, collect special types of herbs and avoid killing any of the small creatures that infest the adjoining cliffs and meadows. **Cedeira**, a few kilometres to the south, is an enchanting little fishing port, partly medieval and partly quite modern, watched over by the remains of a 200-year-old fortress. It has a scenic road back to the major route 6km (4 miles) south of Mera, and a longer way round past a succession of sand dunes and inviting beaches to Ferrol.

Ferrol is, first and foremost, a naval base and has been since the eighteenth century. However, it was also quite important during the Middle Ages when its strategic position, 6km (4 miles) from the open sea, made it a safe haven for warships and merchantmen alike. The ancient quarter, clustered round the Curuxeiras dock, is moderately atmospheric and there are some nice houses in the more modern section, laid out in the grid pattern with a not very interesting cathedral and the Parador de Ferrol in the Plaze Eduardo Pondal. That having been said it certainly does not rate very highly in the happy holiday stakes. On the other hand, it makes a convenient base from which to visit a handful of interesting places in the vicinity.

The N651 is a busy road with a useful turning off at **Pontedeume** whose remarkably long bridge over the Río Eume was built at about the same time as the dilapidated palace in the centre of the town. The ruined Castillo de Andrade on a nearby hill is marginally older and so is the ancient Cistercian Monasterio de Monfero roughly 20km (12 miles) to the south-east along the minor LC152. It is an enormous pile, attributed in part to Juan de Herrera, who was Philip IIs favourite architect, and is worth seeing for its Baroque façade and most attractive cloister. To visit the monastery enquire from the priest.

Determined sightseers have other options open to them in the neighbourhood of Ferrol and Puentedeume. Two examples are the overgrown ruins of Caaveiro, a monastery founded by San Rosendo on an outcrop of rock beside the Río Eume, and the unusual San Miguel de Breamo chapel in the opposite direction, dating from 1137. However, most visitors are inclined to give both these possibilities a miss and spend more time in **Betanzos** where the Romans built their city of *Brigantium Flavium* on the remains of a Celtic settlement. Later it became a busy port handling produce from the surrounding area but when the ria silted up it lapsed into comparative obscurity. Three Gothic churches bear witness to its former prosperity. The aptly named Santa Maria del Azogue (St Mary of the Market), relies for attention on its decorative façade while the Church of Santiago, built by the Tailors' Guild in the fifteenth century, contributes a carving of St James Matamore on horse-back. The Church of San Francisco was part of an earlier monastery founded by Count Fernán Pérez de Andrade whose territory included both Betanzos and Puentedeume. He is buried in a splendid tomb near the west door, supported by a bear and a wild boar, guarded by hounds and decorated with hunting scenes. The rest of the town is equally interesting, crammed with antiquated buildings like the 400 year-old Town Hall and the eighteenth-century Palace of the Archives.

On leaving Betanzos it is a little difficult to decide where to go next. A small scenic road makes straight for **Sada**, half way up the ria, which has nothing in the way of historic attractions but plenty of opportunities for swimming, sailing and walking. It is rather short of hotels at the moment but makes up for this with a trio of modest campsites. The NV1 through Betanzos provides motorists with an easy run to either Lugo or La Coruña whereas the enterprising C540 blazes its own trail southwards towards the splendid **Sobrado de los Monjes Monastery**. This vast complex, 9km (6 miles) along the LC232 from Corredoiras, was founded in the tenth century but was allowed to deteriorate very badly until a group of Cistercian monks took on the formidable task of restoring it.

The church is memorable chiefly for its Rosary Chapel, the sacristy designed by Juan de Herrera and the Medallion Cloister. The Chapel de La Magdalena has survived from the Middle Ages, along with the chapterhouse and a huge kitchen with a monumental fireplace. In days gone by the monastery provided food and accommodation for pilgrims on their way to Compostela, less than 60km (37 miles) distant by the shortest route. This tradition is still preserved by the monks who have twenty-eight rooms for paying guests, offering hospitality to both men and women in addition to the usual guided tours.

There are several back ways through to Compostela but it does not take much longer to drive down from Corredoiras to **Melide** on the N547, which has two Romanesque churches and the Pedra de Raposo dolmen, and then follow the ancient pilgrim route to the city. The only places of any interest on the way are **Arzúa**, with its La Magdalena church, and **Labacolla**

The magnificent façade of the Cathedral at Santiago de Compostela

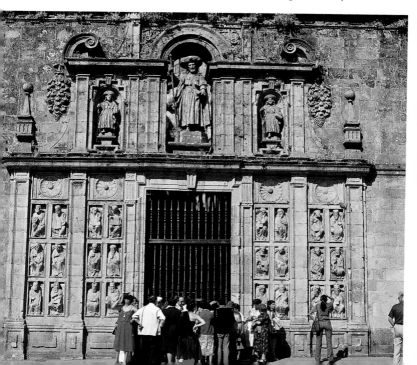

where dusty travellers could wash and brush up before tackling the last few kilometres separating them from what they firmly believed was the shrine of the Apostle, James the Elder. Sceptics have serious doubts about this, pointing out that there are too many discrepancies in the story, too many occasions on which the relics were either lost or mislaid, and anyway *compostela* is the Latin for cemetery and not derived from *Campus Stellae*, the Field of the Star. These arguments carry little weight with dedicated pilgrims who still arrive in their thousands to celebrate the Feast of Santiago on 25 July. They no longer wear the heavy capes, sandals and broad-brimmed hats decorated with scallop shells, or carry the long staves favoured by their predecessors, but they still queue up to climb the steps in the cathedral to kiss the robe worn by the statue of the saint.

Whether or not St James visited Spain before he was beheaded in Jerusalem and his body brought back in a stone boat and buried in Galicia is open to question. Perhaps it really was discovered in AD813 with the help of a star, removed for safekeeping from its tomb in the cathedral when Drake attacked La Coruña, went missing for nearly 300 years and was unearthed accidentally by a local workman. At all events the Vatican was satisfied and the bones, together with those of St Theodore and St Athanasius, were enshrined in a crypt built into the ninth-century foundations below the high altar. They are virtually all that remains of the original church, constructed over the remnants of a Celtic settlement and a Roman burial ground before being destroyed by Al Mansur.

The present cathedral in **Santiago de Compostela** gets a rather mixed reception from visitors. Some describe it as magnificent, others find it inspiring while a minority quarrel with the claim that it is one of the most beautiful churches in the country. The main Obradoiro façade, facing the Plaza de España, is unquestionably Baroque, massively carved and flanked by two slender, soaring towers. Beyond the entrance the Portico de la Gloria is a superb piece of twelfth-century sculpture by Master Mateo, its triple arches encrusted with smiling, animated figures and worn smooth in places by the fingers of millions of pilgrims. The nave and the transept are unexpectedly austere, contrasting sharply with the great silver shrine on the high altar containing a richly attired statue of the saint.

Most of the side chapels were added in the sixteenth century and each has its own individual attractions which may be anything from gold and silver work to Matamore in full cry at the battle of Clavijo. The *botafumeiro*, reputed to be the world's biggest incense burner, is kept in the library off the somewhat muted cloister. On holy days it is suspended over the transept and needs eight strong men to keep it swinging properly. It dates from the beginning of the seventeenth century, although the idea is believed to have been introduced to sweeten the atmosphere during the Middle Ages when pilgrims who were short of money tended to sleep in the cathedral. The chapterhouse and the upper galleries are hung with tapestries, some of them quite viewable, but the archaeological section of the museum below ground level, and filled with bits and pieces discovered during the excavations, is of little interest. The finely carved Goldsmiths Door leads on to the Plaza de la Quintana, overlooked by the clock tower that separates it from the Puerta Santa or Holy Door, which is opened whenever the 25 July falls on a Sunday.

The most obtrusive building bordering on the cathedral is the Hostal de los Reyes Católicos, set at right-angles to it on the Plaza de España. It was built in the fifteenth century by Ferdinand and Isabel as a pilgrim hostel, with four cloisters and a beautiful Gothic chapel, used occasionally these days for concerts. In comparatively recent years it has up-dated both its image and its furnishings, increased its prices out of all recognition, and is now what one appreciative guest described as 'not so much a hotel as an experience'. Also facing this most imposing square are the eighteenth-century Town Hall and the Palacio Gelmirez which was originally the bishop's palace. Among the state apartments open to the public is the huge synod hall decorated with scenes from Alfonso IXs wedding feast. No mention is made of John of Gaunt who, as Pedro the Cruel's son-in-law, laid claim to the crown in 1386 and had himself crowned King of Castile and León in the cathedral.

The San Martin Pinario Monastery, connected to the Plaza de España by the Gelmirez Passage, has a splendidly ornate church opening on to the Plaza San Martin. In olden days the monks, following their saint's example, provided new clothes for down-and-out pilgrims who promptly deposited their rags on an iron cross nearby. The Casa de la Troya, off the Calle Azabacheria, a stone's throw away, is a hostel for students some of whom form themselves into bands of strolling minstrels and entertain visitors with medieval serenades. Progress being what it is they also produce records and cassettes and offer them for sale in the Plaza de España, which makes a pleasant change from the more usual kinds of souvenirs.

Santiago de Compostela is not a large city but it has quite a few other churches and a variety of religious houses. Among them is the Convento de Santo Domingo on the Puerto del Camino, said to have been founded by St Dominic, which uses its cloister for the ethnological Museo do Pobo Galego. The Monasterio de San Pelayo on the Plaza de la Quintana specialises in sacred art while the twelfth-century church of Santa Maria del

Sar was provided with buttresses about 200 years ago to prevent it falling over. Its only remaining cloister gallery is well worth seeing on account of its beautifully carved arches. The best view of the city is from the Passeo de la Herradura, off the Calle de Pombal, which was originally a fairground but is now a pleasant park. There are any number of hotels in every category in addition to the Hostal de los Reyes Católicos and plenty of restaurants, cafés and bars, especially in the Calle del Franco behind the Colegio San Jerónimo.

Anyone who is interested in gardens should make a point of visiting **Pazo de Oca,** 25km (15½ miles) to the south-east along the N525. Strictly speaking it is on the other side of the border with Pontevedra but it is an enjoyable drive and the grounds behind the grey stone mansion are very lovely with their mixture of trees and shrubs, terraces and flowers as well as a pond and lake. By driving back for about 3km (2 miles) to the Río Ulla, which is also the provincial border, it is possible to take a shortcut along a minor road that follows the course of the river to **Padrón** at the head of the Ría de Arousa. According to legend this was the village where Santiago's followers put his body ashore and to prove it the stone pillar to which their boat was moored is kept under the altar in the parish church. From here it is only about 20km (12 miles) to Santiago de Compostela up the N550, and a further 72km (45 miles) to La Coruña. However it is much more interesting to follow the C550 all along the coast to Cape Finisterre provided there is enough time available.

This route starts off along the northern shore of the Ría de Arousa to **Ribeira**, which is more of a fishing port than a holiday resort, and then turns sharply up the other side of the Sierra de Barbanza to **Noya**. It is a nice little waterside town, called after Noah who is supposed to have anchored the Ark close by, on the slopes of a sacred Celtic mountain, while his dove flew off in search of an olive branch. Long after he had sailed on to Mount Ararat and the flood waters had receded the Celts built dolmens all over the area including the remarkable specimen known as Anxeitos near the mirador on Monte Barbanza. Noya has a medieval bridge and two quite fetching churches, San Martin which has the air of a fortress and a fine rose window, and the fourteenth-century Santa Maria de Noya whose cemetery is full of unusual gravestones.

Muros, on the opposite side of the ria, is a pretty little seaside town whose narrow streets and typically arcaded houses are clustered together round a small harbour. The local parish church owns a mysterious crucifix which is said to have been recovered from the sea and whose figure of Christ has unusually long hair which, according to some, is still growing. From Muros there are a number of small hamlets attached to excellent beaches all the way up the coast to **Cée**, a small industrial town with a modest hotel on the Avenida Fernando Blanco. Its nearest neighbour is **Corcubión**, a busy little fishing port, crowded with visitors during the summer months who are attracted mainly by the beaches but also in the hope of finding something of interest washed up along the shore. Their expectations were fuelled by the discovery in 1986 of a galleon that is thought to have gone down in the fifteenth century. Divers brought up bronze cannon, gold coins and other articles which are now on display in the museum in Ferrol.

The road continues round the bay to **Fisterra**, the last village before Cape Finisterre, 'the cape at the end of the world'. Quite apart from its legends about lost cities Finisterre, through its name, perpetuates one of our most popular misconceptions. Far from believing that the cliffs were the last outpost on earth, that the world ended somewhere beyond the horizon and that Columbus was bound to disappear over the edge, a great many intellectuals already knew quite well that the earth was round. However, less well informed travellers would make a special journey to the coast in order to contemplate what seemed to them to be quite literally the gateway to eternity.

The lighthouse at the end of the promontory is also the end of the road so it is necessary to drive back to Cée, after which the C552 deserts the shoreline and makes its way across country through Carballo to La Coruña, a distance of 97km (60 miles). However, anyone who has a soft spot for out-of-the-way places and some extra time to spare would undoubtedly enjoy exploring the network of minor roads that make contact with isolated hamlets either on or just inland from La Costa de la Muerta, the Celtic Coast of Death. There are plenty of dolmens to be visited, secluded beaches, picturesque rias, tiny fishing villages and grim headlands which can only be reached on foot.

Leaving aside the more inaccessible places, **Muxia**, on the Ría de Camariñas, has both the pilgrim church of Nuestra Señora de la Barca which has a splendid retable, and two large rocks that have been credited with supernatural healing powers for many hundreds of years. Meanwhile **Camariñas**, on the far side of the ria, has three small *hostales* of no particular moment, a wide beach and a road through the pine trees to Cabo Vilán. Visitors on the lookout for souvenirs could well find something suitable in either Muxia or Camariñas, both of which are justly famous for their handmade lace.

Laxe, somewhat further up the LC433, is a pleasant fishing village, set in dolmen country with a Romanesque church and the remains of a Celtic city, founded in the sixth century BC at Borneiro not all that far away. On the other hand **Malpica** was one of the old whaling ports and is still much more interested in fishing than it is in casual visitors. This, to all intents and purposes, is the end of the road because the low lying sand dunes to the east have plenty of potential but only a few hamlets and very small byways indeed. However this should not present any problems because it is only 17km (11 miles) inland to Carballo and a further 35km (33 miles) back to La Coruña.

LUGO

The fact that Lugo was named after the Celtic sun god Lug gives some indication of what to expect from both the province and its capital city, occupying a strategic position between La Coruña and Asturias on the Bay of Biscay. It is a great place for myths and legends and is said to be pitted with ancient burial grounds and haunted by spirits who skulk in the mountains waiting to pounce on lonely travellers. It certainly has its dolmens and small, round, thatched stone huts where any ancient Celt would feel at home, but these are outnumbered by picturesque medieval villages, little Christian churches and large monasteries, or what remains of them, as well as sturdy fortifications and busy fishing ports. There are railway links with Madrid and León, Vigo, Orense and La Coruña, express trains to and from Zaragoza, Barcelona, Bilbao and Irún and a fairly wide selection of buses.

Major roads pass through on their way to the northern and western coasts and down to Portugal, connected by secondary roads and dozens of the smaller variety which may not be in very good condition.

Lugo has been a provincial capital since Roman times and, as a result, attracted unwelcome attention from the Moors and the Vikings, both of whom set it on fire. The city was visited by pilgrims on their way to Santiago de Compostela 107km (66 miles) away, it got involved in the Peninsular War and took part in all the local uprisings before settling down to concentrate on agriculture. Today it is both peaceful and prosperous with quite extensive suburbs, attractive shopping streets and an ancient quarter totally encircled by some of the most eye-catching defensive walls in Spain. They were built originally by the Romans but had to be constantly improved and strengthened until they reached a uniform height of about 9m (30ft) reinforced by more than eighty towers and pierced by four gateways, known as Carmen, La Falsa, Miña and Santiago. There is a sentry path along the top and a modern road right round the outside which is worth driving along at least once before joining the inevitable queue of cars waiting at the traffic lights at one of the entrances.

The first place to head for is the cathedral on the Plaza Santa Maria. It started life towards the end of the twelfth century but was constantly remodelled, refurbished and re-decorated, one comparatively recent addition being the round Chapel of the Virgin of the Big Eyes which is less than 300 years old. The Romanesque nave is lined with galleries complimented by enormous carved wooden altarpieces and decorative tombs, with a door in the south transept leading to the cloister. On the opposite side of the Plaza de Santa Maria a road leads down beside the episcopal palace with its wrought iron balconies and distinctive coat-of-arms to the delightful Plaza del Campo. Here the fountain in the middle is overlooked on all sides by old houses, surrounded in their turn by atmospheric little alleys. The slightly larger Avenida del Ruanueva passes the Church of San Francisco a short stroll away which is said to have been founded by St Francis on his return from a pilgrimage. Its cloister is now part of the Provincial Museum, full of Celtic and Roman exhibits, ceramics and coins, stonework and everyday articles used by the local countryfolk.

Lugo's most prestigious hotel is the Gran Hotel Lugo on the Avenida Ramón Ferreiro, which has a good restaurant, swimming pool and garage space for cars. The Méndez Núñez in the Calle de la Reina, has none of these advantages but is well placed in the old city, not far from the Plaza de España. Visitors with tents and caravans are accommodated at the nearby La Parada campsite which is fairly basic but is the only officially recognised one in the neighbourhood.

About 15km (9 miles) south-west of Lugo, on a minor road off the N640 to Orense, **Santa Eulalia de Bóveda** is a remarkable relic from the distant past, discovered less than 100 years ago and excavated not long afterwards. It consists of a Celtic temple that was adapted by the Romans and later converted to Christianity. There is a horseshoe arch decorated with the figures of dancers, a small sunken pool and murals of birds and foliage on the few remaining walls. Some people think that Prisciliano, the region's first saint, was buried there after he had been decapitated at the end of the fourth century. Another school of thought maintains that it was his remains, and not those of St James, that were discovered and enshrined at Santiago de Compostela, but nobody can prove which theory, if either, is correct.

Apart from the countryside itself there is not much in the way of tourist attractions in the southern half of the province. However a pleasant mini-excursion after leaving Bóveda would be to continue along the N640 for about 20km (12 miles) and then turn off on to the C535 to **Portomarin** on the banks of the Río Miño. Part of the old village was flooded in order to create an elongated dam but it still has a Romanesque church and facilities for a variety of water sports. **Sarria**, 24km (15 miles) down the road is a fairly predictable old town with two optional routes back to Lugo city. The shorter one heads for Becerreá on the NV1, which commands one of the few roads into the Reserva Nacional de los Ancares as it spills over into León and is far better suited to walkers than to motorists. The longer way round takes in **Samos** whose Baroque cloister was part of the ancient abbey of San Julian. It then wriggles across with comparative ease to O Cebreiro, the site of an antiquated chapel that was the scene of an unsubstantiated miracle. Some time during the thirteenth century, a local priest complained about having to celebrate mass when there were no pilgrims in the congregation, and especially when it consisted of a single shepherd. Immediately the bread turned to flesh and the wine to blood, after which his services were extremely well attended. The area is bleak and uninviting and includes the Puerto Pedrafita where weather conditions forced Sir John Moore to abandon his equipment, horses and camp followers as the army retreated to La Coruña. From here the NV1 follows the Río Navia almost to Becerreá and then makes its own way back to Lugo.

Motorists en route for the coast from Lugo have two main options open to them. The N640 crosses the agreeable Sierra de Meira with its wooded slopes, widely spaced flint homesteads and the Río Eo, a favourite haunt of salmon fishermen, as far as the Ría de Ribadeo where it doubles back into Asturias. A secondary road continues along the western side of the ria to the port of **Ribadeo** which was an important trading centre in the eighteenth century. Its legacy from those days includes some rather nice old houses, a self-important Custom House and the Church of Santa Cruz which has a splendid view. Foremost among the local hotels is the Parador de Ribadeo, just on the outskirts of the town overlooking the water. It is built upside down with its bedrooms on the lower floor, some of them having their own balconies. The restaurant provides ample quantities of fish and other local produce, and although there is no swimming pool the beach is not too far away. From here the coast road follows the railway line past a couple of small beaches and a second grade campsite near Benquerencia, to join the N634 just south of Foz.

Motorists who opt for the alternative route will find a shortcut off the NV1 at Rabade which cuts down the driving time to Vallalba on the N634. Although it is not a very prepossessing town **Villalba** is an excellent place to stop on account of the large, comfortable Hotel Villamartin on the Avenida Tierra Llana, with a tennis court and a swimming pool in the garden, and the small Parador Condes de Villalba, Valeriano Valdesuso. This is installed in an octagonal tower left over from a medieval castle and still protected by a drawbridge, memorable for its thick

St Martin's Monastery,
Mondoñedo

An elegant square in
Ribadeo

stone walls and traditional furnishings.

Mondoñedo, 34km (21 miles) to the north-east, has nothing quite so romantic to offer although the Mirador de los Paredones, 2km (1 mile) along the road to Viveiro, is pleasantly situated and makes a good base from which to explore the town. Here, pride of place goes to the cathedral, built of golden stone with two eighteenth-century Baroque towers and a lovely rose window that is older by some 500 years. Unfortunately the interior is rather dark but nevertheless has some fine murals and the famous statue of the English Virgin, rescued from St Paul's Cathedral in London during the Reformation to escape the wrath of Henry VIII. The Altarpiece of the Holy Relics has its own fragment of the True Cross while a variety of other treasures are kept in a museum off the cloister. There are statues, paintings and some not very remarkable church plate as well as a collection of furniture and a thirteenth-century drawing room. In addition to all the old houses with their wrought iron balconies, the picturesque little alleys and an elderly stone fountain, both the hospital and the large Convent of Santa Catalina behind the cathedral are worth a glance in passing.

Vilanova de Lourenzá, some 9km (6 miles) to the north, is known chiefly for the Monastery of San Salvador which has a Baroque façade and the chapel of Santa Maria de Valdeflores. The Conde Osorio, who founded the monastery, is buried inside, his tomb having a special hole through which dedicated pilgrims can touch his bones. There is nothing quite so macabre about the Monastery of San Martin de Mondoñedo, a massive building in rural surroundings on the LU152 roughly a mile from the coast, whose proudest possession is a very early Romanesque church. **Foz**, quite close by, is an attractive deepsea fishing port that was a whaling station in the Middle Ages. Augmenting the general atmosphere and some long sandy beaches on the far side of the headland, its only brush with antiquity is a Celtic burial ground at **Fazouro**, a few kilometres along the coast. Beyond Burela, which also earns its living from the sea, the N642 swings inland to Cervo whose modest claim to fame lies in its proximity to the Royal Ceramic Factory at Sargadelos. This was previously the site of an iron factory whose main function was to provide the army with cannons before it turned its attention to more decorative matters. The articles it turns out are quite unusual and on the expensive side, but it is interesting to see some of the older ceramics on display in the manor house where Goya is said to have stayed while he was painting a portrait of the owner.

The next port of call is **Celeiro** on the Ría de Viveiro, known principally for its tasty line in shellfish. The surrounding area is pretty rather than spectacular, sandwiched in between the mountains and the sea, its approach roads shaded by pines and eucalyptus trees. **Viveiro**, at the head of this substantial ria, was fortified in bygone days but has dispensed with all its old walls apart from the Charles V gateway, complete with carved turrets and the emperor's coat-of-arms. It is still a busy fishing port with a growing interest in tourism. Among the local attractions are two ancient churches — Santa Maria del Campo and San Pedro — as well as one that was originally part of the Convent of San Francisco, distinguished by its slender arched windows and adjoining cloister. The coast road to the west, over the medieval La Misericordia bridge, pays its respects to Covas, skirts round a brace of sandy beaches facing the little Isla Coelleira that once belonged to the Templars, and reaches the Ría de Barqueiro. This is a particularly beautiful inlet fed by the Río Sor which forms the boundary between Lugo and La Coruña.

Viveiro has a few modest hotels and the unexpectedly down-market Aguadoce campsite, all of which are crowded during Holy Week and for the Naseiro Romeria at the end of August. The town takes its religious obligations very seriously but also lets its hair down during the summer festivities with folk songs and dances, to the accompaniment of Galician bagpipes and the aroma of fish being cooked in the open air. From Viveiro the scenic C640 struggles manfully through the mountains to the Puerto de Gañidoira and Cabreiros, an overall distance of 47km (29 miles) where it leaves the C641 to cover the next 15km (9 mile) stretch to Villalba on the way back to Lugo city.

ORENSE

Orense, in the south-east of Galicia, shares a fairly lengthy border with Portugal, from Zamora in Castilla y León to a point on the Río Miño where it hands over its frontier duties to Pontevedra. It is an average-sized province without a great deal to say for itself although the scenery varies from beautiful man-made lakes and hillsides cloaked in vines to snow-capped mountains where it is possible to ski in the winter. Historically Orense has been concerned in most of the major events involving the region from the time of the Celts and the Romans. There are some ancient monasteries, a sprinkling of small towns with interesting old churches, mineral springs with attendant bottling factories and a few cattle that either work in the fields or provide milk and good quality beef, some of which is exported.

Orense, the provincial capital, was known to the Romans as *Aquae Urentes* on account of the hot springs which still flow through the fountains, giving off clouds of steam in cold weather. The three main springs, called Las Burgas, are just off the Avenida General Franco on the edge of the old town whose narrow streets and little squares separate them from the cathedral. Here the main structure and the chapterhouse date from the thirteenth century but the much decorated Santisimo Cristo chapel was added some 300 years later. According to legend the figure of Christ, which has a real head of hair and a beard, was one of a number carved by Nicodemus who was instructed to throw them into the Mediterranean. At least two statues found their way through to the Atlantic and were washed up on the shores of the Iberian peninsula, in this case near Cape Finisterre. The Romanesque Pórtico del Paraíso, at the west end of the cathedral, is very similar to the Pórtico de la Gloria in Santiago de Compostela and vies for attention with the ornate early sixteenth-century retable above the high altar. The museum, housed in the chapterhouse, is full of beautiful items, some of which are extremely old. The Treasure of San Rosendo chess pieces were carved out of rock crystal in the tenth century, in addition to which there are vestments and church plate, statues and one of the first books to be printed in Galicia.

A stone's throw from the cathedral, on the opposite side of the Plaza Mayor, the Museo Arqueológico y de Bellas Artes (Archaeological Museum) was once part of the episcopal palace. It divides its attention between prehistoric finds, Roman leftovers and items of sacred art, including a carved seventeenth-century Stations of the Cross, before turning to ethnology with such everyday items as kitchen equipment and local pottery. Just round the corner, the Plazuela de la Magdalena takes its name from the cross with its figure of Mary Magdalene, presided over by the Church of Santa Maria la Madre built in 1722. A good deal further away the old Puente Romano over the Río Miño was constructed 700 years ago on foundations laid down by the Romans. It has been superseded by a modern bridge on either side that point the way to Vigo, 101km (63 miles) to the west and Santiago de Compostela which is only marginally further away along the N525.

Anyone planning to spend a few days in Orense in order to explore the surrounding country has a choice between the Gran Hotel San Martin, Curros Enriques 1 and a number of small establishments which are quite acceptable. However it might prove a trifle difficult to visit all the outlying places of interest in a single day because, although generally quite close to hand, they are most inconveniently placed for would-be sightseers without much time to spare. For instance, the wine growing region of Ribeiro, centred on the typically attractive little town of Ribadavia, is about the only place to visit in that direction before crossing into Pontevedra on the way to Vigo.

The Monasterio Santa Maria la

The Monastery of St Rosendo was originally a staging post for pilgrims on their way to Compostela

A horreó or granary used to store crops

Real de Oseira, some 45km (28 miles) due north of the provincial capital, off the N525, has an isolated spot all to itself. Most of the original buildings are in ruins but there is a twelfth-century church, considerably up-dated nearly 400 years ago, whose sacristy was originally the chapterhouse. The monastery was given a new façade in 1708 with a large Baroque doorway beyond which there is a splendid stairway and two quite impressive cloisters. It also keeps fifteen rooms for male guests only.

The minor road leading to Santa Maria la Real swings round to the right, crosses the N540 at La Bar-rela and then heads south towards the Río Miño and the gorges of the Río Sil. However these can be reached much more easily and quickly from Orense along the N120 with a turning off to the equally world-weary San Esteban de Ribas do Sil Monastery on a rocky spur against a backdrop of granite mountains. From here a scenic but rather time-consuming little road passes the Embalse de Santo Estevo and the reservoirs along the Sil valley to make contact with the main road to León at Castro Caldelas. This provides the only access to Manzaneda from Puebla de Trives and the nearby ski slopes, already well on the way to becoming a popular winter resort. There are nearly a dozen different runs, ski lifts and a chair lift and a handful of hotels including the Queixa. It is open all year like the modest Nieves campsite at Puebla de Trives.

Motorists travelling south from Orense can take either the N525 to Allariz or the less frequented N540 to **Celanova.** This is well worth the extra time involved in order to see the large Benedictine monastery of San Salvador. It was originally a staging post for pilgrims on their way north to Compostela, founded in AD936 by San Rosendo, who would very probably have worshipped at the Mozarabic chapel of San Miguel. If closed enquire from the caretaker. There is also a seventeenth-century church with a dom-ineering altarpiece and a beautiful Baroque cloister as well as galleries and staircases which have been carefully restored. The even earlier church of Santa Comba, overlooking the lake at Bande, 16km (10 miles) down the road, was built by the Visigoths and has been extremely well preserved. A minor road links Celanova with Allariz which has its own church of Santiago and the Convento de Santa Clara, founded by the wife of Alfonso X.

Having got this far there are excellent reasons for carrying on to **Verin,** 69km (43 miles) from Orense, a delightful old town on the vine covered slopes of the Tamega valley a few kilometres from the Portuguese frontier. Its narrow streets, arcades and ancient houses embossed with coats-of-arms and protected from the weather by glassed-in balconies, are straight out of the Middle Ages. Monterrei Castle, 4km (2 miles) to the west, was an important stronghold during the wars between Spain and Portugal. Originally it consisted of the thirteenth-century church, a palace, a hospital, a monastery and several houses, all protected by three lines of fortifications, added at various intervals. The whole place was abandoned in the nineteenth century except for a few residents who refused to leave their homes and kept an unpracticed eye on the ruins. Now it has a modern neighbour in the adjoining Parador de Monterrey, with its comfortable rooms, a swimming pool in the garden and some extensive views.

PONTEVEDRA

Pontevedra is a province which concentrates almost entirely on its Atlantic seaboard, leaving Orense and Lugo to worry about what is happening outside the back door and the Río Miño to guard its frontier with Portugal. Like La Coruña to the north, it has a deeply indented coastline with sheltered harbours, pleasant beaches, a few small fishing communities and at least one potentially Mediterranean-style holiday resort. The countryside is quite uniformly green and agreeable but with nothing exceptional to tempt sightseers away from their chosen patches of sea, rocks and sand.

The main route from La Coruña, through Santiago de Compostela, Pontevedra and Vigo to the Portuguese frontier, is shared between the *autopista* and the N550 with two main roads leading off to the east, namely the N541 from Pontevedra and the N120 from Vigo, that come together shortly before reaching Orense. There are no roads of any real importance with the exception of the C550 that hugs the coast almost continuously from north to south, missing very few places of interest en route. Trains from La Coruña call in on their way to Portugal, regular services operate between Pontevedra and Vigo and there are adequate buses connecting many of the larger centres.

Pontevedra insists that it was founded by Teucer who, like his legendary uncle Ajax, took an active part in the siege of Troy. Thereafter the city appears to have been ignored by all and sundry, leaving it free to build up its trade and fishing interests and give birth to an occasional explorer like Pedro Sarmiento de Gamboa who sailed across the Atlantic in the sixteenth century and wrote about it in his *Voyage to the Magellan Straits*. The area where they lived before the river silted up and the port facilities were transferred to Marín is tucked away between the more modern quarters and the Puente del Burgo on the road in from north.

The old town is quite small and picturesque with winding streets, little squares, a few fountains and old houses whose glassed-in balconies are frequently described as crystal galleries. The Church of

Santa Maria la Mayor at the far end of the Calle Isabel II, built in the sixteenth century by the Mariners' Guild, has an interestingly carved west front that includes the figures of both seamen and fishermen, but not a great deal to see inside. Because of the slight confusion caused by one-way streets in addition to alleys reserved for pedestrians, it is easier to walk than drive half a dozen blocks or so to the lovely little Plaza de Leña and the main section of the Museo Provincal (Provincial Museum). This has taken over two eighteenth-century town houses joined together by an arch and contains something of interest to nearly everyone. There are prehistoric exhibits for the archaeologically minded, including what is known as the Celtic Golada Treasure, as well as articles from a typical house of days gone by and a collection of Sargadelos pottery dating from the nineteenth century. Nautical matters are dealt with just as thoroughly, ranging from equipment used by sailors and fishermen to the admiral's cabin on board *Numancia* where plans were finalised for the attack on Callao, in Peru, in 1866. Items left behind by the Romans, a variety of old tombs and some early stone carvings are on display in the ivy-covered remains of the Convento de Santo Domingo on the Alameda, a short walk away. The two most interesting churches in the city are within a stone's throw of each other near the Plaza de la Herreria. The Church of San Fran-cisco is larger with a Gothic façade whereas La Peregrina is shaped like a cockleshell and is dedicated to the Pilgrim Virgin who is the local patron saint.

Although there are plenty of hotels and campsites all along the coast, anyone who prefers to make daily excursions from a central base need look no further than the atmospheric Parador Casa del Barón on the Plaza de Maceda. One or two other options are available, usually without restaurants, but this is not a serious drawback because there are a few good places to eat in the vicinity. The most convenient campsites are at Sangenjo, 18km (11 miles) away on the northern shores of the Ría de Pontevedra, the best equipped being the Cachadelos. However, there are a handful of second grade sites to choose from and an equally large selection at O Grove on what amounts to an island attached to the coast by a narrow isthmus.

Both **Sangenjo** and **O Grove** are popular holiday resorts, boasting a predictable collection of seaside hotels and restaurants, pleasant sandy beaches and some of the best weather in Galicia. The former has facilities for a variety of water sports whereas the latter is connected by a bridge to the little wooded island of A Toxa, or La Toja, where there is a modest spa and a golf course to match. However there is nothing modest about its Gran Hotel, with tennis and a heated swimming pool and access to the 9-hole golf course.

After calling at O Grove the C550 doubles back slightly and then makes for **Cambados**, notable chiefly for its splendid Plaza de Fefiñanes and the Parador del Albariño, housed in a country manor surrounded by gardens with a restaurant that is widely known for its seafood. From here the road bypasses Vilanova on its way to **Vilagarcía de Arousa**, a medium sized town whose Vista Alegre Convent, straddling the approach route, was founded in the seventeenth century. Here a minor road to the south is joined by a forest path after 4km (2 miles) which climbs up to the Mirador de Lobeira where there is a commanding view across the large Ría de Arousa. The C550 offers nothing else of note as it accompanies the Río Ulla for a few kilometres before joining the N550 on the border with La Coruña. This proves to be very convenient for motorists in search of a direct route back to Pontevedra about 36km (22 miles) to the south.

South of the provincial capital drivers have a choice of three different roads to **Vigo**, the most prestigious fishing port in Spain. The quickest is the *autopista*, the N550 is slightly longer with a turning off at Redondela along the southern shore of the Ría de Vigo, whereas the longest, the C550, trundles round the edge of the Peninsula de Morrazo, visiting an occasional fishing village along the way. Bueu offers plenty of opportunities to explore the semi-deserted beaches on either side but Cangas and Moaña are more interested in day trippers who arrive by ferry from Vigo after crossing the ria in less than a quarter of an hour.

Apart from its hillside position overlooking a deep roadstead, protected by the Cies Islands with their trio of lighthouses, Vigo is rather disappointing. Admittedly there is an old fishermen's quarter, a selection of elderly mansions and a castle fortress with a view across the bay, but very little else of interest. The Celts had a settlement on the top of the hill, the Greeks and the Phoenicians were regular visitors and Sir Francis Drake attacked it twice within the space of 5 years. However, like so many of the galleons returning with treasures from the New World, they have all vanished without trace, leaving the way clear for the port to develop its many industrial interests. There are several large, comfortable hotels, some excellent restaurants, a municipal museum in the seventeenth-century Pazo de Castralos in the Parque Quiñones de Leon and a small zoo but this is hardly enough to satisfy the average holidaymaker. On the other hand the nearby beaches are most inviting, gently shelving with fine golden sands. Early risers will find an exuberant fish auction near the waterfront and the morning market in the Rua de Pescaderia is a good place to buy oysters or mussels which are grown on ropes suspended from wooden platforms in the estuary.

The majority of people in search

The old town of Túy with its ancient fortress doubling as a cathedral

Vigo is the most prestigious fishing port in Spain

of relaxation seem to find **Bayona**, 21km (13 miles) down the coast, infinitely preferable. It is an attractive little port overlooking a large, sheltered bay into which the *Pinta* sailed in 1493 with the news that Columbus had discovered San Salvador. Ships laden with treasures made constant use of the harbour during the sixteenth and seventeenth centuries but they have now been replaced by fishing boats and pleasure craft while highrise blocks across the water at the Playa América bear witness to its growing importance as a holiday resort. The old fortress of Monte Real with its tower and battlements rises out of the cliffs above the town. It was once the governor's residence but has recently found space in the park for the Parador Conde de Gondomar. It is modern, although built in the style of a large country mansion, with some rooms on the ground floor and a choice of restaurants in addition to a swimming pool and tennis in the grounds. Children have a play area and there are lovely beaches within walking distance with opportunities for fishing as well as bathing or just lying in the sun. It is one of the more expensive paradores so anyone who has to economise would be advised to try one of the smaller hotels, leaving those with tents or caravans to find a space at one of the first grade campsites, known as the Bayona Playa and the Playa América.

From Bayona the C550 continues down the coast past Oya with its privately-owned thirteenth-century monastery of Santa Maria la Real. Here the most colourful events take place on the second Sunday in May and the first and second Sundays in June when wild horses are rounded up and driven into specially prepared corrals in the nearby hills to be branded and have their tails and manes cut. The village is only some 13km (8 miles) from **A Guarda** on the tip of Spain's Atlantic seafront and separated from the mouth of the Río Miño by Monte Santa Tecla. This is a most obtrusive mountain which was inhabited from the Bronze Age until about the third century AD. A good deal of the settlement has been excavated, revealing the foundations of primitive houses separated by rough paths and protected by defensive walls. One or two reconstructed huts complete the picture with the help of a stone circle that undoubtedly had a deeply religious significance in pagan times and a small museum filled with bits and pieces that were discovered on the site.

After a quick trip round Monte Santa Tecla the C550 changes direction and sidles up the northern bank of the Río Miño to **Túy**, one of the two main gateways into Portugal from Galicia. The town also insists that it was founded by an ancient Greek warrior, in this case Diomedes, and points to discoveries made on Monte Aloia to substantiate its claim. At all events there were certainly people living in the area before the Romans added a township of their own which, in turn, was adopted by the Visigoths and destroyed by the Moors. *Tude*, as it was called in those days, was rebuilt by the Castilians not long afterwards in order to keep up a spasmodic battle across the river with the Portuguese town of Valença do Minho just opposite. The bridge linking the two was constructed in 1884 and since then has been used regularly by townspeople on shopping expeditions and travellers on their way along the coast.

Túy is a most attractive old town whose ancient fortress has doubled as a cathedral since the thirteenth century without changing its initial character to any great extent. The west front was given a decorative porch but even that was designed to play its part in an attack, while the sentry path above the cloister has an uninterrupted view of the river. The interior is functional rather than decorative although the choir stalls are carved with events in the life of San Telmo, the patron saint of sailors. British seamen rechristened him St Elmo and kept a sharp lookout for any sign of St Elmo's Fire, a strange light that was said to appear at the masthead and was certain to bring good luck. In fact, he was a Portuguese Dominican called Pedro González Telmo who lived in a house adjoining the fortress and died there in 1240. Its position is marked by a shrine, the San Telmo Chapel, containing a reliquary and an alcove in the crypt, much visited by pilgrims in search of a miracle.

The Church of San Bartolomé, dating from the tenth century, was the original cathedral and is said to be one of the first churches to be built in Galicia. The town also has its full quota of narrow streets and elderly houses but the Parador San Telmo is an excellent reproduction of a stately manor with a pleasant garden and a swimming pool. Túy is 29km (18 miles) from Vigo and 48km (30 miles) from Pontevedra along the N550. However, anyone with time to spare can follow the Río Miño as far as the border with Orense and then take the long way round through A Caniza on the N120, the main highway from Orense to Vigo. A further option is the C531, a turning to the right just up the road, which meanders for about 60km (37 miles) across the Sierra del Suido to Pontevedra city.

Additional Information

LA CORUÑA (Province)
Ferrol

Arsenal
Open: 4-6pm. Enquire at the entrance or from S A Zono Maritima.

La Coruña

San Carlos Fort
Open: 10am-1.30pm and 4-7pm summer, 10am-1.30pm and 2-6pm winter. Gardens open: 9am to sundown.

Torre de Hercules
Lighthouse open: 10am-1pm and 4pm to sundown. Closed Sunday.

Santiago de Compostela

Cathedral Museums
Open: 10am-1.30pm and 4-7.30pm May to October. 11am-1pm and 4-6pm November to April. Closed Sunday and holiday afternoons.

Gelmirez Palace
Plaza de España
Open: 10am-1.30pm and 4-7pm April to September.

San Pelayo Monastery
Plaza de la Quintana
Open: 10am-1pm and 4-7pm summer only.

Santa Maria del Sar Church and Museum
Calle Castron D'Ouro
Open: 10am-1pm and 4-6.30pm. Closed Sundays.

Santo Domingo Convent
Puerto del Camino
Open: 10am-1pm and 4-7pm. Closed Sunday afternoon.

Pazo de Oca Gardens
25km (15½ miles) south
Open: 9am-1pm and 3-8pm summer, 10am-1pm and 3-6pm winter.

Sobrado de los Monjes Monastery
Open: 10.15am-12.45pm and 3.15-6.45pm.

LUGO (Province)
Lugo

Provincial Museum
Church of San Francisco
Open: 10.30am-2pm, sometimes
4-7pm. Closed Sundays and
holidays.

Mondoñedo

Cathedral Museum
Open: 11am-1pm and 4-7pm July
to mid-September, 12noon-1pm
mid-September to May.

ORENSE (Province)
Orense

Cathedral Museum
Open: 10am-1pm and
3.30-7.30pm summer, 11am-1pm
and 4.30-6.30pm winter. Closed
Sunday mornings.

PONTEVEDRA (Province)
Pontevedra

Provincial Museum
Plaza de Lena

Open: 11am-1pm and 5-8pm.
Closed Sunday and holiday afternoons.

TOURIST INFORMATION CENTRES

La Coruña
Dársena de la Marina
☎ 981 22 18 22

Lugo
Plaza de España
☎ 982 23 13 61

Orense
Curros Enriquez
☎ 988 23 47 17

Pontevedra
General Mola
☎ 986 85 08 14

Ribadeo
Plaza de España
☎ 982 11 06 69

Santiago de Compostela
Rua del Villar
☎ 981 58 40 81

2
Asturias and Cantabria

Asturias may be small but it is certainly not insignificant, with a reputation for sallying forth like David against any Goliath who appears on the horizon. The Iberian tribe of Astures made the Romans feel unwelcome nearly 2,000 years ago and only softened its attitude towards the Visigoths after Pelayo and his band of followers had routed the Moors at Covadonga in AD718. This minute Christian enclave, known as the Kingdom of Asturias, went on to liberate much of the surrounding area, transferred its court to León and set about the formidable task of recovering Castile.

In due course León and Castile amalgamated, to be joined later in wedlock with Aragón, and together the Catholic Monarchs Fer-dinand and Isabel completed the Reconquest, thereby enabling their grandson Charles V to inherit a united Spain. Asturias was naturally part of it but ceased to play a leading role, even though each heir-apparent has been known as the Prince of Asturias since the title was suggested by John of Gaunt when his daughter married the son of Juan I in the fourteenth century.

The province was well represented when Spain developed its newly-ac-quired territories in central and south America, turned its attention from agriculture to mining in the nineteenth century and staged a revolt in 1934, raising an army of 30,000 men to safeguard its independence. It was Franco who sent in troops from North Africa to deal with the uprising, with the result that he got no help from that quarter during the Civil War and even had to contend with a certain amount of opposition after he had been officially acknowledged as Head of State. These days it is fighting just as hard against all the more blatant aspects of tourism such as highrise buildings, over commercialisation and the threat of extensive developments in its section of the Picos de Europa, one of the wildest and most beautiful mountain regions in the country.

Visitors are welcome in Asturias. The N634 highway runs along the seaboard from Unquera on the border with Cantabria, making only a slight deviation through Oviedo, and on to Ribadeo, a resort at the mouth of the Río Eo which separates the province from Gal-icia. An *autopista*, shaped rather like a champagne glass with its stem resting on Oviedo, links the capital with Gijón on the east and Avilés on the west of the Cabo de Peñas as it juts out into the Bay of Biscay. The N630 connects Oviedo and León 121km (75 miles) to the south, with an *autopista* branching off just short of the boundary through a series of tunnels that make easy work of the mountainous area round the Puerto de Pajares. There are any number of secondary roads, most of which are scenic, that follow a host of small rivers linked by an occasional shortcut which complicates matters still further.

Oviedo is linked by rail with Madrid as well as Barcelona, Zara-goza and a number of provincial capitals in Castilla y León. There are also quite frequent trains to Santander, and others along the coast to El Ferrol del Caudillo in Galicia. Coaches venture as far afield as Brussels, Geneva, Paris and Zurich as well as Madrid, Sevilla, Barcelona and Valencia while buses travel all over the province leaving the Picos de Europa to companies using jeeps or Land Rovers.

Apart from a fairly wide selection of hotels in Oviedo the majority of comfortable establishments are to be found in resorts along the coast. However there are any num-ber of rooms available in private houses, especially up in the mountains, and something like thirty different campsites, at least two of them providing bungalows as well. The Asturians enjoy their food which is tasty but tends to be relatively simple. The best known of the traditional dishes is *fabada*, consisting of white beans and pork, which is tinned and exported to several places in America. Other stews are made with the same white beans (*fabes*) added to clams or partridge. Hake cooked in cider is also extremely popular and easier to find than a delicious concoction of fish and seafood known as *caldereta*. Finally there is the ubiquitous rice pudding, topped with sugar, and *cabrales*, an exceptionally strong cheese that looks a bit like Roquefort. Nearly everyone drinks the local cider which is invariably dropped into the glass from a distance instead of being poured out in the ordinary way, and is by no means as innocuous as it looks. Most of the local fiestas are essentially religious celebrations. At Llanes folklore plays an important part in the feasts of Mary Magdalene and San Roque, Candás pays an annual tribute to Christ with bullfighting on the beach on 14 September whereas the pilgrimage in memory of the Holy Martyrs of Valdecina at Mieres on 27 September is said to be the oldest event of its kind in the province.

Oviedo is both the ancient and the modern capital of Asturias, spreading out in every direction from the large central Parque de San Francisco with all that remains of the old city a mere block or two away. It started life as a Benedictine monastery on a hill called Ovetum but was destroyed by the Moors and had to be rebuilt by Alfonso II at the end of the eighth century. Nearly everything that survived from those early days was obliterated during the savage fighting which characterised the

Asturias and
Cantabria

Costa Verde

0	10	20	30	40 mil	
0		35		70 kr	

Museum of Gaita
Roman Baths

Ribadeo — Luarca — Cudillero — Salinas — Luanco — Avilés — GIJÓN — Villaviciosa — Ribad

Pola de Allande — Tineo — OVIEDO — Valdedios — Cangas de On

Cangas de Narcea

Tito Busti Cave
El Buxo Cave

Pícos de Trea
Europa of the

ASTURIAS

* Cámra Santa
Archaeological Museum
Santullano Church
Santa Maria del Naranco
and San Miguel
de Lillo Curches

ta Verde

| Altamira Caves
| Diocesan Museum

| Prehistory Museum
| Fine Arts Museum
* Menéndez y Pelayo Library

Costa Verde

Cueva del Pindal

Ethnology
Museum

SANTANDER El Sardinero

Vidiago

San Vincente
de la Barquera

Santillana
del Mar

Pedreña

Santoña

Castro-
Urdiales

N634

Comillas

Muriedas

N634

Laredo

nas de
brales

Torrelavega

Peña
Cabarga

S531

S561

Limpias

N62

S224

C625

Yermo

N611

S521

Lebeña

Covalanas
Caves

N634

Potes

S580

S572

S510

Ramales de
la Victoria

C6318

osgaya

C627

CANTABRIA

N623

S570

C629

nte Dé

C628

Reinosa

C627

Retortillo

Embalse
del Ebro

C626

Cervatos

BU550

Embalse de
Aguilar
de Campoo

N611

Rio Ebro

N623

miners' revolt in 1934 and the subsequent upheavals of the Civil War when the local garrison opted for the Nationalists while the rest of the province sided with the Republicans. Some buildings have been restored, in addition to which there are some attractive old streets bordering on the Plaza Mayor.

The cathedral dates in part from the fourteenth century and stands on the site of an earlier church constructed by Alfonso II. The massive tower was added 200 years later, at the same time as the carved altarpiece was installed. This is rivalled, if not surpassed, by the Baroque chapels on either side and especially the shrine of Santa Eulalia, the patron saint of Asturias, who is buried there. The El Castro chapel with its statues of Peter, Paul, Andrew and James and a band of ancient musicians is the royal mausoleum while lesser mortals were consigned to St Leocadia's chapel near the cloister.

The Cámara Santa was built by Alfonso II as a shrine for holy relics which belonged to the Visigoths and were recovered from Toledo after that city was captured by the Moors. It still has most of its treasures including the Cruz de la Victoria, a travelling altar and some gold and silver that was recovered after being stolen in 1977.

One or two ancient buildings near the cathedral survived both the miners' revolt and the Civil War, among them the Casa de la Rúa, the old university and the convent of San Vicente which is now the city's Archaeological Museum. It has some interesting exhibits from prehistoric times as well as items that were commonplace in the kingdom of Asturias, ancient musical instruments, coins and medals. Two of the most attractive squares are the Plaza de Porlier, near the university, and the Plaza de Daoiz y Velarde a short distance away, where the daily market is held almost in the shadow of the Baroque palace of the Marqués de San Feliz. Regardless of these diverse attractions some people maintain that Oviedo's prize possessions are three small churches — the Santullano, or San Julián de los Prados, a stoic little hangover from the ninth century on the road to Gijón, and the marginally younger Santa Maria del Naranco and San Miguel de Lillo on a hillside 4km (2 miles) north-west of the city. All are outstanding examples of uncluttered, pre-Romanesque architecture and have fortunately been preserved rather than over-enthusiastically restored.

A number of comfortable hotels, are scattered about in or near to the old quarter with a choice of several places to eat in the vicinity. On the other hand, visitors who would prefer a parador by the sea need look no further than **Gijón**, 29km (18 miles) to the north. It is a busy port with strong industrial connections which, like Oviedo, had to be largely rebuilt after the Civil War.

Despite the Parador El Molino

Veijo, adjoining the Parque de Isabel la Católica, a variety of other hotels and restaurants and the long sandy Playa de San Lorenzo, the town cannot really be regarded as an ideal holiday resort. Nevertheless it has an atmospheric old fishermen's quarter on the slopes of the Santa Catalina headland separating the beach from the harbour, just a trace of Roman baths installed at the time of Augustus, the Museo de la Gaita which specialises in bagpipes and the seventeenth-century Revillagigedo Palace on the Plaza del Marqués. Golfers will find both an 18-hole golf course and the 9-hole Club La Barganiza which the port shares with Oviedo. Provisions are made for tents and caravans at the Gijón campsite and a fistful of alternatives quite close by.

Villaviciosa, 30km (19 miles) to the east of Gijón on the ria of the same name, is the place where Charles V landed by mistake in 1517 when he arrived to claim his Spanish inheritance. It is an attractive town that has retained much of its original character, partly surrounded by apple orchards which supply a large cider mill on the way to the beach at El Puntal and the fishing village of Tazones. Anyone in search of ancient churches has only to explore the countryside all round. **Valdediós**, 7km (4 miles) along the C638, is said to have the best selection within easy reach, including the somewhat dilapidated thirteenth-century Church of Santa Maria and San Salvador,

dating from AD893. The best beaches are to be found in the vicinity of Colunga on the N632, a coast road that joins the main route on the far side of Ribadesella. Between these two coastal resorts a secondary road wanders off into the Reserva Nacional de Sueve where the wild horses are descended from those used by the Romans when they were patrolling the area.

Ribadesella stages international kayak races along the Río Sella which can be followed in a special train provided for the purpose on the first Saturday in August. The Tito Bustillo Caves are within walking distance for anyone in need of exercise. They were inhabited more than 20,000 years ago and contain a number of rather indistinct paintings, as well as galleries festooned with stalactites.

Further south, on the N625, **Cangas de Onis** takes great pride in being the first capital of Christian Spain with the Capilla de Santa Cruz which is said to have numbered the kings of Asturias among its necessarily restricted congregation. It all started with a dolmen in the Bronze Age that has been incorporated into every subsequent building, starting as long ago as AD437 and persisting into the twentieth century when the chapel was rebuilt after the Civil War. There is nothing controversial about the splendid twelfth-century bridge over the Río Sella, the 400-year-old palace of the Asturian Assembly or the up-

Twelfth-century bridge over the Ría Sella, Cangas de Onis

The magnificent scenery and colourful landscapes of the Picos de Europa can only be attained by walking

dated Church of Santa Maria. The Cueva del Buxu, 2km (1 mile) east of Cangas de Onis, has its own collection of prehistoric art but although the hillside cave is open to the public the number of people allowed in on any given day is strictly limited.

Beyond the road up to the Cueva del Buxu there is a turning off in the opposite direction to **Covadonga**, scene of one of the most important events in Spanish history. After the Moors had captured Toledo and overrun most of the country a local chieftain called Pelayo, who claimed to be a member of the Visigoth nobility, organised a revolt against the invaders. A small armed force was dispatched from Córdoba to deal with the problem and was defeated. The Christians immediately rallied behind Pelayo who set up his court in Cangas de Onis but this made so little impression on the Moors that they chose to ignore it. One glance into a crystal ball would have been sufficient to warn them that the early seeds of Asturian defiance were in reality the prelude to the ultimate Christian victory in 1492.

In 1877 work started on the vast red basilica crowning the Montes de Cueto with a bronze statue of Pelayo and his famous Cross of Victory on the esplanade outside. The cave nearby, where he is said to have fought off a particularly vicious Arab attack, has been turned into a shrine dedicated to the Virgin of the Battlefield. Pelayo, who died in AD737, his wife and Alfonso I are buried close to the enamelled altar and a highly venerated, although relatively modern, statue of the Santina Virgen who is the patron saint of Asturias. Over the years it has become a place of pilgrimage, especially on 8 September when a special procession is held in her honour. The Tresoro de la Virgen (Treasure of the Virgin) is full of offerings including an outstanding diamond-encrusted crown.

Covadonga has its own nature reserve in the western section of the Picos de Europa, the Hotel Pelayo, and a determined little road up to the Mirador de la Reina and two isolated lakes — the Lago de Enol and the Lago de la Ercina — where there is a convenient motel. For motorists this is literally the end of the road and anyone who wants to start exploring must set out on foot, although there are a few tracks suitable for jeeps.

There are very few roads through the Picos de Europa, most of which end abruptly or degenerate into stony tracks, and practically no points of contact between those that do exist. As a result it is impossible at the moment to explore the whole area by car. However this does not mean that everyone has to be a mountaineer or a rock climber to enjoy the magnificent scenery and colourful landscapes that could hardly have been improved upon by Salvador Dali. There are footpaths suitable for even the most timid visitor out for an afternoon stroll, longer trails that would appeal to fell-walkers and still more demanding routes where a good head for heights is useful and occasionally essential. Anyone planning a hiking holiday — the best time being between June and October — would be well advised to apply to the Federación Asturiana de Monatañismo, Calle Melquiades Alvarez 16, Oviedo, for up-to-the-minute information.

It would be impossible to cover all the various alternatives in a few short paragraphs but one walk at least deserves an honourable mention. A broad, well-defined footpath follows the Río Cares east of Covadonga for about 13km (8 miles), gouged out of the mountainside along the Garganta Divina (Divine Gorge), suspended between the foaming water hundreds of feet below and the snow-capped peaks that seem to be reaching for the stars. The village of Cain at the southern end is fairly typical, with a rough track linking it with Posada de Valdeón on the LE244.

Less ambitious sightseers can retrace their original route to Covadonga through Cangas de Onis, and rejoin the N634 to inspect what remains of the Asturian coast east of Ribadesella. The C6312 heads in the opposite direction towards **Arenas de Cabrales** offering further possibilities for exploring the deep ravines, meagre pastures and sharply defined peaks. Thereafter it is a relatively easy run up to Panes, which offers some modest accommodation, and along the Río Deva to the coast.

Apart from some pleasant beaches and unobtrusive little coves there is not a great deal to see on the way back to either Gijón or Oviedo. However about 2km (1 mile) from Pimiango it is worth climbing up to the Cueva del Pindal, a prehistoric cave in the cliff overlooking a small creek. It contains a number of animal paintings including a realistic elephant, mainly dating from Palaeolithic times. In winter it is necessary to collect the key from the village. Vidiago, beyond La Franca, also has a comparable attraction called Peña Tu, an odd megalithic idol dating from the Bronze Age. **Llanes** is the only place of any size before Ribadesella. It has just a trace of its ancient fortifications, a number of small hotels and campsites.

The pattern repeats itself along the coast beyond **Avilés**, an elderly town to the north-west of Oviedo whose seventeenth-century charms are overshadowed by one of the largest steelworks in Spain. Its somewhat motley collection of mansions and churches are only mildly interesting with the possible exception of the Santo Tomás de Cantobery, one of the first to be dedicated to Thomas Becket after his murder in Canterbury Cathedral. The nearby resort of **Salinas** has a clutch of small hotels and a long beach but the fishing village of **Cudillero**, a little further down the N632, is much prettier. There are one or two prehistoric caves in the neighbourhood such as San Román, down the C632 apiece from Soto del Barco, after which it is possible to join the N634 on a cross country run of about 51km (32 miles) through Salas to a point on the coast just short of **Luarca**. This is an old whaling port at mouth of the Río Negro with a trail of white houses, a clutch of basic hotels, a sheltered harbour and a plentiful supply of bridges.

Several little roads in various states of repair thread their way up into the mountains but the most interesting excursion is probably down the Navia Valley almost to the border with Galicia. This route winds about all over the place, calling at a selection of small hamlets, but as hardly any of them have either a café or a garage it is as well to set out with a full tank, and a supply of food and drink.

Among the attractions along the way are the sparse remains of a Celtic village near Coaña and some memorable panoramic views over a series of dams and reservoirs. At the agricultural centre of Grandas de Salime the C630, off to the left, makes its way through arid country to the high Puerto del Palo, drops down to the village of Pola de Allande, tucked away in a fertile valley, and proceeds in a slightly more sedate fashion to the hilltop town of **Tineo** which has a splendid view all to itself.

Alternatively, a minor road from Pola de Allande negotiates the gorges round the Puenta del Infierno to visit **Corias** whose bridge linking the two sections of the community was built originally by the Romans. The 900-year-old monastery lived a reasonably quiet life before it was burned down and then reconstructed in the nineteenth century. It does not look very inviting from the outside but makes up for this with surprisingly ornate altars in the church. A kilometre or two down the road **Cangas de Narcea** has little of interest to offer anyone except hunters, fishermen and hikers, although it is reasonably well placed for motorists on their way back to Oviedo. The most obvious route bypasses Tineo to join the main highway near Salas, 47km (29 miles) from the provincial capital. However, anyone with more far reaching ideas can opt for a much longer way round via the Puerto de Leitariegos to connect with either the *autopista* or the main León-Oviedo road just south of the magnificent Pajares Pass on the border between the two provinces.

CANTABRIA

Cantabria is a strip of territory sandwiched in between the Bay of Biscay and the mountains of the Cantabrian Cordillera, merging into the Basque lands of the Costa Vasca to the east and the Asturian Costa Verde further west. It probably sees as many tourists as any other province on this stretch of coast, but very few pause to draw breath before heading south into Castilla y León towards Madrid and Andalucia. On the other hand it has been popular since the turn of the century with Spaniards escaping from the searing heat of the meseta to spend their summer holidays on its long sandy beaches.

Much of the area has been populated since local artists began to draw on the walls of their caves in prehistoric times but it is singularly short of ancient buildings, hilltop forts and decorative churches. The Romans made a half-hearted attempt to subjugate the inhabitants and then apparently decided that it was scarcely worth the effort. The Moors adopted much the same attitude when they ran into fierce local resistance, the Templars gave it a modicum of attention and Charles V looked in briefly towards the end of his reign en route for the monastery at Yuste in Extremadura.

Nobody paid much attention to the interior of the province, with the result that there are comparatively few medieval villages that are worth making a special trip to

Cudillero is a quaint fishing village

visit. Nevertheless the countryside is green and pleasantly hilly, peppered with smallholdings and reputed to have more cattle to the hectare than anywhere else in Europe. Strangely enough most of them are invisible, spending all their time in byres while the owners traipse backwards and forwards with cartloads of freshly cut grass to keep them happy.

Because Cantabria is the source of so much dairy produce the majority of local dishes include milk and butter, sometimes with the addition of fresh cheese. Fish also appears regularly on menus. *El arroz santanderino* is a rice dish made with milk and salmon, squid is chopped up and fried when it is known as *rabas*, and *la quesada* is a distinctive sweet consisting of fresh cheese, butter and honey which must always be served soon after it is made. The province borrows a number of other recipes from its neighbours and observes some of their religious celebrations. However the coastal resort of San Vicente de la Barquera pulls out all the stops for its Folia ceremony on the Sunday after Easter when leading roles are played by the Picayos group and the Charles V dancers.

Santander, as the capital of Cantabria, has an airport with daily flights to Madrid and Barcelona, a ferry service to Britain, and train services to Madrid, Palencia, Segovia and Valladolid, as well as being on the narrow gauge line that connects Bilbao with Oviedo. There are bus routes in and around the city. Motorists are well served by the N634 which runs along the coast to provide an almost uninterrupted link between the French frontier and La Coruña on the Atlantic seaboard. In addition the N623 heads straight for Burgos 154km (95 miles) to the south, leaving the N611 to make for Palencia where it joins the N620 for the last part of the journey to Valladolid, a total of 250km (155 miles).

Apart from two paradores and a few hotels in Santander and the nearby holiday resorts there are not a great many places to stay in Cantabria, but those that do exist are conveniently placed for visitors who want to explore the less frequented inland areas. On the other hand the coast on either side of Santander has a higher density of campsites than any other stretch along the Bay of Biscay. They range from first class to quite adequate, some remain open throughout the year and at least one, the Camping Caravanning Mogro to the west of the provincial capital, offers bungalows.

Although Santander is by no means a newcomer as far as seaports are concerned it is essentially a modern city overlooking a large bay. The whole place changed completely after it was hit by a tornado in 1941. Giant waves washed over the quays followed by a fire that raged all night, destroying most of the city and leaving 20,000 people homeless, but by some miracle nobody was killed. A totally new town rose like a phoenix out of the ashes, built more or less on the grid system with four or five-storey blocks, gardens fringing the Paseo de Pereda and a specially constructed pleasure boat harbour.

The cathedral was one of the very few buildings to be restored after the disaster. It still has its twelfth-century crypt, now known as the Santisimo Cristo, with a glass floor separating it from the remains of an even older Roman construction. The only other relics from the distant past are housed in the Museo Provincial de Prehistoria y Arqueologia (Prehistory Museum) on the Calle Juan de la Cosa quite close to the pleasure boat harbour. The exhibits include axeheads, decorated bones and other items unearthed mainly in the El Pendo caves and dating from about 8000BC, as well as copies of prehistoric wall paintings. There is also a section devoted to coins and various artifacts discarded by the Romans. The Menéndez y Pelayo Library on the Calle Rubio contains thousands of books collected by the famous philosopher and critic who lived in the Casa Museo just opposite. The Museo Municipal de Bellas Artes (Fine Arts Museum) specialises in contemporary paintings but nevertheless has works by Mengs and Zurbarán in addition to a series of Goya etchings.

El Sardinero, the only suburb to escape the 1941 disaster, is within easy reach of several beautiful sandy beaches on either side of La Magdalena Point where Alfonso XIIIs palace is now part of the International University. This was founded after World War I and runs summer courses for part-time students interested in Spanish culture. Visitors with less academic pretensions are equally well catered for, both in and around the city. Apart from the large casino there are any number of organised entertainments including a festival of drama, music and dancing in August, following the July Festival of Bullfighting held in honour of St James. Facilities are available for all kinds of water sports and there is an 18-hole golf course at **Pedreña** on the far side of the bay. Like Somo, a trifle further on, Pedreña owes much of its popularity to the seemingly endless stretch of golden sands, easily accessible by road but much more quickly by using the motorboats that operate a service every 15 minutes from the city.

Santander has a choice of hotels in every income bracket but even so it is as well to book a room in advance during the high season when everywhere tends to get rather crowded. For anyone in search of a campsite the best option is the Bellavista which remains open 12 months of the year. The Cabo Mayor near the Great Cape lighthouse and the Virgen del Mar have fewer facilities but are equally convenient.

There are several places to visit within easy reach of Santander, the nearest of them being **Muriedas**, 7km (4 miles) away on the road to

Burgos. Here the Casa de Velarde, whose owner made a name for himself during the War of Independence, has been turned into an ethnological museum. The house, standing in its own grounds, is full of homely articles from all over the province as well as items that belonged to Pedro Velarde, some on display in his former bedroom.

It is at this point that the N634 parts company with the Burgos road and swings eastwards round the bay to El Astillero, beyond which there is a turning off to the **Peña Cabarga**. It is a magnificent vantage point with a road and lift to the summit and a monument recalling the seamen of Castile who played their part in opening up the New World. From here onwards a variety of minor roads off the N634 set out purposefully for the beaches round Pedreña and Somo, the Cabo de Ajo and a handful of small but up-and-coming coastal resorts, each with its attendant campsite. The Church of Santa María at **Bareyo**, is extensively restored but still in possession of a font is said to have belonged to the Visigoths. If closed, enquire in the village. The best beaches are at Ris and Noja.

This particular stretch of coast ends at Santoña, an elderly fishing village whose impressive fort was the local French military headquarters during the Peninsular War. A narrow estuary separates **Santoña** from **Laredo**, a thriving holiday playground with enough highrise buildings to accommodate the thousands of visitors who con-

verge on it every year but, for some obscure reason, not nearly enough hotels. The port was established by the Romans after a decisive sea battle and fortified later by Alfonso VIII. The old quarter with its narrow streets has broken out in a rash of bars and discotheques which are extremely popular with visitors but do little to improve the medieval atmosphere. Its centrepiece is the very viewable thirteenth-century church of La Asunción whose matching lecterns in the sacristy were a present from Charles V.

Laredo is only 49km (30 miles) from Santander along the N634 and is linked to Santoña by two minor roads through the marshlands that leave the main highway at Gama and Cicero respectively. Its nearest neighbour, give or take the odd seaside hamlet, is **Castro-Urdiales**, known as *Flavio Briga* in the days of the Romans. It is an extremely picturesque fishing port with a ruined castle built by the Templars, which now doubles as a lighthouse, and a large, business-like Gothic church. The town is mildly industrial but well aware of its potential as a coastal resort. The bay is ideal for boating and sailing, the Hotel Miramar, Avenida de la Playa is right on the beach and there are several different restaurants to choose from. The whole town lights up for the Coso Blanco celebrations on 25 June which include a parade of floats, a battle of flowers and a colourful fireworks display.

Although it is possible to find a

Collecting grass for cattle which are kept in byres

The marina at Santander was designed entirely for pleasure craft

minor route back through the mountains it is easier to return via the N634 to Colindres on the Río Asón and then turn south towards **Limpias**. There is nothing very spectacular about this village except for the crucifix in the local church which is said to have shed miraculous tears in 1919 and has been an object of pilgrimage ever since. On the opposite side of the river a tortuous little road clambers uphill to the sanctuary of La Bien Aparecida whose Virgin has been regarded as the patron saint of Cantabria for nearly 400 years.

Anyone who is more interested in caves than churches will find an interesting collection a few kilometres away at **Ramales de la Victoria** where there is also an excellent restaurant with a handful of rooms for its guests. The Cuevas de Covalanas (Covalanas Caves) are about 3km (2 miles) from the village in a cliff overlooking the Gándara valley and contain both rock formations and a number of wall paintings said to be more than 10,000 years old. A great many more caves have been discovered in the mountains round Puente Viesgo, just off the N623 roughly 30km (19 miles) south of Santander. The limestone hillsides are honeycombed with them but only a few are open to the public. El Castillo, in particular, was liberally decorated with the outlines of animals, strange patterns and the imprint of hands.

Still further south there is a turning off the N623 to the right along the northern shore of the Embalse del Ebro to **Reinosa**, an industrial centre which has every intention of becoming a modern tourist resort. The reservoir, which has replaced a prehistoric lake, is well suited to all kinds of water sports, the large Reserva Nacional de Saja with its woods and streams is almost on the doorstep and winter sports enthusiasts can ski 25km (15½miles) away at Alto Campóo where there are mountain huts in addition to the Corza Blanca Hotel. The nearby Pico de Tres Mares (Three Seas Peak), gets its name from a trio of rivers that find their way by diverse routes to three different seas. The Híjar joins the Ebro en route for the Mediterranean, the Pisuerga is a tributary of the Duero which flows into the Atlantic whereas the Nansa simply follows its own course unaided into the Cantabrian Sea, which is part of the Bay of Biscay. There is a chairlift up to the top that operates during the summer months for anyone who wants to admire the memorable views.

Other places to visit in the vicinity include **Retortillo** with its Romanesque church and exceedingly sparse remains of *Julióbriga*, a city dating from Roman times, and **Cervatos** whose ancient collegiate church is intricately carved with lions and eagles as well as erotic figures that would do justice to a bawdy house. Equally unexpected are the number of dolmens in the area round Suano and a pool shaded by poplars near Fontibre which, according to the signposts, is the source of the Río Ebro.

The quickest way north from Reinosa is along the N611, even allowing for a short pause at **Yermo**. Here the twelfth-century church of Santa Maria pays due attention to St George and the Dragon, investigates the deadly sins with tremendous gusto and provides a home for ancient statues that it inherited from its predecessor. If closed, enquire at the house behind the church. Beyond **Torrelavega**, a very undistinguished town in every respect although it has a selection of hotels, a secondary road leaves the main highway to visit **Santillana del Mar**, almost invariably described as the most beautiful village in Spain.

Time has dealt kindly with Santillana del Mar which, despite its name, is some 3km (2 miles) from the sea. Apart from its newer suburbs the village is really little more than two main streets on either side of a collection of small, cobbled alleys where a number of resident dairy farmers still keep their cows on the ground floor. Santillana is a corruption of Santa Juliana whose remains were brought back from Asia Minor, where she was martyred, and entombed in the twelfth-century Collegiate Church. This is constructed mainly of honey-coloured stone with a beautiful old cloister, some fine stone and wood carvings and an interesting altarpiece that is younger by about 500 years.

The village was an important ecclesiastical centre in the Middle Ages and has retained more than its fair share of ancient towers and medieval mansions. Among the most eye-catching are the Casa de los Hombrones in the Calle de las Lindas, the tall men in question being the two knights who support its coat-of-arms, and the Abbot's House where the insignia of all the most important local families were incorporated into the central crest. The Convent of the Poor Clares on the other side of the village sets aside part of its old building to house the very informative Diocesan Museum with exhibits from all over Cantabria. The Barreda Bracho mansion in a quiet cul-de-sac facing the cobbled Plaza de Ramón Pelayo is now the Parador Gil Blas. The old section is pleasantly atmospheric with oak beams, rafters and tapestries on the walls but it also has an annex built in 1986. There are a few other hotels including the nearby Altamira, which is also a converted mansion, private homes and a first grade campsite that remains open throughout the year.

The famous Cuevas de Altamira (Caves of Altamira) are about 3km (2 miles) from Santillana del Mar. However, because their prehistoric wall paintings have deteriorated alarmingly over the past 100 years or so, viewing is restricted to a bare handful of people on any given day. Anyone who is really interested and is able to plan months in advance should write to the Centro de Investigación de Altamira, Santillana del Mar, Santander for permission to spend a few minutes in what has been called the Sistine Chapel of Quaternary Art. The most ancient drawings are merely black outlines while the later, more sophisticated paintings include natural pigments that may be yellow, red or brown and make use of the uneven rock surface to produce a three dimensional effect. The various animals range from bison and wild boar to deer and can be anything up to 1.6m (5ft) long. The family's living quarters, identified by bones and primitive utensils, were almost invariably at the mouth of the cave but these early home decorators would also work in less accessible places by the light of a fire whose flickering shadows bring scenes like a graphic stampede to life. Because most visitors are only allowed into the museums and an attractive cave full of stalactites a film has been made to give them some idea of the paintings of Altamira, the first to be discovered and so far rivalled only by the Grotte de Lascaux and one or two caves in the Vézère Valley in France.

From Santillana del Mar a pleasant road westwards runs more or less parallel with the coast to **Comillas**, a small fishing port that had all the ingredients necessary to ensure its success as a nineteenth-century holiday resort. Alfonso XII had a palace here which meant that the members of his court were obliged to provide themselves with suitable accommodation for the summer months. In addition to the rather nice old mansions, a large university and two delightful beaches, there is a strange pavilion designed by Antonio Gaudí. El Capricho, as it is called, is an outstandingly colourful building banded with rows of square tiles, each embossed with a yellow and brown sunflower, separated by stylised green foliage. The same flowers, alternating with plain green tiles, smother an extraordinary tower above the main entrance, supported on four squat columns at the top of a trio of stone steps, with his first spiral snail staircase inside. Another innovation was a series of little bells hidden in the sash channels that rang out whenever the windows were opened. After remaining empty for quite a while it is now a restaurant called, quite naturally, El Capricho de Gaudí. It is by no means difficult to find on the Barrio de Sobrellano, near the pink neo-Gothic palace and chapel built by Gaudí's friend Joan Martorell for Antonio Lopez y Lopez, the first Marqués de Comillas.

The most westerly seaside resort in Cantabria is **San Vicente de la Barquera**. It stands well back from the foreshore on a hillside overlooking the somewhat marshy estuary of the Río Escudo with a long causeway across the ria to an extensive beach and the convenient El Rosal campsite nearby. It is essentially a picturesque fishing port with a brace of unremarkable little hotels, several attractive old houses and just a hint of its original

One of several beautiful sandy beaches at El Sardinero

The Ethnology Museum at Muriedas

An ancient gateway leading to Comillas University

Picos de Europa

walls. The pink-tinted church of Nuestra Señora de los Angeles in the medieval quarter dates from the thirteenth century and contains several old tombs, the most viewable of which belonged to the Inquisitor Antonio Corro.

From San Vicente de la Barquera it is only 12km (7 miles) to Unquera on the border with Asturias. Here a secondary road, the N621, keeps company with the Río Deva through Panes and along the incredibly narrow gorge of La Hermida to the village of **Lebeña**. This is admirably sited in a fertile valley surrounded by orchards and vineyards and keeps watch over a fascinating little Mozarabic church, built in the ninth century and tucked away at the foot of a cliff. **Potes** just down the road, is larger and more tourist conscious. It has a bus service, a variety of hotels one of them with a swimming pool, a few shops, a weekly market, some pleasant walks and excursions by jeep up into the hills. It is a charming small town of elderly wooden houses occasionally decorated with coats-of-arms, offset by two medieval towers, the Torre de Orejón de la Lama and the Torre del Infantado now occupied by the Town Hall.

The **Monasterio de Santo Toribio de Liébana**, roughly 3km (2 miles) to the west, was founded in the sixth century and became so important that Turibius, the Bishop of Astorga, presented it with a splinter from the True Cross which he acquired during a visit to Jerusalem. It was placed in a silver gilt crucifix and is kept in a sanctuary off the cloisters.

Beyond the village of **Turieno**, where the local riding stable organises trips up into the mountains, the road wends its way still further into the Picos de Europa. It calls at **Cosgaya**, whose Hotel Del Oso, has facilities for tennis and swimming as well as a useful restaurant, and Espinama where it is possible to hire jeeps and Land Rovers, before coming to an abrupt halt at **Fuente Dé**. This is a short drive from Espinama, the site of the Parador del Río Deva, a large modern building at the foot of a massive grey rock escarpment with a cable car up to the top.

The whole area is ideal for holidaymakers who want to spend their time out in the open air. Serious mountain climbers in search of a challenge will find it on a number of sheer rock faces as well as a pinnacle known as the Naranjo de Bulnes. Long distance hikers are advised to wear heavy boots and carry warm clothes, a waterproof cape and a sleeping bag in addition to food and water if they plan to spend the night in a mountain refuge. It should be possible to buy maps published by the Federación Española de Montañismo from a shop in Potes and get a little extra advice from the Town Hall or the tourist office in the Plaza Jesus de Monasterio. For less ambitious walkers there are tracks which may be relatively easy or fairly difficult, as well as paths designed for people who only want to take a gentle stroll to admire the magnificent wild flowers or indulge in a spot of bird-watching. There are plenty of salmon in the local rivers but would-be fishermen require a licence and are bound by the national rules governing such things as the minimum weight and the size of the catch, which is usually limited to three a day. All the necessary permits and information are obtainable from the National Institute for the Conservation of Nature (ICONA) whose nearest headquarters are at Rodriguez 5, Santander

☎ 942 21 20 52.

Both Cantabria's share of the Picos de Europa and the adjoining Reserva Nacional de Saja are sadly lacking from the motorist's point of view when it comes to finding a short cut suitable for the average family car. However there are one or two scenic roads along the river valleys including an alternative route north to Cabezón de la Sal on the N634 about half way between San Vicente de la Barquera and Torrelavega with a choice between the *autopista* and the N611 for the last 27km (17 miles) to Santander.

ADDITIONAL INFORMATION

PLACES OF INTEREST

ASTURIAS
Cangas de Onis

Cueva del Buxu
2km (1 mile) east
Open: 10am-1pm and 4-8pm
April to September, 10am-1pm
and 3-7pm October to March.
Closed Monday.

Covadonga

Tresoro de la Virgen (Treasure of the Virgen)

In the basilica
Open: 10am-8pm in summer,
10am-6pm in winter.

Gijón

Museo de la Gaita (Museum of the Gaita) and *Bagpipe Museum and Workshop*
Open: 10am-7pm Monday to Friday.

Roman Baths
Beyond fishermen's quarter
Open: 10am-1pm and 4-6pm.
Closed Sundays and holidays.

Luanco

Maritime Museum of Asturias
Opens: 11am-1pm and 5-7pm in
summer.11am-1pm and 4-6pm in
winter.

Oviedo

Archaeological Museum
Convent of San Vicente near
cathedral
Open: 10am-1pm and 4-6pm
weekdays. 11am-1pm Sundays
and holidays. Closed Mondays.

Cámara Santa
In the cathedral
Open: 10am-1pm and 4-7pm
summer, 10am-1pm and 4-6pm
winter.

**Santa Maria del Naranco and
San Miguel de Lillo Churches**
4km (2 miles) north-west
Open: 9.30am-1pm and 3-7pm
summer, 10am-1pm and 3-5pm
winter. Closed Sunday afternoons. If one is locked enquire at
the other.

Santullano Church
On road to Gijón
Usually open: 10am-1pm. If
closed enquire at the presbytery.

Ribadesella

Tito Bustillo Caves
On the outskirts
Guided tours 10am-1pm and
3.30-6.30pm April to September.
Closed Mondays.

CANTABRIA
Muriedas

Ethnology Museum
Casa de Velarde
Open: 11am-1pm and 4-7pm.
Summer, 10am-1pm and 4-6pm
winter. 11am-1pm Sundays and
holidays. Closed Mondays, Good
Friday and Christmas Day.

Ramales de la Victoria

Cuevas de Covalanas
(Covalanas Caves)
Guided tours 10am-1pm and
3.30-7.30pm. Closed Mondays.

Santander

**Museo Municipal de Bellas
Artes** (Fine Arts Museum)
Open: 11am-1pm and 5-8pm.
Closed Sundays and holidays.

Menéndez y Pelayo Library
Calle Rubio
Open: 9am-5.30pm. Closed
Saturdays, Sundays and
holidays.

**Museo Provincial de
Prehistoria y Arqueologia**
(Prehistory Museum)
Calle Juan de la Cosa
Open: 10am-1pm and 5-7pm.
Closed either Sunday or Monday.

Santillana del Mar

Cuevas de Altamira (Altamira
Caves)
View only by writing well in

advance. Museum open:
9am-1pm and 4-6pm summer,
10am-1pm and 4-5pm winter.
Closed Mondays and Sunday
afternoons, 25 December
and 1 January.

Collegiate Church Cloister
Open: 9am-1pm and 4-8pm June
to September, 10am-1pm and
3-7pm October to May. Closed
February and Wednesdays from
mid-September to mid-June.

Diocesan Museum
Convento de Regina Cocli
Open: 10am-1pm and 4-8pm
summer, 9am-1pm and 3-6pm
winter. Closed February and
Wednesdays in winter.

ASTURIAS
Cangas de Onis
Ayuntamiento
Avenida de Covadonga
☎ 985 84 80 05

Gijón
Marqués de San Estebán
☎ 985 34 60 46

Oviedo
Plaza Alfonso II El Castro
☎ 985 21 33 85

Ribadesella
Carret de la Piconera
☎ 985 80 00 38

CANTABRIA
Santander
Plaza Porticada
☎ 942 31 07 08

Santillana del Mar
Plaza Mayor
☎ 942 81 82 51

3
Castilla Y León

Castilla y León is one of the largest autonomous regions in Spain with even more provinces than Anda-lucia. There are nine of them altogether — Ávila, Burgos, León, Palencia, Salamanca, Segovia, Sor-ia, Valladolid and Zamora. La Rioja, as a kind of honorary member, makes it up to ten. It consists mainly of the Duero Basin fringed by mountains where wooded areas and rocky escarpments are at variance with the plains of the meseta, devoted for the most part to growing wheat. There are quite a few lakes, the majority of them created by barrages across the more reliable rivers; pockets of vineyards, mainly in La Rioja; large ranches where fighting bulls are raised and small holdings that are more suitable for sheep.

Much of the area is under-populated, sprinkled with isolated hamlets that have remained almost unchanged since the Middle Ages. On the other hand there are some magnificent cities, steeped in history and richly endowed with ancient buildings, as well as small fortified towns, defiant castles clinging to their respective hilltops and Roman bridges that were utilised by medieval pilgrims on their way to Santiago de Compostela. The region boasts one of the most beautiful cathedrals in Europe and one of the Continent's greatest hotels, the tallest Roman aqueduct in existence anywhere and minute stone dwellings of the type used by the ancient Celts. Despite all this it sees comparatively few tourists and consequently has avoided falling into the highrise, steel and concrete trap that is the hallmark of so many popular holiday playgrounds.

Historically the region can be described as the birthplace of the Spanish nation. It was the first to pit its strength against the Moorish invaders, driving them back by degrees until they were finally defeated at Granada in 1492. One by one the local kingdoms had already amalgamated, usually through judicious marriages. In 1479 Ferdinand became king of Aragon and Isabel finally put an end to her niece Juana's claim to the throne of Castile, leaving the two Catholic Monarchs as the joint rulers of a united Christian country. This did not put an end to its problems, especially as the nation's capital was officially moved down to Madrid by Philip II in 1561. It was plagued by wars, revolts, religious differences and other troubles, culminating in the Civil War which broke out in July 1936. The Nationalist headquarters were established in the region and before long controlled all the northern territories. A provisional government under Francisco Franco was set up in Burgos and it was from La Isla Palace in the city that he announced the official cease-fire on 1 April 1939. The return of the monarchy after his death in 1975 was followed by a new Constitution which created a number of autonomous regions including

Castilla y León, thereby perpetuating its ancient associations within the framework of a modern democracy.

All the provincial capitals are linked by major roads and various forms of public transport. Each has its own comfortable hotels and less up-market establishments as well as a variety of restaurants. The basis of original Castilian cooking is the chickpea, introduced into Spain by the Carthaginians, which found its way into nearly every stew with pieces of meat and cabbage. However, lentils and large white beans called *alubias* are almost as popular, especially in recipes calling for things like pig's ear or ox tail. At the same time the area is known as the Land of Roasts, famous for its lamb and suckling pig which are particularly outstanding in Segovia. Castile also has some excellent fish, mainly trout and cod. The *bacalao al ajo arriero*, called after the mule drivers who introduced it into places as far away as Andalucia, is made from cod and garlic, but other things to try are stuffed partridge and quail. León is noted for its crusted pies and salt pork with turnip tops while Salamanca produces a rice dish called *chanfaina salmantina*, delicious roast kid and a variety of cheeses.

With so much history to its credit Castilla y León has plenty to celebrate. The best known festivals include religious processions such as those marking Holy Week and Corpus Christi, as well as a week of festivities in Segovia in June. However there are any number of less publicised events which attract a great deal of local attention. Wives rule the roost on St Agatha's Day (5 February) in Miranda del Castañar in Salamanca and a week later at Zamarramala in Segovia where the celebrations end with the burning of a rag doll. Soria lights bonfires in San Pedro Manrique on the night of San Juan in June, but for some reason dedicates them to the Virgen de la Peña, and maintains that the men who walk through the embers barefooted are completely unharmed afterwards. Meanwhile the Visigoth cathedral of Baños de Cerrato in Palencia celebrates the occasion with a special mass. On 22 June Anguiano in La Rioja pays tribute to Mary Magdalene with one of the most original demonstrations from Spanish folklore. Colourfully dressed dancers on stilts negotiate the church steps and then race down the hill, only to reverse the whole process on the last Saturday in September. The Assumption is marked by an open-air mystery play at La Alberca in Salamanca on 16 August, followed by traditional dancing on 8 September in Miranda del Castañar, Saldaña in Palencia and Alaejos in Valladolid. Bulls play an important role in a number of celebrations throughout the year. The most ancient is thought to be bull running through Cuéllar in Segovia on the last Sunday in August but there are similar events in Ciudad Rodrigo at Carnival time, cross country displays at Fuentesaúco in Zamora on 2 July and Soria's ancient Feast of San Miguel bull festival at Medinaceli on the nearest Saturday to the 13 November.

Castilla y León does not really make the running where souvenirs are concerned. The most obvious are the sweet Yemas de Santa Teresa from Ávila, caramels from Logroño, La Rioja wines and local jewellery in Salamanca. Less obvious are woollen blankets in Ávila, pottery and embroidery from the market in La Alberca and a variety of strictly practical items turned out by resident craftsmen in some of the larger villages. Typical souvenir shops have opened in most provincial capitals and there are plenty of markets

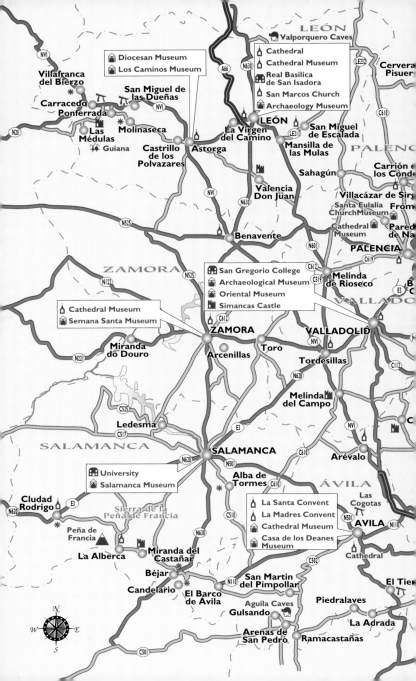

Castilla y León

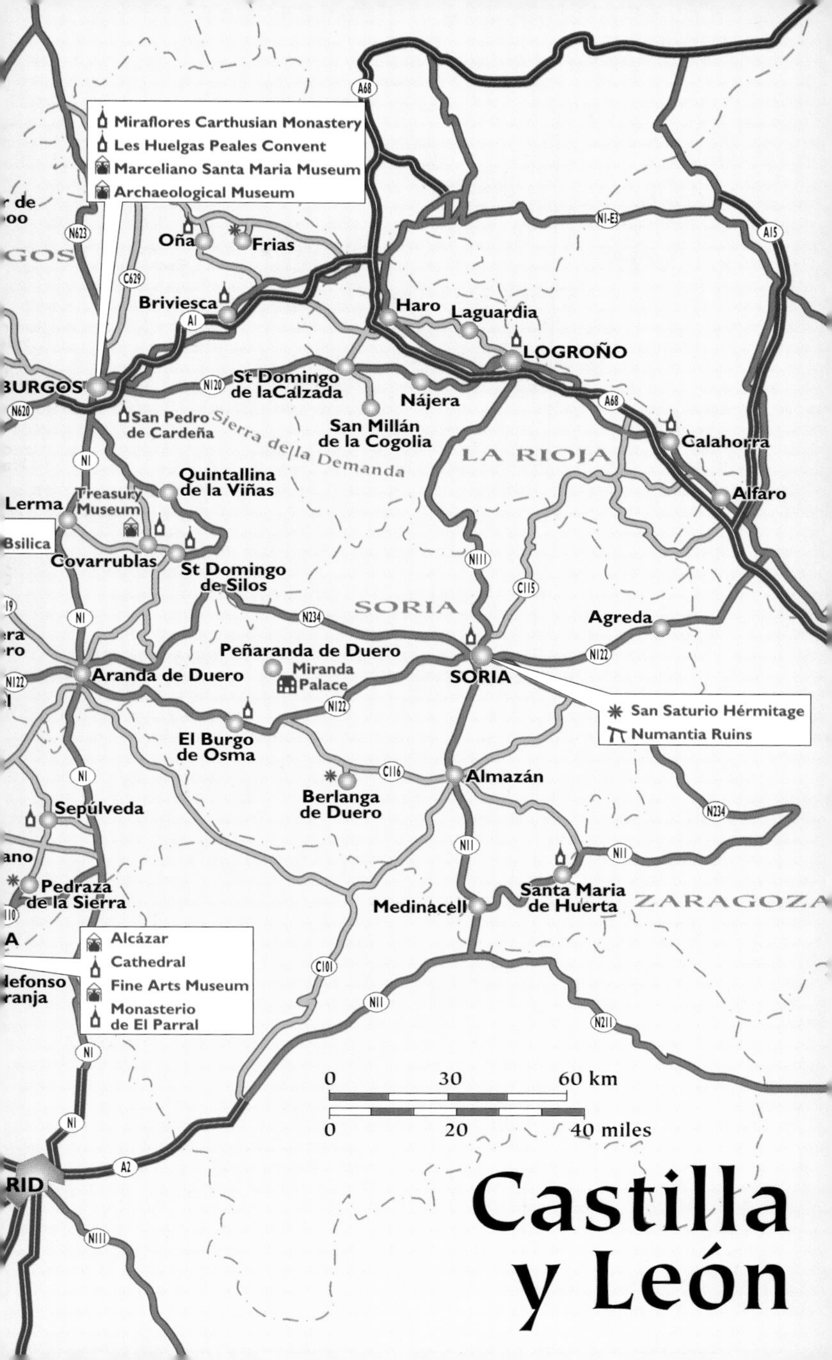

Miraflores Carthusian Monastery
Les Huelgas Peales Convent
Marceliano Santa Maria Museum
Archaeological Museum
A68
N1-E3
A15
N623
C629
A1
N120
N620
N1
N111
C115
N234
N122
C116
N11
C101
N211
A2
Oña
Frias
Briviesca
Haro
Laguardia
LOGROÑO
BURGOS
St Domingo de laCalzada
Nájera
San Pedro de Cardeña
Sierra della Demanda
San Millán de la Cogolia
LA RIOJA
Calahorra
Alfaro
Quintallina de la Viñas
Lerma
Treasury Museum
Bsilica
Covarrublas
St Domingo de Silos
SORIA
Agreda
Peñaranda de Duero
Miranda Palace
Aranda de Duero
SORIA
San Saturio Hérmitage
Numantia Ruins
El Burgo de Osma
Almazán
Berlanga de Duero
Sepúlveda
Pedraza de la Sierra
Medinacell
Santa Maria de Huerta
ZARAGOZA
Alcázar
Cathedral
Fine Arts Museum
Monasterio de El Parral
0 30 60 km
0 20 40 miles

supplying everything necessary for people staying on one of the campsites, the majority of which are within easy shopping distance of the adjacent towns.

ÁVILA

The province of Ávila is a small, somewhat under-populated region in the south of Castilla y León between Madrid and Salamanca. The scenery, for the most part, is quite pleasant, its undulating hills breaking up here and there into rocky outcrops which may sometimes be mistaken for the ruins of an ancient fortress. The road to Segovia, to the north-east, has little to recommend it whereas the Sierra de Gredos in the south definitely has its moments. These include lakes and grottoes, small villages, mountain goats, trout streams and some well-tended orchards in the valleys. The best time to explore is in the spring because the winters can be harsh with high winds, rain and snow that barely has time to melt before the onset of what is frequently an uncomfortably hot summer.

Ávila city is the highest provincial capital in Spain, the site of a Roman outpost and later the scene of frequent battles between the Christians and the Moors. After Toledo had been reconquered in 1085 Alfonso VI consolidated his position by building a second line of defence south of the Río Duero. As well as other fortifications this entailed the creation of massive ramparts on the old Roman foundations at Ávila. They are some 3m (10ft) wide and an average of 10m (33ft) high, with battlements, towers and eight fortified gateways spaced out at intervals over a distance of some 2½km (1½ miles). As the result of a little assistance in the fourteenth century they have survived intact, enclosing one of the most conscientiously unrestored medieval towns in the country. When Charles V transferred his court to Toledo the local nobility lost no time in joining him leaving Ávila to begin its long period of hibernation which lasted well into the twentieth century.

The only other event of any moment in Ávila was the birth of Teresa de Cepeda y Ahumada in 1515. At the age of 18 she became a Carmelite nun in the Convent of La Encarnación, living there peacefully for nearly 25 years. One day on the staircase she had a vision during which an angel pierced her heart with a burning arrow. Thereafter she became even more devout, reintroducing rules of the Order which had been allowed to lapse, writing, travelling extensively, founding new convents and carrying on a long correspondence with St John of the Cross. She was canonised 40 years after her death in 1582 and made a Doctor of the Church by Pope John in 1970.

It is impossible to move very far in the city without being reminded of Santa Teresa. Streets, squares, hotels, cafés and even arches are named after her. A convent was built to replace the house where she was born and the nuns still turn out quantities of sugared egg yolks called *Yemas de Santa Teresa* which can be bought from almost any shop in the neighbourhood.

One of the first places to visit in the old town is the cathedral, part church and part fortress, with an apse that protrudes out through the ramparts on to the Calle San Segundo. The exterior is plain and businesslike, totally at variance with all the later decorations inside. These range from statues, wrought-iron pulpits and sculptured panels to the alabaster tomb of Cardinal Alonso de Madrigal, a theologian who was Bishop of Ávila in the fifteenth century. On the far side of the sacristy the museum contains a variety of items including a portrait by El Greco and a giant monstrance fashioned by Juan de Arfe in 1571.

The chapel of La Santa Convent was built in the seventeenth century on the site of the bedroom where Santa Teresa was born. It is aggressively Baroque, highly commercialised and usually crowded with sightseers inspecting the various relics, among them her small whip and an amputated finger. It was common practice in those days to dismember the bodies of saints and distribute the pieces among various religious centres where they were sometimes credited with supernatural powers. The convent is situated on the Plaza La Santa, near the south gateway, within easy strolling distance of several ancient mansions. The most eye-catching are the nearby Nuñez Vela Palace, the Guzmán Tower on the Plaza General Mola and the Polentinos Palace which now serves as a barracks.

There are just as many places to visit outside the walls starting, perhaps, with the large San Vicente Basilica near the gateway leading to the Avenida de Portugal. This marks the site where St Vincent and his sisters Sabina and Cristeta are alleged to have been murdered at the time of Diocletian. However other accounts maintain that the saint was martyred in Valencia. At all events his graphically carved tomb under the lantern tower tells the whole tragic story. A rock in the crypt is said to have been the place where the saint and his sisters died and where their bodies were hidden during the Moorish occupation. It also contains an ancient icon known as Nuestra Señora de la Soterana or Our Lady of the Underground. It was while she was praying down in the chapel that Santa Teresa had another vision in which she was told to remove her shoes. The sandals that she wore became the hallmark of her new order of barefoot Carmelites.

A few blocks away, on the Plaza de Italia, the sixteenth-century Casa de los Deanes is the home of a comprehensive regional museum. The exhibits include a number of Celtic *verracos*. These stone animals, usually bulls or bears, marked the graves of warriors and leading members of the community, even under the Romans. Other

A street in Ávila

Throughout Spain houses are adorned with flowers

items on display range from archaeological discoveries to ceramics from Valencia and Spanish furniture to traditional costumes and examples of local crafts. In addition the Fine Arts Museum on the first floor has a very viewable collection of medieval pictures.

Further along the ramparts, beyond the protruding apse of the cathedral, the delightful thirteenth-century Church of San Pedro has some fine stained glass but nothing else of any real consequence. It looks out over the arcaded Plaza Santa Teresa at the Puerta de Alcázar, the main entrance to the walled city. In the opposite direction, along the Avenida del Alférez Provisional, the Dominican Monastery of Santo Tomás was founded in the fifteenth century. At various times it was the site of a university, provided an important centre for the Inquisition and was used as a summer residence by Ferdinand and Isabel. Their only son, Don Juan, who died when he was 19, is buried in the church. His expertly carved tomb is the work of Domenico Francelli who also created the mausoleum for the Catholic Monarchs in the Capilla Real in Granada. The three cloisters are complimentary. The first is simple and was reserved for novices, the Silent Cloister beyond is small and decorative whereas the Royal Cloister is larger but surprisingly understated. Stairs lead up from the Silent Cloister to the choral gallery which is worth seeing for its Gothic stalls whose carvings owe a great deal to the Moors. There are also steps up to the gallery of the high altar where it is possible to take a closer look at the superb St Thomas Aquinas retable, the work of Alonso Berruguete who studied in Italy with Michelangelo.

Another place of interest is the little Hermitage of San Segundo, poised between the ramparts, the Avenida de Madrid and the Río Adaja. It is believed to contain the remains of St Secundus, a disciple of St Peter, who was the first Bishop of Ávila. Visitors who want to follow more closely in the steps of Santa Teresa have a longish walk ahead of them. La Encarnación Convent, where she spent her first years as a nun, is on the Calle de la Encarnación, which leads off the Avenida de Madrid to the north. Although it has its fair share of religious memories most people gravitate towards the staircase where she had her first vision. The Convent of San José, also known as the Convento de las Madres, is on the Calle del Duque de Alba, outside the walls beyond the Plaza de Italia. It was founded by Santa Teresa in 1562, the forerunner of many similar establishments created during her lifetime. Apart from the tombs in the Guillamas Chapel there is a small museum with some predictably ghoulish relics and a replica of the simple room where she did a great deal of her writing.

Visitors to Ávila should have no problems as far as travelling is concerned. There are regular trains and buses to and from Madrid the journey in either case lasting about

2 hours. The city also has rail links with Salamanca, Santander and Burgos, in addition to bus services to Segovia and Salamanca. Motorists have a choice between the N110 which passes through on its way to Segovia 67km (42 miles) to the north-east, the N501 from Salamanca 98km (61 miles) away, the nearby N601 to Valladolid and the N403 to Toledo. There are several different road links with Madrid, in the region of 110km (70 miles) to the south-east. The quickest is obviously the A6 autopista or the N601 which cross-es the N110 at Villacastin but the A505 is more interesting, especially as it calls at El Escorial en route.

There is plenty of evidence that the countryside round Ávila was well populated in prehistoric times. **Las Cogotas**, somewhat off the beaten track near the village of Cardeñosa about 6km (4 miles) to the north, was originally a Celtic settlement although little has survived the passage of more than 2,000 years. Time has been much kinder to **Arévalo**, 55km (34 miles) due north of Ávila, which has not changed dramatically since Isabel the Catholic was a girl. She was born at Madrigal de las Altas Torres 24km (15 miles) away but spent much of her childhood in the fortress which still dominates the town. Among its main attractions are the beautifully preserved Plaza de la Villa, the Church of Santa Maria and the Alcocer Arch leading to the picturesque Plaza Real.

Travellers who enjoy being out of doors and have the necessary time to spare will find even more places to visit in the south of the province. **El Tiemblo**, roughly 50km (31 miles) down the N403 on the way to Toledo, weighs in with a selection of Celtic *verracos*, at a site called Los Toros de Guisando, and the elongated Embalse de Burguillo which is a good place for sailing. Meanwhile a minor road past Los Toros de Guisando ignores San Martin de Valdeiglesias, which has little to offer apart from a small restaurant, and joins the C501 for a trip into the Sierra de Gredos.

This often scenic route to the west calls at a number of hamlets like **La Adrada** with its modest ruins, the attractive hill village of **Piedralaves** and **Ramacastañas** where the main attractions are the nearby Cuevas del Aguila. Only one of the caves is open to the public but it is large and colourful with guided tours that can be expected to last for more than half an hour. **Arenas de San Pedro**, in the heart of a pine forest, is a pretty little town clustered round a small castle. It is a popular centre with holidaymakers who plan to spend their time walking or climbing in the mountains, fishing for trout, visiting nearby lakes and villages or shooting in the Coto Nacional Park during the hunting season. Visitors bringing tents or caravans with them can choose between the Los Galayos campsite at **Guisando**, an old hill village on the scenic but minor route to the west, and the

Prados Abiertos site at Mombeltrán on the C502 further north. Both are open throughout the year.

The C502 follows the zig-zag course of the old Roman road across the sierra through Mombeltrán with its ancient castle up to the Puerto de Pico, a mountain pass with a view across to the Tiétar valley, after which the scenery becomes rather more severe. A short way along the road a turning off to the left (the C500) calls at **San Martin del Pimpollar**, where there is a more basic campsite, before pausing at the Parador de Gredos. It was opened in 1928, the first of what soon became a countrywide chain of comfortable state-run hotels, and offers its guests a view from the terrace as well as facilities for tennis and swimming.

The road presses on beyond the parador to **El Barco de Ávila**, which also has its old castle and is conveniently placed on the N110 for the return trip to Ávila, a distance of about 80km (50 miles).

BURGOS

Burgos is one of the larger provinces of Castilla y León but seems to get fewer compliments than many of its neighbours and considerably less attention than it deserves. This could well be due in part to the fact that Franco had his headquarters here during the Civil War, which certainly did not endear it to any Republican supporters, either at home or overseas.

More than a quarter of a century later it became synonymous with the infamous trial of a group of Basque Nationalists which raised such an international outcry that the death sentences were never carried out. On the other hand the region has always been somewhat aggressive, sure of its place in the scheme of things and willing to back its convictions with force if necessary.

To all intents and purposes the city of **Burgos** dates from the end of the ninth century when Diego Porcelos built a castle on the Río Arlanzón as a first step towards ousting the Moors from the remainder of the country. The area allied itself to the newly-formed Christian kingdom of León and then thought better of it. Fernán González, one of the local nobility, proclaimed himself Count of Castile and the head of an independent region with Burgos as its capital. This was a shrewd move. Less than 100 years later, in 1037, one of his descendants decided to call himself King Fernando I and promptly married the heiress to the kingdom of León. Once the northern states had been unified they redoubled their efforts to dislodge the Moors and 50 years later Alfonso VI was able to move his court down to Toledo, although Burgos retained its status as an alternative capital.

Everything changed with the reconquest of Granada in 1492. Its leading position was assumed by Valladolid until Madrid was declared the official capital by Philip

II in 1561, thereby leaving Burgos free to devote all its energies to art and commerce instead of politics and war. Despite this the city emerged as an important French stronghold during the War of Succession when it successfully withstood a determined attack by Wellington in 1812. Napoleon's brother, who had been manoeuvred on to the Spanish throne as Joseph I, showed his appreciation by blow-

The Fuegos artificialea display illuminates the sky above Burgos City

ing up the city when his army was forced to retreat in June of the following year.

A great many buildings were damaged beyond repair in the course of the Peninsular War but somehow the cathedral managed to survive. It is one of the largest and finest in Spain, sharing top honours with León, Sevilla and Toledo, but is so crammed with artistic delights of one kind or another that it gives the impression of being more of an ecclesiastical museum. The structure itself was built on different levels between the thirteenth and fifteenth centuries, starting with the nave whose cornerstone was laid by Ferdinand III, assisted by Maurice the Englishman in his capacity as Bishop of Burgos. The first addition was the cloister with an upper gallery that is level with the main pavement, allowing plenty of scope for steps and small enclosed areas. This was followed by the Constable's Chapel, the spires and a large proportion of the interior decoration.

A preliminary walk round the cathedral is full of interest, ranging from the Puerta Alta de la Coroneria dating from 1257 and the adjoining Pellejeria portal, past the ornate west façade with its balustrades and rather unexpected Stars of David, to the southern entrance, or El Sarmental portal. This doorway, where the four Evangelists are shown busily working on their manuscripts, leads to the transept where El Cid and his wife Jimena were reburied below the beautiful lantern in 1921. Their unobtrusive funeral stone is completely overshadowed by the tomb of Bishop Maurice whose effigy is made of wood encased in copper and enamel. The choirstalls of carved walnut are fascinating, combining biblical scenes with bacchanalian type merrymaking. Beyond the huge supporting columns, the famous Golden Staircase is shaped like a star, emphasised by its magnificent bannisters.

Each chapel has its own highly individual contents and distinctive forms of ornamentation. One of the most unusual is the Capilla del Santo Cristo where the figure of Christ on the cross is covered in buffalo hide to resemble human flesh, an illusion emphasised by the addition of real hair and fingernails. It is situated near the west door, almost opposite a sixteenth-century mechanical clock, known as the flycatcher because an open-mouthed devil is involved in striking the hours. Various other bishops and leading personalities are also buried in the cathedral.

The cloister is rather over-populated with statues, the most memorable of them being Christ at the Column by Diego de Siloé in the sacristy. The chapterhouse boasts a Mudejar ceiling inlaid with ivory and a variety of other treasures including a set of medieval Brussels tapestries. The church plate, together with some ancient manuscripts and precious documents, including El Cid's marriage contract, are lodged for safekeeping in

St Catherine's Chapel. It takes the better part of an hour to wander round the cathedral but even longer to examine everything properly. Extra time is needed to visit the little church of San Nicolas de Bari, more or less opposite. The things to look for, apart from the Virgin and her escort of angels, are various episodes in the life of St Nicholas, especially his voyage to Alexandria and his preoccupation with saving children from the gaping cauldron, as well as an unusual angle on the Last Supper.

The French made a thorough job of destroying Burgos Castle which is now nothing more than a collection of ruins set a little apart from the city beyond the Arco de San Esteban. It was here that England's Edward I married Eleanor of Castile. The ceremony took place some 200 years after El Cid and his wife, the redoubtable Jimena, celebrated their wedding in the palace before he fell foul of her cousin, Alfonso VI, and was banished from the kingdom. His ancestral home has completely disappeared but there is a characteristic statue of him on horseback between San Pablo Bridge and the Plaza Muguel Primo de Rivièra. However this is not the main entrance to the old city which is distinguished by the amazingly white and much decorated Arco de Santa Maria slightly further down the river. It was once part of the medieval walls but during the sixteenth century took on the guise of portrait gallery for the rich and famous. Charles V is very much in evidence along with El Cid, Diego Porcelos, a pair of tenth-century judges and Count Fernán González, the far-sighted Count of Castile. Anyone strolling through the massive arch into the Plaza del Rey San Fernando would be wise to keep an eye open for the municipal water cart that sprays the cobble stones whether or not there are sightseers within range.

The Casa del Cordón on the Calle Santander, which is one of the main shopping streets, is so called because of the rope motif inspired by St Francis' girdle carved over the door. The palace was designed as the official residence of the Constables of Castile and was associated in more than one respect with the Catholic Monarchs.

Burgos has two museums, neither of them very conveniently placed. The Archaeological Museum across the river in the attractive Casa de Miranda is largely concerned with religious matters ranging from the tomb of Juan de Padilla to decorative altarpieces. On the other hand the Marceliano Santa Maria Museum, slightly out on a limb in the elderly Monasterio de San Juan, takes its name from a local painter who died in 1952. Well over a hundred of his works are on display in the remains of the building that was once part of the Benedictine Order. The city is, in fact, a great place for monasteries, including two splendid examples on the outskirts — Las Huelgas Reales Convent a mile or so to the west on the N620 and the Cartuja de Miraflores, marginally further away to the east.

In its early days Las Huelgas was the summer residence of the kings of Castile but in 1187 Queen Eleanor, the daughter of Henry II of England, persuaded her husband to turn it into a very superior nunnery. The inmates were all members of noble families whose abbess soon became the most influential woman in the kingdom apart from the queen herself. The convent owned large quantities of land and several towns and villages besides accumulating a very respectable fortune. Part of this was spent on entertaining royal visitors, some of whom were so impressed that they decided to be buried in the church. Unfortunately most of the tombs were desecrated by the French, who never missed an opportunity to search for hidden treasure, but there is still plenty left to admire.

The iron and gilt pulpit is a case in point, not so much for its artistic qualities but because it was designed to revolve so that the sermon could be addressed to either the choir or the congregation, who were separated by a screen. In addition to a variety of tapestries and the statues of Alfonse VIII and Queen Eleanor in the body of the church, the Gothic cloister still has the remains of what must have been a beautiful Mudejar ceiling. The chapterhouse contains the silken flap of an Arab tent, captured by Alfonso at the battle of Las Navas de Tolosa in 1212, and Don Juan's banner from the battle of Lepanto in 1571. It was the venue chosen by Franco for the first meeting of his provisional government at which members were obliged to swear an oath of loyalty to the party and their future head of state.

The earlier Romanesque cloister was part of the original palace with its Moorish overtones and a legendary statue of St James in the private chapel. This was specially constructed so that his sword arm would move and it is said that Fernando III was the first monarch to be dubbed a Knight of the Order of Santiago by the effigy, a privilege thereafter reserved for princes of the blood. The Museo de Ricas Telas is equally well known for its collection of priceless fabrics, medieval court dress and regalia, recovered in part from the tomb of the Infante Fernando de la Cerda, the son of Alfonso X, which, for some reason, was overlooked by the French. These days there are less than fifty nuns living in the convent who pay their way by taking in washing, selling pastries and providing accommodation for eight female guests in their specially updated hospice. So many women, including visitors from America, are anxious to experience life in Las Huelgas that no one can book in for more than a week. This can be done by writing to the Hermana Hospedera or contacting her on the convent's telephone.

The Miraflores Carthusian Monastery, surrounded by its own park, makes no such provision for guests but visitors are welcome to look round the impressive Abbey

Church. It was founded as a pantheon for Juan II and Isabel of Portugal but was still under construction when the king died in 1474. The work was completed by their daughter, Isabel the Catholic, who commissioned Gil de Siloé to create the exuberantly sculptured mausoleum in the centre of the apse. It takes the form of an eight pointed star with canopies and pinnacles, cherubs and coats-of-arms, all of which seem to give Juan II food for thought while his wife takes refuge in a book. The tomb of the Infante Don Alfonso, whose early death left the path to the throne clear for his sister Isabel, occupies a recess in the north wall. The young prince is shown as attractive, devout and, presumably, fond of birds and animals. Elsewhere in the church there are some attractive paintings and a statue of St Bruno, the choirstalls are expertly carved and the high altar glistens with gold, reputedly a present from Columbus on his second return from the New World.

Also in the vicinity is the Hospital del Rey, which Alfonso VIII built for ordinary pilgrims, while 10km (6 miles) to the south the Monasterio San Pedro de Cardeña was where El Cid left his family when, as an exile, he offered his services to the Moorish king of Zaragoza. Initially he and his wife were buried here but after the tombs had been broken into by French troops their bones were recovered and transferred to Burgos cathedral. The monastery sets aside about thirty rooms for guests — one of the few to provide accommodation for both men and women as well as married couples. This allows more than enough time to inspect the original tombs, the Cloister of Martyres where a great many monks were beheaded during a Moorish raid in the tenth century, and the grave of El Cid's horse Babieca just outside the gate.

Visitors who would prefer something more luxurious can retrace their steps and book in at the Landa Palace on the outskirts of Burgos some 4km (2 miles) down the road to Madrid. A generation or so ago Jesús Landa opened what he described as an inn, bought a semi-ruined medieval tower and transferred it to the site as the first step towards creating a first class hotel with an exceptional restaurant. He and his wife struck up a firm friendship with Michel Guerard, whose similar establishment at Eugenie-les-Bains in south-west France is justly famous throughout that country. With his help Landa's dream soon became a reality and after his death a few years ago continued to prosper in the hands of his daughter and her husband Santiago Alameda. The king of Spain's suite has gold fittings in the bathroom and a bed that belonged to Isabel II, the vaulted Castilian diningroom is lit by a three-tier chandelier and serves both French and Spanish dishes, while anyone using the indoor pool can swim through an entrance to the vault at one end into its open-air counterpart surrounded by immaculate lawns.

Burgos cathedral is one of the largest in Spain

The cluttered gardens of the college at Covarrubias

Naturally such attractions do not come cheaply so anyone who has to watch their pesetas would find a comfortable alternative in the Hotel Condestable, Vitoria 8 just off the Plaza Miguel Primo de Rivera, or the even less up-market Norte y Londres on the Plaza Alonso Martinez. This has the advantage of being within easy shopping distance of the Calle Santander and a short walk from the Plaza José Antonio, the attractive main square which is the setting for most official celebrations. One particularly outstanding religious festival in Burgos is Corpus Christi, introduced into Spain during the fourteenth century. Pope John XXII had decreed that the Holy Sacrament should in future be carried in solomn procession on a specified day after Whitsun. As a result the monstrance on its elaborate cart is escorted through the streets to the cathedral by members of the clergy, government officials, soldiers in full-dress uniform and schoolchildren. After the service boys dressed as medieval pages, enormous figures of the Catholic Monarchs and other gigantes of various descriptions introduce a lighter note which is the signal for traditional songs and dances and general merriment.

The countryside round Burgos has little to recommend it. The high plateau can be unpleasantly windy and is rather tedious in places, although there are some compensations. The N620 to Valladolid, 125km (77½ miles) away, can be quite spectacular when the extensive fields of sunflowers on either side of the road are in full bloom. In the opposite direction the N120 is nicely wooded for part of its 144km (89 mile) run to Logroño and there are a number of places to visit within striking distance of the *autopista*, the quickest route northeastwards to Bilbao, a distance of 156km (97 miles). The same applies to the N1 which heads straight for Madrid 239km (148 miles) to the south. Getting to and from Burgos by train or bus is equally simple. The city is on the main line linking Madrid with Irún on the French frontier south of Biarritz and has regular connections with other provincial capitals in Castilla y León as well as with Barcelona, Córdoba and Málaga on the Costa del Sol. It is also in daily contact by bus with Madrid, Santander and San Sebastián in addition to many other towns throughout the region.

There is nothing much to see in Burgos province to the west of the provincial capital nor, for that matter, between the city and **Briviesca**, 42km (26 miles) along the road to Vitoria Gasteiz in the Basque country. This is a quiet, modest town on the banks of the Río Oca, only really worth visiting in order to see the extraordinary Baroque altarpiece in the Santa Clara chapel. For anyone anxious to deviate from the beaten track a moderately scenic road calls at one or two entirely forgettable villages on its way to **Oña**. Here the main attraction is the St Saviour Monastery church, founded in 1011 by Count Sancho of Castile. Several members of his family are buried in the chancel but their tombs and the fifteenth-century cloister are the only survivors from its early days. Further along the road a turning off to the right crosses the Río Ebro, providing a cross-country route to Bilbao and an opportunity to inspect the attractive Losa valley and a rather odd church above the village of San Pantaleón de Losa. It was built about 800 years ago and decorated with unidentifiable heads and legs while the figure of a man carrying what appears to be a fishing net replaces a pillar at the west door.

As there are very few roads in this area, and only one rather inconvenient minor connection with Miranda de Ebro via the N625, the majority of motorists prefer to ignore the deviation at Briviesca in favour of the much more direct N1, or even the *autopista*. The town itself is not particularly endearing and has nothing to offer in the way of tourist attractions. On the other hand the Hotel Tudanca on the main road is modern and quite comfortable with a restaurant, a snack bar, ample parking and an adjoining shop that sells items like wine, cured hams and chocolates in addition to ceramics and souvenirs. The hotel also provides a base from which to visit the large Sobrón Dam and the extremely picturesque village of **Frias** further up the river. It is a delightful jumble of narrow, cobbled streets, some half-timbered houses and others precariously balanced above a cliff face, bearing a striking resem-

blance to the famous hanging houses of Cuenca. There is also a medieval bridge, an ancient gateway and an elderly castle with a commanding view down the valley.

There is even more to see and explore in the south of the province, especially for anyone heading towards Soria on the N234. Archaeologists in particular would be interested in the ancient hermitage associated with **Quintanilla de las Viñas**, a little over 3km (2 miles) off the main highway, but they would also have to be reasonably energetic. It was apparently built by the Visigoths and is beautifully carved both inside and out, skillfully indicating their belief in Christianity without offending the pagan gods. Before setting out it is necessary to collect the key from a house marked Turismo in the village, where a guide is also available if necessary.

Some 24km (15 miles) further down the N234 there is a turning off to **Santo Domingo de Silos** whose isolated Benedictine monastery is said to date in part from the eighth century. Other sources maintain that it was founded by Fernán González in AD919. At all events the original structure was destroyed by Al Mansur, who went on to capture León and Pamplona and remove the bells from Santiago de Compostela which he promptly transferred to the mosque at Córdoba. A monk called Dominic supervised the rebuilding of the monastery which then provided food and shelter for pilgrims until it was deserted in 1835. Less than 50 years later a group of Benedictine monks from Poitou moved in and cleaned up the buildings which include an outstanding Romanesque cloister, an eighteenth-century church and a special wing containing predictably spartan accommodation for roughly twenty male visitors.

People are encouraged to join any of the conducted tours during which the monk in charge draws their attention to all the finer points in the church and cloister. The former is impressive but not spectacular except during Mass, celebrated exactly as it was in the Middle Ages and especially memorable for the ethereal quality of the Gregorian chants. The cloister is a sculptor's delight, a contrast in styles and subjects depicting plants, mythical creatures, birds and animals, many engaged in anything from courtship dances to ferocious battles. Other pillars draw on the New Testament for inspiration, especially the Resurrection, Christ's meeting with Doubting Thomas, the Ascension and Pentecost.

Opening off the cloister are the old pharmacy and a small museum containing among its ancient treasures a valuable Mozarabic manuscript and a chalice that belonged to St Dominic who is buried in the north gallery. The chapterhouse has nothing out of the ordinary to offer but the adjacent Virgin's Door that was once part of the old monastery church is worth a second glance.

St Benedict would undoubtedly approve of the arrangements made for guests, about 2,000 of whom spend some time at the monastery in the course of a year. Their cells have what has been described as an intermittent supply of hot water; breakfast is at 9.45am, dinner is served in the refectory at 8.30pm, half an hour before the main gates are locked for the night, and everybody goes to bed at 10pm.

During the day the monks work on the farm, leaving the visitors to their own devices. Some spend the time resting or studying while others take the opportunity to explore the countryside all round. There are enough ruined castles and fortified villages to keep them fully occupied in addition to the Yecla Gorges 5km (3 miles) away. This is a rather extravagant title for a narrow but abnormally deep cleft in the limestone, created by a particularly energetic little rivulet that still froths and tumbles far below. The monastery is not an hotel and nor does it offer travellers a bed for the night. However the Tres Coronas de Silos in the Plaza Mayor provides an alternative for anyone who is ineligible or feels disinclined to occupy a cell.

The Hotel Arlanza, Plaza de Doña Urraca in **Covarrubias** is another option, also housed in an ancient mansion, the only drawback being that it closes during the winter months. The village is situated on the banks of the Río Arlanza, surrounded by woods and vineyards and within easy driving distance of both the monastery and the N234. It still has some of its old ramparts, a tower that vaguely calls to mind the famous Pyramid of the Sun in Mexico and a fourteenth-century church where Fernán González and his wife are buried. If the church is closed, enquire at the house by the entrance. There are well over a dozen other medieval tombs as well as an interesting collection of paintings in the Treasury Museum.

Just as Covarrubias is associated with Fernán González so **Lerma**, 23km (14 miles) to the west on the N1, is inevitably linked with the Duke of Lerma, a court favourite in the reign of Philip III. He was probably no worse than any of the other royal advisers at that time who spent money like water. At least part of his illgotten gains were used to beautify the town before he was ousted by his son, the Duke of Uceda. Beyond a fortified gateway in the ramparts narrow streets lined with antiquated houses converge on one or other of the abnormally large squares. It has no outstanding buildings or fascinating little churches, and even the ducal palace looks uninviting, to say the least of it, but the town is an interesting example of urban planning in the late sixteenth century.

South of Lerma on the N1 to Madrid, **Aranda de Duero** has grown up at the intersection of the N1 and the N122 which links Valladolid with Soria, Zaragoza and the Mediterranean. This makes it a convenient stopping place for motorists heading in almost any direction.

Apart from one or two hotels in the town there are places to spend the night on each of the four main roads. One obvious choice would be the Motel Tudanca, 6½ km (4 miles) to the south which has both a restaurant and a cafeteria. In addition there is a first class, although not luxurious, campsite called the Costaján, to date the only one of this calibre in Burgos province apart from the Fuentes Blancas on the outskirts of the provincial capital.

As far as local attractions are concerned there is little of real moment except the Church of Santa Maria and the nearby village of **Peñaranda de Duero**. This is an attractive little place on a tributary of the Río Duero, known principally for its Palacio de los Miranda (Miranda Palace) half-timbered houses and fifteenth-century pillory, all concentrated on the Plaza Mayor. The palace alone is worth a visit, mainly on account of its typical Renaissance façade, grand staircase, decorative ceilings and superior fireplaces. Burgos is 83km (51 miles) away.

LEÓN

León, one of the most historic regions of Old Castile, is a fairly large province, bordered by Galicia and Asturias, as well as by Palencia and Zamora separated by a fistful of Valladolid. Part of it was once a huge lake surrounded by mountains but this disappeared soon after the dinosaurs, leaving the way clear for an influx of settlers during the Bronze Age. Very few Celtic remains have been discovered but there is plenty of evidence of Roman occupation, especially in El Bierzo where they changed the whole atmosphere and colour of the landscape in their search for alluvial gold. It is believed that other foreigners settled here from time to time, possibly Phoenicians who were brought in as slaves and Berbers left behind when the Moors were driven out. However it was the Knights Templar who built castles and fortifications during the Middle Ages while pilgrims created the well-worn Universal Route to Santiago de Compostela, now replaced by the N120 and the NVI.

Part of León is typical meseta country but there are also mountainous areas, woods full of trees such as chestnut, oak, beech and walnut, meadows, orchards and vineyards. Barrages across some rivers have created large lakes which have not so far been turned into holiday playgrounds and coachloads of tourists are virtually unknown apart from those rushing through to more widely publicised resorts. This leaves much of the province free for trout fishermen and people who enjoy walking, visiting nature reserves or discovering half-forgotten communities where, until quite recently, the villagers lived in houses that owed more to the ancient Celts than to anybody else. Small mining towns have grown up here and there, in sharp contrast to the ancient monasteries that have survived at intervals along the pilgrim route. The most magnificent of these has been turned into a parador, with an archaeological museum attached, in León. The best times to visit are the spring and the autumn.

The city of **León** has been cosmopolitan since its very early days when the Romans fortified the site they called *Legio Septima* because the Seventh Legion was stationed there. The Moors moved in briefly but were driven out by the kings of Asturias who chose it as their new capital in AD913 as a prelude to the reconquest of the rest of the Iberian peninsula. As time went by Christian refugees from Andalucia and other territories dominated by the Arabs helped to swell the population before the region was united under Ferdinand I of Castile. He preferred to establish his court in Burgos, thereby leaving León slightly out on a limb. Not that the city was particularly bothered. It became a Mecca for pilgrims on their way to Santiago de Compostela, built a lovely cathedral and recouped its fortunes through farming, mining iron and anthracite and establishing a useful hydro-electric system. It is connected by train with Madrid and various provincial capitals and has regular bus services to Madrid and a number of other important towns including Santander. Where motorists are concerned León is on the N630 from Oviedo to Zamora and the N601 to Valladolid 139km (86 miles) to the south-east, while the N120 through Astorga has an uninterrupted run to Vigo on the Atlantic coast, a distance of 367km (228 miles).

The old town of León is set well back from the river, partly enclosed at one end by the remains of its medieval ramparts. The Calle Generalísimo Franco slices through the middle, separating the Barrio Humedo district from the area beyond the cathedral. However it does have its merits such as the quiet, arcaded Plaza Mayor, a fourteenth-century façade and tower that were once part of the palace of the Condes de Luna and the recently restored Church of Nuestra Señora del Mercardo in the attractive market square.

One of the glories of León is undoubtedly its cathedral, considered by many people to be the most exquisite in Spain and one of the finest in Europe. Building started in the early thirteenth century on the site of three earlier versions and continued for about 200 years. It has some quite unusual features, especially on the west front where no attempt was made to match either the towers or their steeples. Saints and sinners are depicted with equal enthusiasm at the Last Judgment but the best statues were reserved for the south portal.

The most remarkable thing about the cathedral is its stained glass windows, more than 250 of them, jewel coloured and magnificent with the sun shining through. The rose window over the west door is among the oldest whereas those in the nave deal with less biblical matters and were added some time later. A certain amount of glass is also used in the chancel, giving an uninterrupted view past the alabaster carvings to the high altar below which is a shrine containing relics of San Froilán, the patron saint of the city. There are some rather fine Gothic tombs in the nearby chapels and the cloister as well as an altar to Nuestra Señora del Dado, so named because a gambler is said to have thrown his dice as an offering, hitting the Christ Child and drawing blood. The Cathedral Museum has a variety of other exhibits including a tenth-century illuminated bible, a representative collection of sacred art and a staircase that once led to the chapterhouse.

The cathedral has a worthy companion in the Real Basilica de San Isidoro, built into the ramparts a short walk away on the Plaza de San Isidoro. They take their name from the eleventh-century Archbishop of Sevilla, one of the most learned men of his day who pointed out at considerable length that the coming of Christianity had little or nothing to do with the fall of Rome. When he died his remains were removed from Sevilla and are now buried near the high altar.

Very little exists of the original church, founded by Ferdinand I, partly as a shrine for the archbishop and partly as a royal pantheon. Most of the building was redesigned, redecorated and modernised during the Middle Ages but fortunately the pantheon escaped almost untouched. The two small chambers with their early frescoes and expressively carved capitals are among the earliest examples of their kind in the country. The tombs were broken into and the library burned by the French during the Peninsular War but a number of priceless articles had been removed to places of safety and are now on display in the treasury.

A number of small chapels are scattered like confetti in this area, one or two forming an integral part of the medieval ramparts that run from San Isidoro, with a couple of sharp right-hand bends, and along the Avenida de los Cubos to end at the cathedral. From here the Calle Generalísimo Franco heads straight for the river past the Renaissance Palacio de les Guzmánes and a large square building known as Les Botines. It was designed by Antonio Gaudí in 1891 for a friend of his patron Eusebio Güell and derives its name partly from *botin*, the Spanish word for bounty, because some pots of money were unearthed on the site. It is by no means as colourful or as striking as his famous creations in Barcelona but nevertheless includes

---

The twelfth-century San Marcos Monastery is Leóns third great architectural masterpiece

more than one hint of things to come. He even managed to incorporate a statue of St George and the Dragon over the entrance, demonstrating his loyalty to Catalunya through its patron saint.

From the Plaza Guzmán el Bueno, so called in honour of the heroic defender of Tarifa in 1292 who was born in León, the Avenida de la Condesa de Sagasta follows the river up to the Plaza de San Marcos. This is the site of the city's third great architectural masterpiece, the Monasterio de San Marcos, founded in the twelfth century by the Knights of the Order of Santiago as a haven for pilgrims on their way to Compostela. Some 400 years later Ferdinand the Catholic replaced the original buildings with a splendid construction that was improved still further by his grandson Charles V.

These days it is divided up between the Church of San Marcos, decorated with cockleshells, the Archaeological Museum and the outstanding Hotel de San Marcos which is almost a museum in itself. The exterior decorations span the centuries by featuring such famous personalities as the Roman emperors Trajan and Augustus, biblical characters, Isabel the Catholic and Charles V as well as events in the militant life of St James. The museum is comprehensive with prehistoric discoveries, bits and pieces discarded by members of the Seventh Legion and items of sacred art, the most memorable of which is an eleventh-century ivory known as the Carrizo Crucifix.

They are splendidly housed in the cloister where both the chapter-house and the sacristy have exceptionally fine ceilings.

The Hotel de San Marcos is well up to standard with nearly a mile of carpeted corridors that act as a showcase for reproductions of Spanish furniture through the ages. The main salon is vast with both a polished marble floor and a painted ceiling and there is also a night club, a choice of restaurants and a terrace overlooking the river. As it is generally regarded as one of the world's great hotels the prices are very reasonable by international standards, but it is possible to find comfortable accommodation in the city at around half the amount. The modern Hotel Quindós, Avenida José Antonio is a case in point, as is the even more moderate Hotel Paris in the Avenida Generalísimo Franco. There are a number of campsites round about.

Anyone who chooses the rather modest Esla campsite at **Mansilla de las Mulas** on the N601 18km (12 miles) south of the city, is well placed when it comes to visiting a number of historic places in the surrounding area. The village itself has managed to preserve some of its twelfth-century walls and towers but **San Miguel de Escalada** along a minor road to the northeast is both older and more interesting. A party of monks, expelled from Córdoba by the Moors at the end of the ninth century, chose it as the site for a large monastery which quite naturally incorporated several ideas they had picked up in Andalucia. Although most of the buildings have now disappeared the church has survived to become one of the most fascinating of its kind in the country. The nave and aisles below their wooden vaulting date from AD913 and make full use of typical horseshoe arches and Visigoth and Arab ornamentation. The exterior gallery was added later but was designed to blend in with the existing structures.

Some 18km (12 miles) further down the N601 a turning off to the right leads to **Valencia de Don Juan** whose photogenic Gothic castle has been adopted as the logo for the provincial tourist office. Here the Pico Verde campsite is well equipped and within striking distance of the vineyards and bodegas of Valderas, near the point where León joins both Zamora and Valladolid. On the other hand, a few kilometres beyond the turning off to Valencia de Don Juan on the N601, the N120 makes tracks in the opposite direction for **Sahagún**, yet another temporary refuge for pilgrims in the olden days. Much of its ancient monastery is in ruins but there are two small medieval churches and an antiquated bridge over the Río Cea. However, the Convento de Sahagún still maintains its age-old reputation for hospitality by providing rooms for male or female guests. The nearby Pedro Ponce campsite is adequate with all the basic necessities but no extra frills.

From Sahagún the C611 heads due north along the Río Cea, ignoring most of the little hamlets before it swerves to the left, just short of the large Embalse de Riaño and its adjoining nature reserve that bridge the gap between the Cantabrica Cordillera and the Picos de Europa. There are quite a few scenic drives through the foothills but not many tourist attractions apart from the **Cuevas de Valporquero.** These caves were hollowed out over the centuries by subterranean mountain streams that are still eating their way through soft rock and clay, making the going a bit slippery. At present they cover about 3km (2 miles). There are guided tours lasting up to an hour through various chambers and galleries, past little pools and strange rock formations, many of them stained by minerals that are mined in one or two places in the vicinity. A minor road from Vegacervera, quite close by, links up with the N630 for an easy run of 40km (25 miles) back to León.

Much more time is needed to explore the western part of the province beyond Astorga 38km (24 miles) away. The only place of interest along the first part of the route is **La Virgen del Camino**, a modern sanctuary built in 1960 to replace the previous chapel. Its façade includes a group of bronze statues which makes a change from the more usual stone ones. Further along the road the Don Suero de Quinones campsite at Hospital de Orbigo has a rather tenuous link with Cervantes. In 1434 Don Suero and a small party of friends stationed themselves on the long bridge and challenged every passing knight to prove that his lady was more beautiful than any of theirs. Many accepted the challenge but very few were injured and only one was killed. The escapade attracted attention and became known as the Paso de Honor. Nearly two centuries later Cervantes decided that Don Suero de Quinones was the sort of character he needed to draw on when he created Don Quixote.

Astorga was once a Roman settlement called *Asturica Augusta* and later a Castilian stopover on the road to Compostela but it may have been even more closely associated with the Phoenicians. It was thought that the Maragatos who live in the area were probably of Arab extraction and arrived on the scene during the early Middle Ages. However a certain expert, Dr Julio Carro, has put forward the theory that they are descended from Phoenician slaves brought over by the Romans to work in the gold mines. Apart from intermarrying with the Asturians they had little time for anyone else and earned their living by carrying goods backwards and forwards between Castile and Galicia. They have preserved their own characteristics, customs and traditional dress and still bake the well-known *mantecadas*. On special occasions some of them may appear in their ancient costumes but as these events are relatively few and far between, the only examples a visitor is likely to see are worn by two figures who strike the hours on the town hall clock in the Plaza Mayor.

Comparatively little time is needed for sightseeing in Astorga because its two most noteworthy buildings stand cheek by jowl on the north-eastern outskirts of the town. The cathedral is the older by several hundred years, dating in part from the fourteenth century with a decorative façade that was added afterwards. The interior is agreeably spacious and contains a sixteenth-century retable behind the high altar carved by Gaspar Becerra, an Andalusian who studied in Italy with Michaelangelo. The church plate is kept in the Diocesan Museum along with several Romanesque statues and a tenth-century gold and silver casket that belonged to Alfonso III.

The Episcopal Palace, more or less next door, was designed by Antonio Gaudí in 1889 to replace an earlier building which had been destroyed by fire. It is built of white granite in the form of a square with rounded towers and unusual hooded arches that interconnect outside the main entrance. Both the chapel and the throne room are two storeys high, as originally planned, but the ideas for a central patio and a lofty pyramid-shaped roof were discarded by Luís de Guereta, a young architect who took over when Gaudí resigned following the death of Bishop Grau. Nowadays the palace is home to the Museo de los Caminos (The Museum of the Way), full of

The Episcopal Palace at Astorga was designed by Antonio Gaudí

maps and other reminders of ancient pilgrimages, Roman relics, pictures, figures dressed in medieval pilgrim garb and a thirteenth-century statue of St James on horseback.

The most up-market place to stay in Astorga is the Hotel Gaudí in the Plaza Eduardo de Castro, but there are also two or three more modest establishments in town and the large Motel de Pradorrey 5km (3 miles) away on the NVI towards Ponferrada. This is a moderately pleasing route but not an especially interesting one so motorists with time to spare would no doubt find the minor LE142 somewhat more rewarding. It calls in at **Castrillo de los Polvazares**, a typical Maragato village which is so tourist conscious that it occasionally stages an unusual wedding ceremony for visitors. Although there are a number of other similar hamlets, such as Rabanal del Camino and Santa Colomba de Somoza, the most striking is undoubtedly **Molinaseca**. It boasts a splendid medieval bridge, much used by pilgrims in the olden days, the parish church of San Nicolás and the Calle Real which is very much in keeping with its surroundings.

Ponferrada is so called because

the bridge over the Río Sil was strengthened with iron when it was built in 1082 to speed pilgrims on their way to Galicia. This ore is still mined in the area with the result that Ponferrada has grown into quite a sizable industrial centre which even the inhabitants could hardly describe as beautiful. The most dominant feature is its huge brooding castle, rather the worse for wear but nevertheless an outstanding example of a military fortress in the Middle Ages. It belonged originally to the Knights Templar but was given its towers and impressive gateway after the Order was disbanded in the early fourteenth century. The town also has two very worth while churches, the Basilica de Nuestra Señora de la Encina in the Calle Comenador and the seventeenth-century church of San Andrés in the Plaza del Temple. The former has some excellent carvings and paintings as well as a Gothic sculpture of Our Lady of the Oak while the latter is justly proud of its thirteenth-century Cristo de las Maravillas.

Other local attractions include the old guildhall built by Philip II which is now used as a prison and a splendid gateway, the sole survivor from the ancient walls. At one time steam engines were used by the Minero Siderdúrgica de Ponferrada company to operate a passenger service to Villablino along the pleasantly green Sil valley. Although this has been discontinued a few engines can be seen by anyone who is sufficiently interested to ask for permission.

The area round Ponferrada has a great deal to offer and the Hotel del Temple in a former palace on the Avenida de Portugal is a comfortable base from which to explore at leisure. One most attractive drive southwards is along the LE161 to San Esteban de Valdueza where motorists are faced with a dual option. The right-hand fork climbs up to Guiana, a lonely mountain peak with a memorable view, while the left fork keeps company with the Río Oza through Valdefrancos, becoming increasingly convoluted until it reaches the medieval hamlet of Peñalba de Santiago. Several caves in the nearby Valle del Silencio were once occupied by hermits one of whom, San Genadio, who went on to become Bishop of Astorga, founded the lovely old Mozarabic Church of Santiago in the village.

A more unusual choice for an outing would be **Las Médulas** at the end of a minor road off the N536 at Carucedo. It was here that the Romans spent the better part of two centuries mining for gold. They built canals and tunnels to carry water from streams and rivers and used whole armies of slaves to shift an estimated 300,000,000 tons of earth which was piled up into strange, apricot coloured formations that would not look out of place on Mars. The atmosphere is weird and even faintly sinister, which probably accounts for the belief that witches and demons live among the peaks while the lake, originally constructed by the Romans, is peopled by the inhabitants of an underwater city whose sole object is to guard its hidden treasures.

With so many pilgrim routes threaded through this part of León it is hardly surprising to find that castles and religious houses are unusually thick on the ground. **San Miguel de las Dueñas**, just north of Ponferrada, has a convent with a rather splendid church while **Carracedo**, slightly off the NV1 to the west, is worth seeing for the remains of a Benedictine monastery founded in the closing years of the tenth century. It suffered at the hands of the Moors but was later restored and provided with royal apartments and a chapterhouse, followed by the cloister and a large tower. Once again it fell on hard times after the Dissolution of the Monasteries in 1835 and was left very much to its own devices for close on a hundred years.

A minor road links the village with **Cacabelos,** a small wine town with an exceedingly long history. It was founded by the Romans after they captured the ancient hilltop settlement of *Bergidum*, near Pieros, and was sufficiently important for Pliny the Elder to make it his home for about 18 years. It has an old church and the Santuario de Augustias, an arcaded main square and a reputation for producing cherry brandy that is strong enough to be treated with respect.

From Cacabelos the LE712 presses on northwards, bypassing Vega de Espinareda with its partly ruined Benedictine monastery on the way to Candin and Pereda de Ancares in the heart of the Reserva Nacional de los Ancares Leóneses. This is an enchanting area, seldom visited by anyone apart from hunters, trout fishermen, wild life enthusiasts and a few dedicated long distance walkers. The scenery is fairly rugged, alternating between hillsides doused in broom and heather, woods full of old trees and deep valleys better suited to less hardy varieties like beech, holly and hazel. It is also home to a whole range of birds and animals, among them bears, wolves, wild boar and deer. Some of the more inaccessible communities still occupy their *palloza* houses which have a striking resemblance to the ones already excavated in ancient Celtic villages. They are usually low and circular, built of stone with a single door and a wooden pole supporting the roughly thatched roof that ends almost at ground level.

There are only a few minor roads into the reserve and most of them stop abruptly when they reach some isolated hamlet or other small community. This means that motorists are constantly turning round and negotiate all the same potholes on the way back which requires plenty of time and their undivided attention. If the whole venture sounds daunting it is better to return to the NV1 from Carracedo and cover the last 10km (6 miles) to **Villafranca del Bierzo** in comfort.

In bygone days the town had a special significance for pilgrims on their way to Santiago de Compostela. Anyone who was too exhausted or too ill to complete the journey could get a special dispensation at the Puerta del Perdón, the splendid doorway into the Church of Santiago. It was an arrangement made with the approval of Pope Calixto II who, in the twelfth century, produced what in effect was the forerunner of today's tourist guides.

Villafranca del Bierzo is a delightful, picturesque town with some lovely streets and gardens, a number of fine medieval mansions and its fair share of elderly churches and convents. The Palacio de Arganza, dating from the early sixteenth century, had to be rebuilt after it was severely battered by French troops during the Peninsular War but the convent of La Anunciada on the Calle Rúa Nueva was more fortunate and still has its original church. The convent of San Francisco off the Plaza Mayor is both older and more impressive, showing a distinctly Moorish influence in the nave, whereas the church of Santa Maria in the Calle Quintano was modelled on St John Lateran in Rome.

The Parador de Villafranca del Bierzo on the Avenida de Calvo Sotelo is one of the few hotels in town. It is modern and comfortable without many frills but has adequate parking space and its own restaurant. This is the last town of any consequence before the border with Lugo whose provincial capital lies 101km (63 miles) to the north-east. León is slightly further away at 130km (81 miles) whereas it is all of 403km (250 miles) to Madrid.

PALENCIA

At first sight it is a little difficult to work up much enthusiasm for Palencia unless one happens to be interested in mining, growing grain or inspecting market gardens. It is an oddly-shaped province, sandwiched in between León and Burgos, longer than it is wide, nudging the Cantabrian mountains in the north and stretching southwards across the Tierra de Campos into Valladolid. The capital, though prosperous, is one of the 'if this is Thursday it must be Palencia' sort of places with a long, rather dreary history and nothing much to show for it. The site was occupied by the Celts, largely disregarded by the Romans and the Moors, but it obviously appealed to the Visigoths who settled here long enough to build a church. In 1185 the city was chosen by Alfonso VIII for Spain's first university but even this was transferred to Salamanca when it was only 54 years old. However, Palencia's greatest mistake was to become involved in the Comuneros Revolt against Charles V when he tried to impose absolute rule and a new tax system and paid the inevitable price after the uprising had been crushed and the ringleaders executed in Segovia in 1521.

Regardless of all these misfortunes the city of **Palencia** still has its splendid Gothic cathedral not far from the Plaza Mayor which is sometimes referred to, with considerable justification, as 'La Bella Desconocida' or the Unknown Beauty. It started life in the seventh century when San Antolín, a Visigoth who had been converted to Christianity, was martyred by some of his countrymen and later venerated by others who shared his beliefs. The resulting shrine survived the Moorish occupation after which, according to a popular legend, it was stumbled on by Sancho the Great while he was out hunting. He restored the chapel in 1034 and this was incorporated into the crypt of the new cathedral some 300 years later. The interior has a great deal to offer including two memorable altarpieces, Gothic choir stalls, sculptures attributed to Gil de Siloé and the tomb of Queen Urraca of Navarre who died in 1189. Another attraction is a clock in the transept which has a knight and a lion on hand to strike the hours. The museum, housed in the cloister, has its own collection of treasures, including fifteenth-century tapestries and El Greco's 'San Sebastian'.

Anyone who feels inclined to stay long enough to explore the surrounding countryside would find the Husa Rey Sancho, in the Avenida Ponce de León, well equipped and comfortable with facilities for both tennis and swimming. There are a number of other establishments of various categories dotted about the city in addition to the somewhat more expensive Europa Centro 10km (6 miles) outside on the N610 in the direction of Burgos. This road connects with the N620, the main highway between Burgos and Valladolid, which are 88km (55 miles) and 47km (29 miles) away respectively. Other main routes out of Palencia are the N661 to Santander, a distance of 203km (126 miles) and the N610 to León, 128km (79 miles) to the north-west. Palencia also has rail links with Madrid, Ávila, Burgos, Valladolid and Santander and a few local bus services.

The only place of interest south of the provincial capital is **Baños de Cerrato**, 14km (9 miles) away on the river, whose San Juan Bautista basilica is believed to be the oldest church in Spain still in an excellent state of preservation. It was built as a sanctuary by the Visigoths in AD661, a fact born out by the date which King Recesvinto wisely decided to have carved on one of the main arches.

Somewhat further afield in the opposite direction, on the C613, the village of **Paredes de Nava** was the birthplace of a number of famous personalities in the fifteenth century. Among them was Jorge Manrique, the lyric poet whose *Coplas* on the death of his father is regarded as one of Spain's most famous elegies. He was 10 years older than Pedro Berruguete who was appointed court painter during the reign of Ferdinand and Isabel. His son Alonso, although more interested in sculpture, nev-

Las Médulas was once part of a Roman goldmining area

A scenic camping area at the foothills of the Cantabrian Cordillera

ertheless fulfilled the same function at the court of Charles V. Examples of their work can be seen in the local church of Santa Eulalia although several paintings were stolen from the museum more than 20 years ago and apparently have never been recovered. If the museum is closed, enquire at number 6 Plaza de San Francisco.

From Paredes de Nava the minor P961 provides a shortcut through Villoldo to **Carrión de los Condes**, another stopping place on the road to Compostela. Here the main attractions are the Church of Santiago, whose carved twelfth-century façade includes several local figures such as the cobbler, the architect and the potter, and the Church of Santa Maria del Camino, recalling the Castilian maidens who were demanded as an annual tribute by the Moorish overlords. The ancient Benedictine monastery of San Zoilo, founded in the eleventh century, was largely rebuilt during the Renaissance. It contains the tombs of the two Counts of Carrión who married El Cid's daughters for their dowries, but mistreated both girls on the way home and abandoned them along the roadside. On hearing the news El Cid sent a party of knights to murder both the men, thereby leaving his daughters free to find more worthy husbands.

Villalcázar de Sirga, 7km (4 miles) along the P980, is a small rural community with a large Gothic church built by the Knights Templar to house the statue of Santa Maria la Blanca, who is still in residence although time has not dealt kindly with either the Virgin or the Child. The finely carved tombs of the Infante Don Felipe and his wife are located in the south transept. She appears to be gagged, perhaps to stop her telling anyone that her husband had been murdered by his brother, Alfonso X, in 1271 although, judging from carving round the base of the tomb, he was given a princely funeral.

Some 13km (8 miles) further on, the road joins the highway to Santander at **Frómista**, a favourite stopping place for pilgrims on their way to Compostela. The Benedictine monastery of San Martin has now disappeared but the church, built at about the same time as William the Conqueror was busy invading England, is worth seeing. From here the highway carries on quite pleasantly and uneventfully to **Aguilar de Campoo** in the foothills of the Cantabrian Cordillera, complete with its ruined castle, two attractive little churches and the Santa Maria la Real Monastery just outside the town.

Motorists who have no intention of returning to Palencia, 97km (60 miles) back along the same road, but would enjoy spending some time in the mountains, should turn off along the P212 to the west. It skirts round the Aguilar Reservoir, which is a popular water sports centre during the summer months, in order to reach **Cervera de Pisuerga** which has both a small church and a modern parador. This Parador Nacional de Fuentes Carrionas takes its name from the source of the Río Carrión and is ideally placed for people who are interested in fishing, shooting or walking. It is a chalet-type building, pleasant but not luxurious, well signposted from Cervera de Pisuerga and especially attractive in the spring when all the wild flowers are in full bloom. For anyone travelling with a tent or a caravan there is the two-star Monte Royal campsite at Aguilar de Campoo and another in the same category called El Eden at Carrión de los Condes, as well as El Soto at Saldana, slightly further from the beaten track, all of which are seasonal.

SALAMANCA

Salamanca province has a good deal in common with neighbouring Extremadura, home of the tough, uncompromising Conquistadores who overran vast tracts of south and central America, hot on the heels of Columbus's epic voyage of discovery to San Salvador. The treasures they appropriated, especially from the Aztecs and the Incas, provided Spain with more wealth than even the Emperor Charles V had any right to expect. Much of it was squandered on interminable battles but there was still plenty left over to finance extensive building programmes, enrich churches, provide additional funds for universities and encourage both local and foreign artists and other craftsmen.

The countryside is fairly typical, an enormous chequer board of ranches, fields and pastures where black fighting bulls graze among the holm oaks, sharing the landscape with flocks of sheep and cultivated areas planted mainly with wheat. There are more rivers than one would expect, the largest of which is the Río Tormes that wanders across the province from south-east to north-west, interrupted by two large man-made lakes, flowing past the ancient capital city to join forces with the Río Douro on the frontier with Portugal. The mountains of the Sierra de Bejár are snowcapped during the winter when the weather can be wet and miserable, whereas the summers are usually dry with long hours of sunshine .

Salamanca has railway links with both Madrid and Portugal as well as with other provincial capitals such as Ávila, Valladolid and Burgos, while buses keep the city in constant touch with Zamora, León, Valladolid and Ciudad Rodrigo, in addition to daily express coach services operating to and from Madrid. As far as main roads are concerned the N630 calls in on its way south from Zamora, the N510 is the quickest route to Ávila while the N620 connects Burgos with Fuentes de Oñoro and Vilar Formoso. This is one of the main frontier posts with Portugal and remains open 24 hours a day throughout the year. The area is not very densely populated and many of the outlying villages are blissfully unaware that the country has moved into the twentieth century, but are nevertheless quite happy to welcome the occasional stranger who calls in to admire their archaic buildings and sample the local specialities.

The area has been occupied since prehistoric times, a fact born out by some Neolithic rock paintings in the deep south, within a short distance of the enchanting and increasingly popular village of La Alberca. The region was well known to the Celts, the Romans and the Visigoths and was the point at which the Christians succeeded in turning the tide against the Moorish invaders after nearly 400 years. Thereafter it became disputed territory, fought over by local families, trampled across by Spanish armies en route for Portugal, invaded by the French under Napoleon and liberated by Wellington whose decisive victory in the Arapiles valley, south of the provincial capital, in 1812 marked the last phase of the Peninsular War.

Salamanca, one of the most memorable cities of Northern and Central Spain, was firmly rooted in antiquity even before it was captured by Hannibal in the third century BC. The only tangible evidence of Roman occupation is the old Puente Romano over the Río Tormes, within sight of the dual cathedral rising imperiously above a collection of more modern buildings that separate it from the waterfront. The so-called Old Cathedral was completed in the twelfth century, incorporating the superb Torre del Gallo with its two tiers of windows, a handful of small chapels and an outstanding altarpiece. The colours of its fifty-three individual paintings are unusually brilliant, in sharp contrast to the sombre background of the Last Judgment. In the centre is a twelfth-century wooden statue of the Virgen de Vega, encased in bronze enriched with enamel and gold.

Some of the oldest frescoes are in the Capilla de San Martin while the Capilla de Talavera contains a standard that rallied the Comuneros during their historic revolt against Charles V which was crushed at Villalar in 1521. Among the most interesting tombs is that of Bishop Lucero in the Capilla de Santa Barbara, one member of the clergy who could almost be described as a talisman of university students in search of doctorates. They developed a habit of spending the night before taking the final examination with their feet propped up on those of the bishop in the hope that he would see them safely through the questions fired at them next morning. If he obliged the student would be escorted from the chapel to celebrate by writing his name in bull's blood on the nearest convenient wall in the vicinity. Meanwhile Bishop Diego de Anaya has an intricately carved tomb in the chapel that was named after him, which also contains a beautiful fifteenth-century organ, said to be the oldest in Europe.

When it was decided to build the New Cathedral in 1513 its architect, Juan Gil de Hontánon, excelled himself by designing it as a companion for the old Romanesque church instead of a replacement. It is larger and more ornate, forested with pinnacles on the outside and extravagantly Baroque behind its imposing west portal. There are a number of things to see inside including the choir stalls and a chapel filled to capacity with wooded sculptures of what must surely be nearly every saint in existence. One of the other chapels contains El Cid's 'Christ of Battles' which the famous eleventh-century warrior took with him on his campaigns, as well as the tomb of his chaplain Bishop Jerónimo.

A block or so away, down the Calderón de la Barca, is the main entrance to the university, founded by Alfonso IX in 1218. Some 50 years later, when it had expanded quite considerably under the fatherly eye of Alfonso the Wise, it was considered to be just as important as its counterparts in Oxford, Paris and Bologna. The exceptionally fine doorway was presented by the Catholic Monarchs who appear together in a medallion below the central coat-of-arms. Around this are some oddly assorted bedfellows ranging from church dignitaries to Venus and Hercules.

Inside the main building the original lecture halls are concentrated in a double-storey cloister, its two levels linked by a truly magnificent Renaissance stairway. The curved bannister is a masterpiece of riotous carving: Acrobats and students, musicians and members of the clergy disport themselves among the foliage in company with a *picopardo* who wears a pointed headdress and holds up her skirt demurely with one hand. She is actually one of the prostitutes who were very much part of the university and were governed by its rules and regulations. They were obliged to wear brown dresses, scalloped at the edges, and had their own quarter in the town. At the beginning of Lent every year they were removed to a safe distance and then brought back for the decidedly bawdy Fiesta de las Aguas on Easter Monday. The festival is still part of the city's annual celebrations but these days it is a much more restrained affair.

Foremost among the lecture rooms are the Paraninfo Hall with its seventeenth-century Flemish tapestries and Goya's portrait of Charles IV, the Salinas Hall which still has a portfolio of medieval music, and the Aula Fray Luis de León where the famous poet and theologian held his classes. He was a professor who was arrested by the Inquisition during a lecture in 1573, spent the next 5 years in prison and then returned, picking up where he left off with the words 'As we were saying yesterday... ' Nothing has changed since then.

His canopied chair is still in place and so are the narrow uncomfortable benches covered with graffiti which the students infinitely preferred to lounging on the floor or propping themselves up against the wall as they had always done before. Centuries later the philosopher, Miguel de Unamuno, spent a lot of time in the room among the hearts pierced with arrows, names, initials and sentimental messages which he christened 'Un rosario de amor'. He was rector of the university and a staunch supporter of the Nationalists at the outbreak of the Civil War. However, at a Columbus Day celebration in 1936, he roundly attacked both sides for their atrocities and would probably have been killed on the spot if Franco's wife had not intervened. Despite this he was relieved of his post and died shortly afterwards at his home next door to the oddly-named House of the Dead, apparently from natural causes.

Other buildings which are worth inspecting include the Students' Hospice and the Escuelas Menores, or Lesser Schools, which have their fair share of decorations, both inside and out. Of particular note are the Calderón de la Barca gallery, the cloister and all that is left of the Salamanca Ceiling with its constellations and signs of the zodiac, a relic from the days when the department of astrology was considered to be one of the most advanced in Europe.

Just across the way, on the Plaza Fray Luis de León, Alvarez Abarca House is home to the Salamanca Museum which spreads itself over several rooms but turns out to be rather disappointing. It has some fine ceilings and attractive windows but little else of moment apart from a few archaeological discoveries including a menhir dating from the tenth century BC. The exhibits in the Municipal Museum are just as undistinguished although they are on display in the Torre del Clavero on the Plaza de Colón. This is a free-standing tower left over from a sixteenth-century castle, crowned with turrets and decorated with Mudejar trellis-work.

The surrounding area is full of noteworthy buildings such as the Dominicas-Dueñas on the Gran Via, a medieval convent which allows visitors to inspect its unusual five-sided cloister. The upper gallery takes its theme from Dante's *Divine Comedy* with special emphasis on the Inferno, leaving little or nothing to the imagination when it comes to the more demoniacle aspects of his famous vision. The Convento de San Esteban, just opposite, is infinitely more pleasant but every bit as eyecatching. The rather over-elaborate altarpiece in the church is the work of José Churriguera, who was disinclined to use a simple line if an ornamental one would do, while the cloister restricts itself to medallions and a grand staircase up to the gallery. It was here that Columbus persuaded the monks to support his arguments for a voyage of discovery across the Atlantic. As a result they added their considerable weight to that of the monks of Rabida in an effort to obtain the necessary backing of the Catholic Monarchs, particularly Queen Isabel. The nearby Church of Santo Tomás de Canterbury was built by the English residents of Salamanca and was completed in 1173 when he was also cannonised.

The centrepiece of the city is the Plaza Mayor a present from Philip V in recognition of its support during the War of Succession. It is a huge, empty square surrounded on all sides by elegant buildings made of sandstone that have weathered to a deep golden-brown. The uniform pattern of arcades, separated by three floors of shuttered windows from the upper balustrades, is interrupted by lofty archways over the main entrances, the Royal Pavilion and the town hall. This is a splendid mixture of columns and stone carving with a clock below the central arch of the belltower and statues instead of pinnacles on the balustrade.

The life of the city revolves round the Plaza Mayor with its shops, cafés and bars, tables, chairs, newspaper stands and stone benches that are sometimes occupied by weary travellers, unable or unwilling to find somewhere more comfortable to sleep. In the evening the crowds are serenaded by groups of young minstrels in their medieval black velvet suits and white open-neck shirts, strumming guitars. They are the modern version of the *tuna* students who literally sang for their supper in the Middle Ages. Many of the ancient melodies are included in their large repertoires but these days the singers are more than happy if people show their appreciation in cash instead of food and wine. Occasionally a small crowd may gather round a storyteller who personifies the blind men who once travelled round the villages, providing entertainment and spreading all the latest news.

To one side of the Plaza Mayor is a large covered market filled with stalls of all descriptions where bustling housewives do their morning shopping. Not far away, beyond the area reserved for taxis, is the small Romanesque Church of St Martin while further south, on the Rua Mayor, the Casa de las Conchas is decorated with hundreds of scallop shells, the emblem of St James. This was the brainchild of its owner, Dr Talavera Maldonada, who was a Knight of Santiago and a counsellor at the court of Ferdinand and Isabel. Slightly further afield, the Barrio de San Benito was once the home of Los Bandos, fiery young noblemen whose vendetta started over a game of pelota and lasted for about a hundred years. Nearly every church and mansion in the vicinity has something to offer, such as Ribera's Immaculate Conception in the church of the same name, the tomb of Alfonso de Fonseca in Las Ursulas Convent, the Renaissance palace of Monterrey and the more distant Church of San Marcos whose designers believed that a round building would be better able to withstand an enemy attack.

A certain amount of time is needed to explore Salamanca thoroughly and to this end there are several hotels available in every category. The most obvious is the Parador de Salamanca, a bland, rather unprepossessing building on the far side of the Roman bridge with memorable views across the river to the city centre, roughly 10 minutes' walk away. It is sited on the Teso de la Feria and has two restaurants, a garden and a swimming pool. Alternatively, right at the heart of things is the Gran Hotel, Plaza Poeta Iglesias just across the road from the Plaza Mayor. Among the somewhat cheaper establishments a popular choice is the Hotel Condal, Plaza Santa Eulalia. Meanwhile, beyond the city limits the Regio y Restaurante Lazarillo de Tormes, 6km (4 miles) away on the N501 to Ávila, is in the upper price bracket but has facilities for tennis and swimming and plenty of parking space. It also runs the well-equipped campsite next door, called simply Regio, which is open throughout the year.

South-east of Salamanca, 23km (14 miles) along the C510, **Álba de Tormes** is perpetually linked with the Dukes of Alba and with Santa Teresa of Ávila, some of whose remains are enshrined in the Convento de la Anunciación which she founded in 1571. Everything is deliberately understated, even down to the reconstructed cell where she died 11 years later, now protected by a grille at the end of the church. A large, businesslike keep is all that remains of the ducal castle but there are a clutch of pleasant little Romanesque Mudejar churches, especially St John's with a sculptured detail taken from a somewhat older altarpiece.

South of Alba de Tormes a barrage across the river has created the large man-made lake of Santa Teresa, an ideal place for boating and sailing but so far with too little accommodation to be described as a holiday resort. There is a small hotel at Guijuelo quite close by and the somewhat larger Hotel Colón in **Béjar** a bit further down the road. This is the largest town in the area, built along a rocky outcrop with some very viewable old streets partly enclosed by the remains of its ancient ramparts. Among the various local attractions is the ducal palace, distinguished by two stalwart towers known as the Mirador and Las Cadenas, that once formed part of the Moorish keep.

Candelario, 4km (2 miles) along a minor road to the south-east, is only one of a number of atmospheric villages dotted about the Sierra de Béjar. It is known for its whitewashed houses, flower-filled wooden balconies and the fact that some of the older women occasionally wear their national costumes at the weekend, consisting of black velvet skirts, black shawls, beautifully embroidered blouses and a distinctive hairstyle called *de zapatilla*.

The picturesque setting of Las Batuecas Convent, Salamanca province

The city of Salamanca revolves around the Plaza Mayor

The costumes worn by the inhabitants of **La Alberca**, in the heart of the Sierra de la Peña de Francia, for the celebrations marking the Day of Assumption on 15 August, and the performance of a local mystery play (the Loa) on the 16 August, are no less colourful. The women appear in richly embroidered dresses and aprons, leaving the men to don white gaiters and black waistcoats, their shirts closed at the neck with a gold buckle.

Although La Alberca tends to become rather crowded in August it has seen no good reason to change its way of life or improve the surface of its oddly shaped plaza, cobbled streets and little alleyways. It is full of ramshackle, half-timbered houses, some of which have a distinct list, sells pottery and embroidery at the outdoor market, along with pollen grains and pots of wild honey, and uses bells to warn passersby to avoid any livestock as it is being led out to the surruounding pastures. The local church is a comparative newcomer, having been built in the eighteenth century, but nevertheless it has its idiosyncrasies. On the outside wall two skulls keep watch over a lantern that is lit to warn wayward parishioners that their time for repentance is strictly limited. On the other hand, nobody appears to know very much about the strange, many-coloured granite pulpit, carved with the figures of the apostles. One of the few places to stay is Las Batuecas, near the entrance to the village. In addition there is a perfectly acceptable campsite, the Nava de Francia, not far away.

The countryside round La Alberca is green and pleasant, with forests of oak and chestnuts and plenty of opportunities for people who enjoy walking. Alternatively, an attractive scenic road enables motorists to visit a selection of delightful mountain villages in a relatively short time. It heads due east to Mogarraz beyond which there is a turning off the C512 to **Miranda del Castañar** complete with its ancient castle, some rather nice old houses and the unusual Ronda de la Muralla, a walk that has been constructed through the protecting walls.

Other hamlets along the route are Cepeda, Herguijuela de la Sierra which looks its best when the cherry orchards are in bloom, and Madroñal, known for its cherry festival in July but called after the strawberry trees, or *madroñas*, that are a feature of the area. Meanwhile, north of La Alberca a tortuous but splendidly scenic road climbs up to the **Peña de Francia**. It is the highest peak in the region with panoramic views across to Portugal and over the plains of the meseta. There is a small inn run by the Dominican Monasterio de la Peña at the summit which is open to visitors during the summer.

From Peña de Francia two alternative routes, one of them very minor, strike out across pleasant open country to the historic walled town of **Ciudad Rodrigo**. It owes its existence to the Romans who built the old bridge over the Río Agueda, was occupied by the Moors and recaptured by Count Rodrigo González Girón in the twelfth century. He supervised the construction of new defensive walls on what remained of the Roman foundations to such good effect that the town not only took his name but also became an important fortress on the frontier with Portugal. It was captured by the French during the Peninsular War, only to be besieged and liberated by Wellington with some considerable difficulty in 1812. As a result he was presented with a silver key to the city and was created Duque de Ciudad Rodrigo and a Spanish Grandee.

The walls, extended and strengthened by 1712, stretch for about 2km (1 mile) with a sentry path along the top reached by a number of different stairways. One of the most imposing buildings is the cathedral, founded in 1170 but updated at intervals thereafter and conscientiously restored after the battering it took during the Peninsular War. One of its best features is the thirteenth-century Puerta de la Virgen with statues of the twelve apostles lined up between the columns overhead. Inside there is some attractive stonework as well as beautifully carved choirstalls and a Renaissance altar in the north aisle. The cloister was decorated in stages, resulting in a mixture of Romanesque capitals, grotesque figures personifying some of the deadly sins and a doorway lavishly decorated in what is sometimes described as the Salamancan style. The nearby Cerralbo Chapel on the Plaza del Buen Alcalde is quite different, simple to the point of austerity and very viewable.

Apart from the Montarco palace on the Plaza del Conde, dating from the fifteenth century, there are two other palaces facing on to the uncluttered Plaza Mayor, one of which now serves as the Town Hall. The *alcázar* in the Plaza del Castillo overlooking the river, is home to the Parador Enrique II. It is an impressive building with a keep and crenellated walls, attractive gardens, opportunities for fishing and the undoubted advantage for some visitors of having all its bedrooms on the ground floor.

Ciudad Rodrigo is conveniently sited on the N620, 89km (55 miles) from Salamanca and 27km (17 miles) from the Portuguese frontier. It is also well placed for a return trip to the provincial capital by way of the scenic Arribes del Duero, roughly 70km (43 miles) to the north. One of the prettiest villages set among the canyons, lakes and almond trees near the Río Duero is Saucelle, although motorists without much time to spare would be better advised to leave the SA324 at Lumbrales and head for the Embalse de Almendra instead. This is a huge lake on the Río Tormes which Salamanca shares with the province of Zamora. A secondary road skirts round its southern contours down to **Ledesma** which has an attractive main square, a brace of medieval churches and a bridge to match. Its solitary hotel, attached to a small spa, is only open during the summer but this hardly matters because the river road provides motorists with an undemanding drive to Salamanca city about 34km (21 miles) away.

SEGOVIA

Segovia could in all honesty be described as one of the most amiable provinces in Castilla y León, small enough to explore at leisure but with sufficient variety to make this a thoroughly enjoyable experience. It is tucked away on the far side of the Sierra de Guadarrama some 87km (54 miles) north-west of Madrid, with a remarkably beautiful capital city presiding over the red Castilian countryside and the green valleys of the Río Eresma and the smaller Río Clamores. The sandy plains are speckled with little hamlets and roamed over by herdsmen, flocks of sheep and goats, pigs, modest herds of cattle and working dogs. Gradually the land becomes more undulating as the clumps of trees merge together in ever-increasing numbers until they blend into quite sizeable forests with very few inhabitants apart from birds and small animals.

The ancient city of **Segovia** is instantly recognisable with its fairytale castle that would have captivated Mad King Ludwig of Bavaria, a majestic cathedral and a superb Roman aqueduct, generally considered to be one of the finest examples to have survived anywhere. The site had probably been occupied by the Iberians for more than 700 years when Roman engineers laid down the heavy granite foundation stones during the first century AD. It was a massive undertaking, some 823m (2,700ft) long with close on 130 pillars supporting two tiers of arches on their way across the valley from the Río Frio, 18km (11 miles) away. Although architects and historians give the builders full credit for creating a structure that has existed without the help of either lime or cement for some 2,000 years, there are still people who maintain that it was the work of the devil. The story goes that a young serving wench, who got tired of carrying water up to the city every day, agreed to exchange her soul for the aqueduct, but only if it was completed in a single night. The sun rose before the last block was in place, the contract was declared null and void and the convenient niche, nearly 30m (100ft) above the Plaza del Azoguejo, made an ideal platform for a statue of Hercules. Some of the arches were destroyed by the Moors in the eleventh century but these were reconstructed in due course by monks from El Parral monastery on the orders of Queen Isabel. They naturally took the opportunity to replace Hercules with a statue of the Virgin Mary who still keeps watch from her lofty vantage point. The aqueduct is also the venue for one of Spain's strangest livestock markets. Every Thursday breeders and dealers, farmers and butchers congregate in the vicinity, conducting transactions over copious quantities of local wine and sealing bargains with a formal handshake instead of written agreements. However the most unusual feature is that there is not an animal to be seen anywhere; the whole business is based on trust, as it has been from the very beginning.

The cathedral is younger than the aqueduct by some 500 years, the original church having been burned down during the Comuneros revolt against the Emperor Charles V. He immediately instructed Juan Gil de Hontánon to build a bigger and better one on a new site, midway between the aqueduct and the *alcázar*. It is a superb Gothic construction in golden stone with slender pinnacles, elegant balustrades, a tall square bell tower and a well proportioned dome over the choir. The interior is light, spacious and very dignified without too much in the way of decoration to detract from the overall effect. The small chapels, protected by attractive wrought iron screens, are worth more than a casual glance and so are some of the old tombs. One belongs to the Infante Don Pedro who wriggled out of his nurse's arms and toppled over the wall of the *alcázar* in 1366. Apparently she jumped over after him, although there has been some speculation that it was in fact a punishment imposed to fit the crime. Another tomb belongs to Maria del Salto, a Jewess who was accused of adultery and thrown over a cliff. Knowing herself to be innocent she appealed to the Virgin Mary for help with the result that she floated gently down to earth without even a bruise to show for her unnerving experience. Juan Gil de Hontánon also chose to be buried inside rather than in the new cathedral at Salamanca, which was another of his noteworthy achievements. The ancient cloister belonged to the original cathedral. After the fire it was dismantled stone by stone and reconstructed on its present site, blending in remarkably well with its more modern surroundings.

The *alcázar* can look either romantic or forbidding, depending on the angle; closely resembling a Germanic château at one end but giving a very fair impersonation of a prison in the middle. This is not altogether surprising in view of the fact that it was used as a military academy before a group of disgruntled cadets decided to set fire to it. The existing building rises up from a rocky spur surrounded by antiquated walls and festooned with turrets that would make it a perfect hat-stand for a witches' convention. The site has been fortified since the days of the Roman and Moorish invaders but, although it creates a popular medieval background for several films set in the Middle Ages, the present castle had to be almost entirely reconstructed after the fire of 1862.

In its younger days the *alcázar* had been one of the great royal palaces of the kings of Castile. Alfonso the Wise was particularly fond of it and spent long hours out on the battlements studying the stars. It is said that on one occasion he informed the court that if the Creator had discussed the matter with him the universe would have been designed rather differently. He changed his mind when the royal apartments were hit by a thunderbolt and hurriedly instructed his confessor to apologise on his behalf.

In 1474 Princess Isabel was staying in the castle when her half-brother, Henry IV, died and she was crowned Queen of Castile in preference to her niece, Dona Juana, who renounced her claim to the throne about 5 years later. Among its most famous visitors was Charles I, then Prince of Wales, who was given a magnificent reception in Segovia by Philip IV in 1623. His impression of the city was certainly very different from those of the king's enemies who were usually imprisoned in the Torre de Juan II. Anyone with enough energy to clamber up its 150 steps to the top is rewarded with an exceptional view of the city, the surrounding countryside and the Monasterio de El Parral on the opposite bank of the Río Eresma. These days the interior of the *alcázar* has also been restored to something resembling its medieval splendour with Mudejar decorations, stained glass, large quantities of arms and armour and a parade of more than fifty monarchs in the Hall of Kings.

The old quarter of Segovia is just as determinedly medieval, preserving its characteristic streets lined with elderly and sometimes rather decrepit houses, a handful of decorative palaces and a selection of small but outstanding Romanesque churches. Fortunately most of them are within easy walking distance of the cathedral, encapsulated behind the protecting city walls that still have three of their original seven fortified gateways. Two of the most picturesque streets, the Velarde and the Daoiz, start from the site of the original cathedral at the entrance to the *alcázar* but part company almost immediately, the former heading for the beautiful thirteenth-century church of San Esteban. A stone's throw up the road, past the eyecatching Casa del Hierro, the Iglesia de la Trinidad on the Plaza Dr Laguna is both spacious and expertly restored. Slightly further on, in the Calle San Agustin, a sixteenth-century mansion has been converted into Segovia's not particularly memorable Museo Provincial de Bellas Artes (Fine Arts Museum). This vies for attention with the works of Daniel Zuloaga, housed in the church of San Juan de los Caballeros on the Plaza de Colmenares. He was an artist from the Basque country who was mainly interested in keeping alive the various methods used in making traditional ceramics and achieved considerable success before his death in 1921. Also in the vicinity are four palatial mansions built for members of the local nobility and grouped round the Plaza del Conde de Cheste, not far from the church of San Sebastián.

On the opposite side of the aqueduct, and about the same distance away, is the Casa de Los Picos whose façade is covered with rows of stubby, protruding pyramids. From here the Calle Juan Bravo, named after the man who spearheaded the Comuneros revolt, leads past his old home to the twelfth-century church of San Martin, planted firmly in the middle of its own square. Among its nearest neighbours are the seventeenth-century prison, the Lozoya tower and a number of fine mansions, some of them built in the days when Segovia grew rich on the proceeds of its tanneries, hat manufacturing industry and the production of various textiles. But the city also had other claims to fame. It is said to have printed one of the first books in the country, an ecclesiastical document turned out on a machine imported especially from Heidelberg in the fifteenth century. At one time it was the home of the national mint, transforming South American gold and silver into Spanish currency, and was the headquarters of several important guilds. Foremost among them was the ancient Guild of Meat Roasters whose present members include restaurants like the Mesón de Cándido in the Plaza Azoquejo and the Mesón Duque on the nearby Calle Cervantes, both of which are famous throughout Spain.

Although Segovia has expanded beyond the confines of its ancient walls the suburbs are by no means as aggressive as those of some other provincial capitals. The whole area is a happy blending of open country, modern apartment blocks and comfortable hotels with the added attraction of an occasional Romanesque church, a convent or a monastery. San Millán, on the Avenido Fernández Ladreda, is the oldest and among the best preserved with an arcade whose capitals are carved with local scenes and biblical stories and a Mozarabic tower left over from the eleventh century. However the valley of the Río Eresma on the northern outskirts of the city has rather more to offer, starting perhaps with the Convento de las Carmelitas Descalzas where St John of the Cross is buried. The nearby chapel of Vera Cruz was built by the Knights Templar in 1208 with a circular corridor surrounding a double-storey section in the middle which was reserved for their secret rites. After the Order had been abolished in the early fourteenth century its most precious relic, a splinter from the True Cross, was transferred to the village of Zamarramala, less than a mile away. Nevertheless the chapel still has some of its more recent treasures, including an unusual version of the Last Supper, as well as an excellent view from the top of the bell tower.

Upstream from La Vera Cruz, past the site of the old mint, is the

The alcázar in Segovia city was once a royal palace for the Kings of Castile

The Roman aqueduct in Segovia city is one of the finest examples to be found anywhere

Monasterio de El Parral, founded by the Marqués de Villena. He was a courtier who perfected the art of intrigue, supporting both Queen Isabel and her niece Juana in their running dispute for the crown of Castile while still finding time to father about thirty illegitimate children, some of whom are buried in the church. Although the façade was left unfinished the interior with its abundant carvings and outstanding sixteenth-century altarpiece by Juan Rodriguez has been faithfully restored. The monastery is still surrounded by the lovely woods and gardens that have always been one of its most famous attributes. At the far end of the Paseo de la Alameda a footbridge recrosses the river, lined with willows and poplars, and heads towards the Convent of Santa Cruz with its decorative entrance and emblems of the Catholic Monarchs. From here it is only a short distance to the Plaza San Lorenzo, a picturesque square of half-timbered houses, looking out on yet another small church, as they have done for centuries.

Because Segovia is less than 2 hours drive from Madrid, and is easily accessible by either train or bus from the capital, many people look on the city as a one-day excursion. This allows enough time to visit all the main attractions but is hardly sufficient to absorb the atmosphere, meet the people and sample its most famous dishes. These include suckling pig which, ideally, should be cooked over pine logs in a special oven while ash wood is apparently essential for roasting lamb, another local speciality. In addition there are several kinds of *tapas* and the great white beans from La Granja called *judiones* which appear in several different guises, among them a filling but inexpensive stew in which they are combined with ham and chunks of sausage.

The best way to appreciate Segovia is to wander round without bothering about any arbitrary time limit, spend a night or two in one of the comfortable hotels and plan a few excursions to other places of interest in the province. The Hotel Los Linajes, Dr Velasco 9 is conveniently placed inside the walls a few blocks from the cathedral whereas Los Arcos, Paseo de Ezequiel Gonzáles, and the Acueducto, Avenida del Padre Claret are both within easy walking distance of the aqueduct. On the other hand the Parador de Segovia would be an excellent choice for anyone who would prefer to stay just out of town. It is a modern building on a hill about 2km (1 mile) along the C601 in the direction of Valladolid. It is very well appointed, with small flower-filled patios, indoor and outdoor swimming pools, some ground floor accommodation, plenty of parking space, a good restaurant and a stunning view. Visitors with tents and caravans can book in to the El Acueducto campsite which has most of the basic requirements and is situated just outside the city. As far as fiestas are concerned the week-long feast of St John and St Peter begins on the 24 June, the San Frutos celebrations take place on 25 October and those of Santa Agueda at Zamarramala in early February. For this one day in the year the women of the village ride roughshod over the men in memory of the *alcaldesas* who successfully tempted the Moors out of their stronghold in the *alcázar* so that they could be defeated by the advancing Christian forces.

La Granja de San Ildefonso in the foothills of the Sierra de Guadarrama, 11km (7 miles) to the east of Segovia on the C601, is well known for both its royal palace and its superb parklands. It owes its existence to Philip V, a grandson of Louis XIV of France, who wanted to create something to remind him of Versailles without actually producing a facsimile. The result was highly satisfactory. French and Italian craftsmen adapted ideas to suit the Spanish style, incorporating long lines of decorative windows, a few balustrades and one or two pinnacles, all complimented by predictably formal gardens. A guided tour of the palace itself takes anything up to an hour and includes most of the apartments, galleries and salons. Pride of place goes to a collection of sixteenth-century Flemish tapestries which have an integrated museum all to themselves. The landscaped gardens are just as memorable. Beyond them are extensive woodlands full of chestnut trees imported from France, shaded walks and specially constructed bridle paths.

When Philip V died in 1746 his queen, Isabel Farnese, was forced to leave La Granja de San Ildefonso so she decided to build a country retreat of her own, also within easy reach of Segovia. Her Riofrio Palace is exactly the same distance from the city on a minor road to the south, midway between the N110 to Ávila and the N603 to Madrid. It is large but not as regal, set in a deer park with a splendid courtyard, a monumental staircase, plenty of statues and richly decorated apartments. However its main attraction is the Museum of the Chase, filled with pictures illustrating the history of hunting from prehistoric times to the mid-eighteenth century. Also on display are specimens of many of the birds and animals associated with Spain. The palace is open the same time as La Granja.

Another popular excursion from Segovia is to the huge Mudejar fortress known as **Coca Castle,** 50km (31 miles) to the north-west, near the border with Valladolid. It is an impressive example of medieval military architecture with three perimeter walls, battlements and watch-towers, turrets and an extremely businesslike keep. It was built by Moorish workmen for a member of the tyrannical Fonseca family, who was then Archbishop of Sevilla, on a site which had been both an Iberian settlement and a Roman town. Nothing remains of the early inhabitants but the fortress is well worth seeing, especially as the keep and the small church with its old wood carvings are both open to visitors.

A less militant day's outing, this time to the north-east, provides three contrasting bites at Segovia's historical cherry. The first place of interest is **Turégano**, approached without difficulty along the C603. Both the village and its twelfth-century castle once belonged to the bishops of Segovia. At least one of them, Juan Arias Davila, enjoyed meddling in politics and was therefore obliged to see that his defences were kept in good working order. Two of the three walls he rebuilt in the last quarter of the fifteenth century are still in existence, protecting, among other elderly buildings, an 800-year-old church which, for some reason, was given a belfry borrowed from one of its neighbours in the seventeenth century. From Cantalejo, 16km (10 miles) further up the road, there is a minor turning off to **Sepúlveda**, a typical hill village occupying an attractive site in the Duraton valley. Apart from the ruins of an old castle its proudest possession is the Church of San Salvador boasting one of the most antiquated lateral doors in the country, said to date from 1093 or thereabouts.

The quickest way back to Segovia runs due south to join the N110, with a slight deviation to **Pedraza de la Sierra**, a fortified village of stone mansions which has remained almost unchanged since the Middle Ages. However the twentieth century is beginning to creep up on it. Shops selling antique furniture, scented candles and pottery are starting to appear in its narrow streets and alleys, the dramatic twelfth-century castle has been restored and provides a home for paintings by Zuloaga and concerts are held in the open patio. The Plaza Mayor with its rustic balconies has tables and chairs set out infront of the arcades where the restaurant owners prefer oak to ash when roasting suckling lamb, which is a well known speciality. The local inn, La Posada Don Mariano, is small and cosy while at El Yantar customers can fill their own wine glasses from a thin pipe attached to the barrel. Beyond the fortified gateway the high mountain pastures still provide grazing for cattle, goats and sheep as they did in the days when the village, like the rest of the province, grew rich and powerful on the proceeds of a thriving wool trade. Nowadays the emphasis is rather more on tourism, particularly as Pedraza de la Sierra is only 35km (22 miles) from Segovia city.

SORIA

Soria is one of the lesser known and therefore less frequently visited provinces with the result that it is more of a traveller's joy than a tourist paradise. On the other hand it has all the necessary ingredients for a pleasant, short interlude. The craggy mountains and natural lakes of the Sierra de Urbión, created by ancient glaciers, are best explored on foot although they can also be reached quite easily by motorists, which makes them a favourite haunt of local fishermen. The villages are small but picturesque, some showing the telltale signs of early Roman occupation on Celtic foundations, often overlaid with medieval castles and Christian churches. The winters are cold while the summers can be uncomfortably hot so the best time to explore is in the spring, especially along the Duero valley and up in the mountains. The folded hills provide grazing for sheep driven up from the baking plains of the meseta as they have been for centuries.

The provincial capital **Soria,** is a good place to pause on the way down to Madrid, 225km (140 miles) to the south, on the journey north to France through Pamplona, a distance of 167km (104 miles) from town to town, or eastwards to Barcelona 470km (291 miles) away. It also makes an excellent base for touring the surrounding countryside. Apart from the modern Parador Antonio Machado, adjoining the old castle ruins, there are one or two smaller, less expensive hotels in the city, a sprinkling of acceptable restaurants and the Fuente de la Teja campsite about 2km, (1 mile) away southwards on the N111 which has a restaurant and a swimming pool and is open throughout the year.

Most of the main attractions are concentrated in the ancient city centre below the Parque del Castillo, although San Juan de Duero, founded by the Knights of St John of Jerusalem in the early thirteenth century, is on the opposite bank of the river. Very little remains of the original monastery apart from the church with its Roman mosaic, carved stone capitals and small museum and the ruins of what must once have been a beautiful arcaded cloister. In the opposite direction, roughly 1.3km (less than a mile) downstream beyond a narrow archway, is the San Saturio Hermitage, consisting of an ancient cave with religious associations and a small chapel that was added in the eighteenth century.

The most convenient point from which to set out on a sightseeing tour of Soria is the Plaza Ramón y Cajal near the Alameda de Cervantes Gardens, an attractively wooded park with a bandstand built up in the branches of a tree, a paved patio and space to play *tanguilla* which entails throwing metal discs at a peg in the ground. On the opposite side of the Paseo del Espolón the Numancia Museum houses a variety of items discovered during excavations in Numantia, a Roman settlement 7km (4 miles) to the north-east. Alternatively the Calle Caballeros, lined with attractive old houses, leads to the Church of San Juan de Rabarera whose entrance was recreated from the remains of a church dedicated to St Nicholas. Some two blocks away along the Calle Juan, the Palace of the Counts of Gómara on the Calle Aguirre is an imposing sixteenth-century building with a business-like tower, an ornamental doorway and an elegant inner courtyard. It is now occupied by various government departments including the Courts of Justice.

Slightly further to the north, on the Calle Aduana Vieja, the Church of Santo Domingo was founded by Alfonso VIII and his English queen Eleanor whose figures are included among the intricately carved biblical scenes round the west door. Another religious survivor from the Middle Ages is the Cathedral of San Pedro, consisting of a twelfth-century church with its original cloisters, considerably enlarged and updated 400 years later.

Roughly 7km (4 miles) northeast of Soria, a minor road doubles back from the village of Garray on the N111 to inspect the Roman ruins of **Numantia.** This started life as a thriving Iberian city of 8,000 people which held out against the

Gardens to the royal palace at La Granja de San Ildefonso

Roman invaders for nearly a year in 132BC. Eventually, realising that further resistance was impossible, the townspeople committed mass suicide by burning it down around them. The Romans promptly rebuilt the site into an important garrison and agricultural centre but when they in turn were driven out it was left to moulder on its flat isolated hilltop. Although there have been some excavations and a certain amount of restoration is under way, there is not a great deal to see apart from one or two columns, plenty of foundations and traces of the surrounding walls.

The north of Soria province is rather short of tourist attractions with the exception of the mountains and lakes of the Sierra de Urbión to the west and the little town of **Ágreda** on the border with Aragon slightly further away to the east. This was an important stronghold in the Middle Ages but it has mellowed considerably during the intervening centuries, preserving its ancient palace and the Church of San Miguel, largely rebuilt in the fifteenth century, and acquiring the Convent of La Concepción during the reign of Philip IV 200 years later. However it is a very different story to the south of the capital.

Some 56km (35 miles) to the south-east on the N122, **El Burgo de Osma** is the proud possessor of a beautiful, quite small cathedral. The town was an important religious centre at the time of the Visigoths but their original church was replaced by a Gothic sanctuary in 1232 as a result of a vow made by San Pedro de Osma. The splendid south door with its well-protected statues of biblical characters, a-mong them the Virgin Mary, Moses, Gabriel, Judith and Esther, dates from the same period. The cloisters were added somewhat later whereas the decorative Baroque tower was an eighteenth-century afterthought. The interior is memorable for its elegant nave, the high altar and some fine wrought-iron screens. The cathedral treasures include the decorative tomb of San Pedro de Osma and a collection of illustrated manuscripts, kept under lock and key in the small museum. It is worth spending a short time wandering through the nearby streets and squares, past the old houses and other eighteenth-century buildings like the San Agustín Hospital on the Plaza Mayor, the Bishop's Palace and the old university of Santa Catalina. Searchers after antiquity might also enjoy a brief visit to Ciudad de Osma, a tiny hamlet on the outskirts that marks the site of the Roman settlement of *Uxama Argalae*.

From El Burgo de Osma the C116 strikes out across country with a turning off along the SO104 to **Berlanga de Duero**, dominated by the massive protecting ramparts of its fifteenth-century castle. Unfortunately all but a fraction of the Duke's Palace was destroyed by the French during the Peninsular War but the village still has plenty to offer in the way of medieval gates, elderly houses, arcaded streets and an early Gothic church. Back on the C116 the next place of interest is **Almazán**, which also owes its existence to the Romans but has little or nothing to substantiate this claim apart from a few remnants of the ancient walls. It is an engaging little place with its narrow streets and alleys, three fortified gateways and the sixteenth-century palace of the Counts of Altamira overlooking the Plaza del Ayunamiento. The oldest building in town is the neighbouring Church of San Miguel, built in the twelfth century, which still has its Moorish dome of interwoven arches embellished with carvings recalling the murder of Thomas Becket in Canterbury.

Heading south from Almazán the N111 joins the main Madrid-Barcelona highway near **Medinaceli**, another Roman outpost that was captured and fortified later by the Moors. Its main claim to fame is the triumphal arch built by the Romans in about AD2 to commemorate some important victory. However, as all the inscriptions have been obliterated by time and the elements there is no way of knowing why it was sited on this particular hilltop in the first place. The town, known originally as *Ocilis*, was renamed *Medina Selim* by the Moors because of the salt marshes which are still in production near the village of Salinas de Medinaceli a short distance away. Many of the old buildings in the town were added at intervals after the Recon-quest,

the most recent being the eighteenth-century palace of the resident dukes.

There are two excellent reasons for making a brief excursion along the N11 towards Barcelona, even for motorists who are not heading for the Mediterranean coast. In the first place there is some impressive scenery beyond Lodares as the highway snakes its way through the towering reddish cliffs of the Jalón Gorges to Arcos de Jalón. Thereafter it follows the river in a more sedate fashion across the border into Zaragoza, 1km (½mile) or so after a turning off on the right near the modern Albergue Nacion-al Santa Maria de Huerta, which takes its name from the nearby Cistercian monastery.

The first religious community was established here in 1162 and by the late thirteenth-century much of the building work had been completed. Everything went well until the Dissolution of the Monasteries in 1835 when it was abandoned and left to its own devices for nearly 100 years. A small band of monks returned in 1930 and set about restoring as much of the damage as possible. Today visitors are shown round the magnificent refectory with its Gothic vaulting and a hatch through to the kitchen, mem-orable chiefly for its huge central chimney. The Knights' Cloister is appropriately elegant with a decorative gallery, while the Hostelry Cloister adjoins the old Lay-brothers' Hall, divided by a line of sturdy, functional pillars. The beautifully restored church is quite ornate with a fine wrought-iron screen, Renaissance panelling and ancient tiles on the floor. Among the various treasures are a cope, boots and gloves that belonged to a twelfth-century Archbishop of Toledo, while the outbuildings include both functional storehouses and spacious wine cellars.

True to their tradition the monks set aside eight small rooms for men in search of temporary refuge from the strains and stresses of the world outside. No concessions are made for visitors and there are even one or two basic rules, such as appearing on time for meals and behaving in a suitably restrained manner in keeping with the religious atmosphere. However there is no ban on people of different faiths, nor is there any obligation to attend any of the daily services, although most people seem anxious to take part in them.

Like most of the other monasteries of Northern and Central Spain, Santa Maria de la Huerta makes no provision for female guests so families, and anyone else who is just looking for a bed for the night, would be wise to book accommodation at the Albergue before returning to Soria in the morning. Male travellers in search of peace and comparative solitude can write to the monastery to see if it is possible to make the necessary arrangements in advance.

VALLADOLID

Valladolid is at the very heart of Castilla y León, encased in seven of the eight other provinces with Soria looking on from the sidelines. The countryside is monotonous, excellent for raising sheep and fighting battles, the former having kept the area prosperous for centuries. The weather is not wonderful and the tourist attractions are somewhat limited but, like so many other places in Spain, it has a fair amount to offer the determined sightseer. It is also well supplied with main roads and rivers, the most important being the Río Duero, has a large rail junction at Medina del Campo, an airport within easy reach of Valladolid city, a comprehensive network of bus services and its full quota of thriving industrial interests.

Some people describe **Valladolid** as a lovely university city while others cast it just as firmly in the role of one of the Ugly Sisters. The only reliable solution is to call in, look round and make a personal assessment. It was certainly a popular centre in its earlier years. Pedro the Cruel was married here and so were Ferdinand and Isabel, it was the birthplace of Philip II among others, such as Anne of Austria whose son was Louis XIV of France. Cervantes wrote part of *Don Quixote* in a house on the Calle del Rasto and Columbus died in straitened circumstances at the Casa de Colón.

The Palace of the
Counts of Gómara, Soria
city

A superior example of a
dovecot in Soria

The old centre lies more or less between the cathedral and the river and includes the university, a liberal sprinkling of small churches, some antiquated mansions and the Colegio de San Gregorio on the Plaza de San Pablo. This fifteenth-century college, founded by Alonso de Burgos who was Isabel the Catholic's confessor, has a profusely decorated façade combining a pomegranite tree, to emphasise the reconquest of Granada, with cherubs and savages, branches covered in thorns, religious symbols and heraldic emblems. The patio is just as exuberant; comparatively simple and restrained at ground level but breaking out into an excess of stone tracery, carved columns, coats-of-arms and gargoyles in the gallery. The small chapel, which has also been restored, has carved choirstalls and a Berruguete altarpiece.

Part of the college is now home to the National Museum of Polychrome Sculpture, full of examples gathered in from various churches in the region. Some of the exhibits are rather repetitive but one or two stand out from the crowd, among them the Entombment by Juan de Juni. The Church of San Pablo, which also overlooks the square, was given a very similar façade at the end of the sixteenth century. Apart from a few tombs there is nothing of particular interest inside because all its treasures were looted by French troops during the Peninsular War. Behind the Capitania General, a former royal residence that unwillingly played host to Napoleon at about the same time, a complicated system of one-way streets surrounds the Valverde Palace, the Church of San Miguel and the Archaeological Museum, all of them within a stone's throw of the Plaza de San Miguel. The museum contains a fairly wide range of items in addition to its not-very-inspiring Roman sculptures. There are some early frescoes and medieval paintings as well as pieces of furniture and a collection of tapestries.

On the far side of the San Quirce Angustias, which curves round from the Plaza de San Pablo, a number of different architects had a hand in building the cathedral, with not entirely satisfactory results. They included Herrera, commissioned by Philip II in 1580, Alberto Churriguera who added his own Baroque ideas more than 100 years later and a variety of more recent but less talented renovators. The high altar is colourful and impressive and so are a handful of items in the museum. This is located in the adjoining Church of St Mary Major and is worth a visit if only to see the huge silver monstrance and two portraits that may or may not be the work of Velázquez.

A certain amount of persistence is needed in order to inspect the city's other attractions, mainly because this entails rather a lot of walking with nothing much to see along the way. In the immediate vicinity are the little fourteenth-century Church of Santa Maria la Antigua in the shadow of the cathedral, the university with its eye-catching entrance and, behind it, the Renaissance College of Santa Cruz. The Calle de Cardenal Mendoza, leading off the square, is the quickest way to the Calle Colón and the strangely sad little museum in the house where Columbus died nearly 500 years ago.

A good deal further away in the opposite direction, Cervantes' old home in the Calle del Rastro is simple and unpretentious, having apparently changed very little since he was a local resident. However, as museums go, it is overshadowed by the Oriental Museum in an ancient convent on the other side of the Campo Grande. It is full of beautiful things brought back from the Far East; fragile Chinese porcelain, rich embroidery, carved ivory, pictures, examples of folk art from the Philippines and a great deal more besides. Meanwhile, Simancas Castle, 11km (7 miles) south of the city on the road to Zamora, is really only of interest to serious historians. It was built in 1480, acquired by Ferdinand and Isabel and used by Charles V to house the state archives. These have been added to conscientiously, so that today the eight million or more documents present a complete picture of events in Spain over the past 400 years.

Valladolid is not everybody's idea of a good base from which to explore the surrounding area although it has one or two perfectly acceptable hotels such as the Olid Melia in the Plaza San Miguel. An alternative choice might be El Montico on the N620 5km (3 miles) from Tordesillas, or the Parador Nacional de Tordesillas surrounded by pinewoods on the outskirts of the town. There is nothing atmospheric about it but because it is located near the highway from Madrid to Galicia, as well as being on one of the major routes to Portugal, it would be advisable to book a room in advance. The same applies to the El Astral campsite in the vicinity for the same reasons.

Tordesillas itself can hardly be said to sparkle although it is banked up beside the Río Duero with an unusual, rather rundown Plaza Mayor and the ancient Convent of Santa Clara. The town was assured its place in history on more than one occasion. It was here in 1494 that Spain and Portugal agreed to divide the emerging New World between them, Spain taking everything west of a line drawn beyond the Cape Verde Islands, leaving the rest to Portugal. Since then a number of experts have wondered if the early Portuguese discoverers had travelled further than anyone was prepared to admit because it turned out shortly afterwards that the country had a legitimate claim to Brazil.

The convent was originally a palace built for Alfonso XI but it took holy orders in the fourteenth century when Pedro the Cruel was looking round for a safe retreat for Maria de Padilla, out of reach of his wife Blanche de Bourbon. However its most famous inmate was Juana the Mad who locked herself away, or was imprisoned, here for more than 40 years after the death of her husband Philip the Fair in 1506. She never received any visitors, but whether this was her own decision or on the instructions of her son Charles V is still open to question. The convent looks rather dull from the outside but is, nevertheless, worth a short visit. The patio is most attractive with its variegated tiles and Moorish style arches while the church, converted from the original throne room, combines a beautiful ceiling in the choir with some elderly tombs in the Saldañas chapel.

Medina del Campo, 24km (15 miles) south on the NVI to Madrid, has always been a busy market town, famous for its medieval fairs that attracted buyers from all over Europe. Its most obvious attraction is La Mota castle with its large square keep, much frequented by Isabel the Catholic who died there in 1504, although some reports suggest that she was actually staying in the Dueñas Palace in the Calle Santa Teresa at the time of her death. The greater part of the town was destroyed during the Comunero revolt in the reign of Charles V but the large Plaza de España still has a sixteenth-century church, the old slaughter house and a Town Hall dating from 1660.

From Medina del Campo the C112 crosses the N601 at Olmedo, passes a ruined castle near Iscar and makes a brief sortie into the province of Segovia: at Cuellar the SG223 heads straight for **Peñafiel** on the Río Duero, an overall distance of 86km (53 miles). Here the dominant feature is the massive 600-year-old fortress poised on a rocky spike overlooking three separate valleys. It is considerably longer than it is wide with a proportionately large keep and has been extremely well preserved. The attendant village is memorable for its fourteenth-century San Pablo Church and the Plaza del Coso surrounded by ancient houses whose balconies provided spectators with seats for the regular bullfights staged in the square below.

A minor road from Peñafiel crosses the river on its way to **Pesquera de Duero**, roughly 6km (4 miles) away. Just short of the village is the Bodegas Alejandro Fernández, a thriving winery that is open to visitors who have made a prior appointment. Since it first went into production in the mid-1970s the red Pesquera wines have gained an enviable reputation in America, especially the Reserva Especial which spends 2 years in an oak cask and a further 2 years in the bottle before being launched on to the open market. At the moment a tour of the premises is restricted to the whole process of wine-making, from the area where the grapes are crushed through to the wooden crates used to store the bottles while they complete their ageing process. However plans are afoot to create a wine museum as well as a reception area overlooking the river where visitors will be able to sample the wines while at the same time enjoying a lunch of grilled lamb chops.

Peñafiel is 55km (34 miles) from Valladolid. Motorists leaving the city again have a choice of main routes to all the nearby provincial capitals as well as to Madrid 188km (117 miles) away. Its closest counterpart is Palencia, 47km (29 miles), followed by Zamora 97km (60 miles), Segovia 110km (68 miles), Salamanca 115km (71 miles) Ávila 120km (74 miles) and Burgos 125km (77½ miles). The most distant is León, 139km (86 miles) to the north-west. Apart from being one of the main roads up to the Bay of Biscay this gives motorists an opportunity to pause in **Medina de Rioseco**, an agricultural centre in the Tierra de Campos. It is a pleasing small town with an attractive, if narrow main street and two interesting little churches — a modest prelude to the treasures lying in wait on the far side of the border.

Peñafiel is dominated by the 600-year old fortress

ZAMORA

Zamora wraps itself round the north-eastern corner of Portugal, threaded through by the Río Duero which neatly divides the Tierra del Pan, or bread lands, from the wine growing areas of the Tierra del Vino to the south. Regardless of the fact that tourists are somewhat thin on the ground here the province has three paradores, a number of hotels and hostales, four campsites, a national park and an impressive collection of ancient buildings. Zamora city is on the main railway line from Madrid to Galicia and is connected by bus with Madrid, Salamanca, Valladolid and Barcelona besides being on the N630 which runs from the Bay of Biscay down to Sevilla in Andalucia. At the same time the N122 passes through the city on its way from Bragança, in northern Portugal, to Tordesillas, 30km (19 miles) short of Valladolid, where it joins the main road to Madrid. For motorists heading south to the national capital from Zamora this is an easy run of 246km (153 miles).

The old heart of **Zamora** is contained in an area shaped rather like an ankle-length boot standing on the north bank of the Duero. Although there are plenty of lovely old houses and attractive little churches tucked away in the maze of narrow streets, the most impressive building is undoubtedly the cathedral with its unusual dome, standing in the shadow of the cas-

tle ruins at the very toe of the boot. Parts of it date from the twelfth century but, in common with most others of its ilk, a variety of different styles were superimposed on the Romanesque original. The most eye-catching additions are the wrought-iron grilles, the fifteenth-century pulpits and the beautifully carved choir stalls. These are a study in contrasts with conventionally sedate biblical figures on the backs and somewhat more improper monks and nuns disporting themselves in a bacchanalian fashion on the armrests and misericords. The Cathedral Museum is memorable chiefly for its so-called Black Tapestries, finely woven in Belgium in the fifteenth century to depict such historical events as the Trojan War and the exploits of Hannibal.

Further east towards the instep, past the little church of La Magdalena, the Plaza Canovas is only a block away from the Church of Santa Maria la Nueva whose prize possession is a sculpture of the *Dead Christ* by Gregorio Fernandez. On the Thursday night before Easter it is carried through the streets in a silent torchlight procession marking the anniversary of Christ's last walk to the Garden of Gethsemane. All the tableaux which form part of the city's other Holy Week celebrations are kept in the Semana Santa Museum just opposite. Anyone interested in elderly mansions and picturesque small churches would have a field day in the vicinity, starting with the Casa del Cordón, a stone's throw from the river, before wandering upstream to inspect the nearby Church of Santa Maria de la Orta built by the Templars and the remains of Santo Tomé. Meanwhile the ankle area of the boot, round the Plaza Fray Diego de Deza and the Plaza General Sanjurjo, is full of interest with churches like Santiago del Burgo and mansions such as the Casa de los Momos with its decorative windows. The Parador Condes de Alba y Aliste in the central Plaza Viriato is small and elegant, housed in a fifteenth-century ducal palace with all the appropriate furnishings as well as a garage and a swimming pool.

There are one or two places worth visiting quite close to the city. **Arcenillas**, 7km (4 miles) to the south-east on the C605, has a village church containing a collection of panels portraying the life of Christ that were painted by Fernando Gallego in the fifteenth century for the altarpiece in Zamora cathedral. **Toro**, 33km (20 miles) to the east on the N122, about half way to Tordesillas, is much larger and more historic. Apart from anything else it was the site of Ferdinand and Isabel's victory over her niece Juana in their struggle for the crown of Castile. The best preserved of its Romanesque buildings are the Church of San Lorenzo and the larger Collegiate Church with its lantern tower and carved doorways. Inside there are a variety of painted statues in the nave and a picture referred to as the Virgin and the Fly, supposedly painted by Fernando Gallego and thought by some experts to be an excellent likeness of the Catholic Monarch, Isabel.

Benavente, due north of Zamora, is an old town with a few minor surprises up its sleeve. The church of Santa Maria del Azogue contains some thirteenth-century sculptures while San Juan del Mercado has a twelfth-century carving of the travels of the Magi. The town's Pimentel Palace was burned down by the French during the Peninsular War but has been largely restored and converted into the atmospheric Parador Rey Fernando II de Leon, Paseo Ramón y Cajal.

From Benavente the C620 heads westwards on a somewhat roundabout route to Orense and Compostela. On the way it passes the modest La Estacada campsite at Santa Cristina Polvorosa before calling at the delightful mountain village of Puebla de Sanabria, 110km (68 miles) from Zamora. This is very much an outdoor area, greatly favoured by hunters and fishermen, ramblers and water sports enthusiasts. The Lago de Sanabria in the nearby National Park is a glacial lake surrounded with wooded slopes, fed by little streams and overlooked by two minor roads and the village of San Martin de Castañeda. There are three campsites, the best equipped being Los Robles at Ribadelago, although El Folgoso, nearer to Puebla de Sanabria, is the only one which remains open throughout the year. The

Zamora stands on the north bank of the Río Duero

The cathedral in Zamora city

Parador Puebla de Sanabria is modern and not too expensive but for anyone who is economising the Victoria is quite acceptable.

Motorists who have no intention of retracing their steps to Zamora have two main options — to carry on to Orense, 158km (98 miles) away or backtrack to the C622 which is a convenient shortcut through La Bañeza where there is a further choice between Astorga and León.

LA RIOJA

La Rioja is a small, autonomous province in the Ebro valley on the old pilgrim road to Santiago de Compostela, known first and foremost for its wines. They were being produced before the Romans arrived, received an honourable mention in at least one twelfth-century manuscript and within the next 400 years were being exported to France and Italy. For the most part they are red or rosé with a moderate alcohol content and the ability to travel well to places as far afield as the USA. The province takes its name from the Río Oja, although most vineyards are concentrated along the Ebro, leaving the southern part of the region to produce a variety of early vegetables.

The capital, **Logroño**, is linked by train or bus to several nearby cities including Bilbao, Zaragoza, Burgos and Pamplona: the A68 *autopista* passes the front door on its way from the Mediterranean to the Bay of Biscay and there are major road links with all the surrounding provinces, such as the N111 through Soria that joins the N11 to Madrid, 331km (205 miles) away. Although it marks the spot where ancient pilgrims crossed the Ebro, using a bridge built specially for them by San Juan de Ortega, Logroño is not a very prepossessing city. In fact its rather limited tourist attractions can be visited in the space of an hour or two. They consist mainly of the cathedral, which was very considerably updated in the eighteenth century, the somewhat older Church of San Bartolomé and the Church of Santa Maria de Palacio that was originally part of a palace which Alfonso VII presented to the Order of the Holy Sepulchre in 1130 or thereabouts. There are a clutch of modern hotels some of which only have cafeterias but this hardly matters because La Merced in the Marqués de San Nicolas is an excellent restaurant sited in an eighteenth-century palace.

Anyone approaching La Rioja from the east along the N232, might prefer to spend the night in **Alfaro** where the Hotel Palacios on the Avenida de Zaragoza belongs to the Palacios family who own the adjoining winery. It is reasonably comfortable with a tennis court and swimming pool, in addition to which guests are invited to visit the bodega and inspect the exhibits in the family wine museum, housed in the basement. This contains part of a 54,000 litre American oak fermenting tank that is big enough to walk inside and inspect the bullfighting posters and photographs pinned up on the walls. Other items on display include a number of old tools that were used for making the smaller oak barrels in which the wine is kept for about 12 months before being transferred to bottles for a further year.

Some 27km (17 miles) down the road **Calahorra** is an ancient Celtic town that crossed swords with Pompey before it was starved into submission in 71BC. Here the most outstanding attraction is the cathedral with its impressive sacristy and an elegant Gothic nave. The modern Parador Marco Fabio Quintiliano is one of only two in La Rioja at the moment, and is considerably less atmospheric that its opposite number in Santo Domingo de la Calzada on the opposite side of the provincial capital. However, before heading further west along the N120, there is a pleasant excursion for motorists with time on their hands along the valley of the Río Iregua to the Reserva Nacional de Cameros. The scenery varies from cultivated plots and orchards to massive ochre-red boulders and from wooded hillsides to narrow ravines until it reaches Villanueva de Cameros, a delightful little urban collection of half-timbered houses. From here it is possible to carry on for some 6km (4 miles) and turn off on to the minor, time-consuming LO801 through the reserve as far as the no less tortuous C113 which rejoins the N120 at **Nájera**. The town was once the capital of the kingdom of Navarre and the site of a monastery founded in about 1032. Very little is left apart from the Church of Santa Maria la Real containing the entrance to the cave where an early statue of the Virgin was discovered, and a number of royal tombs. Foremost among them is the tomb of Sancho IIIs wife, Blanca of Navarre, who died in 1158, while the intricately carved choir stalls incorporate a figure of the founder, Garcia III, dressed in armour.

Like Nájera, **Santo Domingo de la Calzada** was an important stopping place on the road to Compostela. It is only 19km (12 miles) to the west along the N120 but has done slightly better as far as preserving part of its ancient pilgrim hostal is concerned. The façade and the main hall have been incorporated into the Parador Nacional Santo Domingo de la Calzada on the Plaza del Santo. The name, St Dominic of the Causeway, dates from the eleventh century when a local anchorite built a bridge over the Río Glera and enlarged his hermitage to provide shelter for the constant stream of pilgrims. A few houses were added and in due course they grew into a town, protected by ramparts, with a Gothic church that was soon promoted to the status of a cathedral.

There is plenty to see inside, including the tomb of the saint and the miraculous sickle he is believed to have used to clear paths through the oaks and undergrowth to make the long journey a little easier. However the most unusual feature is a small Gothic shrine that doubles as a coop for a live cock and hen which are replaced with a fresh couple on 12 May every year. The reason behind this is an odd miracle that, strangely enough, has its counterpart in the Portuguese town of Barcelos. Apparently a young German pilgrim was wrongly accused of theft, found guilty and condemned to death. Some considerable time later he was discovered hanging but still very much alive. The news was rushed to the local judge who was about to start eating. He only laughed, remarking that the young man was just as dead as the roast chickens on the dish in front of him; upon which the birds stood up, the cock crowed and the victim was cut down, seemingly no worse for his very unpleasant experience.

Before leaving Santo Domingo de la Calzada anyone with a soft spot for out-of-the-way places would probably enjoy a brief sortie into the attractive **Sierra de la Demanda**. A cobweb of minor roads and byways south of the main highway is peppered with tiny hamlets, the most interesting of which is **San Millán de la Cogolla** which, incidentally, can also be reached off the C113 a few kilometres from Nájera. The village is known principally for its two antiquated monasteries, Suso and Yuso. The former dates from the early tenth century when it was

partly hollowed out of the mountainside 2km (1 mile) away. It has a distinctly Moorish flavour with horseshoe arches, arcades and a few medieval tombs, the most decorative of which belongs to San Millán. Another contains the remains of Gonzalo de Berceo, the Castilian poet who was the local abbot in the early thirteenth century. Yuso, which is more accessible, was founded by Benedictine monks more than 100 years later and was largely rebuilt in the sixteenth century.

North from Santa Domingo de la Calzada the LO750 makes a B-line for **Haro**, a prosperous old town with some delightful sixteenth-century houses, that is sometimes referred to as the Capital of the Wine Coast. It makes a good base for touring the local wineries, the best known of which is probably the Bodegas Bilbainas which can be visited almost any morning or late afternoon without an appointment. The best places to stay are Los Agustinas, 2 San Agustin or Iturrimurri, 1km (½ mile) outside the town on the N232, which looks a little like an Alpine chalet and has plenty of parking space, a restaurant, a snack bar and a swimming pool. There is also a campsite at Haro which is open all year. Visitors planning to be in town on 29 June would do well to book their accommodation in advance and take some form of protective clothing with them. It is the anniversary of a boundary dispute between Haro and Miranda and is celebrated by all and sundry armed with litres of wine, much of which is sprayed over anyone within striking distance.

As far as sightseeing is concerned the local Church of St Thomas has a finely sculptured doorway. In addition the medieval town of **Laguardia**, a short drive away along the N232 on the opposite side of the river, has both the eye-catching Church of Santa Maria de los Reyes and a very informative Casa del Vino for visitors who want to improve their knowledge of local wines. Thereafter the road rejoins the river at Assa and more or less keeps it company into Logroño.

The choir stalls inside the cathedral at San Domingo de la Calzada

ADDITIONAL INFORMATION

PLACES OF INTEREST

ÁVILA (Province)
Ávila

Casa de los Deanes Museum
Plaza de Italia
Open: 10am-2pm and 4-6pm.
Closed Mondays and some
holidays.

Cathedral Museum
Open: 10am-1.30pm and 3-7pm
summer. 10am-1.30pm and
3-5pm winter. Opens at 11am on
Sundays and holidays.

La Encarnación Convent
Calle de la Encarnación
Open: 9.30am-1.30pm and 3.30-
7pm summer. Closes Tuesdays
and 6pm November to March.

La Santa Convent
Open: 9am-1.30pm and
3.30-9pm.

Las Madres Convent
Calle del Duque de Alba
Open: 10am-1pm and 4-7pm.

Santo Tomás Monastery
Avenida del Alférez Provisional
Open: 9.30am-1.30pm and
4-7pm.

San Vicente Basilica
Avenida de Portugal
Open: 10am-2pm and 4-6pm.

Closed on Sunday.

Ramacastañas

Aguila Caves
Open: 10.30am-7pm summer,
10.30am-1pm and 3-6pm winter.

BURGOS (Province)
Burgos

Archaeological Museum
Casa de Miranda
Open: 9am-2pm and 4-6pm.
10am-1pm Sundays and
holidays. Closed Mondays.

Cathedral
Open: 10am-1.30pm and 4-7pm
June to September. 10am-1pm
and 4-6pm October to May.

Las Huelgas Reales Convent
1½km (1 mile) west.
Guided tours 11am-2pm and
4-6pm. Closed Sunday and
holiday afternoons.

**Marceliano Santa Maria
Museum**
San Juan Monastery
Open: 10am-2pm and 4-7pm
June to September. 10am-2pm
and 4-6pm October to May.
Closed Sundays and holidays.

**Miraflores Carthusian
Monastery**
4km (2 miles) east

Open: 10.30am-3pm and 4-7pm
June to September. 10.30am-
3pm and 4-6pm October to May.
11.30am Sundays and holidays.
Closed Good Friday.

Covarrubias

Treasury Museum
Open: 10am-2pm and 4-8pm
June to September. 10am-2pm
and 4-7pm October to May.
Closed Tuesday October to May.

Peñaranda de Duero

Miranda Palace
Open: 9.30am-1.30pm and
4-7pm summer. 10am-1pm and
4-6pm winter. Closed Sunday
and holiday afternoons.

Santo Domingo de Silos

Monastery
Guided tours 10am-1.15pm and
4.15-6.45pm summer, 10am-
12.45pm and 3.45-6.45pm
winter. 12noon-1.15pm Sundays
and holidays.

LEÓN (Province)
Astorga

Cathedral and Museum
Open: 10am-2pm and 4-8pm
summer, 11am-2pm and 3.30-
6.30pm winter. Closed December
to February.

Los Caminos Museum
Near cathedral
Open: 10am-2pm and 4-8pm

summer, 11am-2pm and
3.30-6.30pm winter. Closed
Mondays in winter.

León

Cathedral Museum and Cloister
Open: 9.30am-1.30pm and
4-6.30pm. Closed Sunday
afternoons.

Real Basilica de San Isidoro
Plaza de San Isidoro
Open: 9am-2pm and 3.30-8pm
summer, 10am-1.30pm and
4-6.30pm winter.

**San Marcos Church and
Archaeology Museum**
Plaza de San Marcos
Open: 10am-2pm and 4-6pm.
Closed Sunday afternoons and
Monday.

Ponferrada

Castle
Open: 9am-1pm and 4-7pm
March to September, 10am-1pm
and 3-6pm October to February.
Closed Saturday afternoons and
Tuesdays.

Valporquero Caves
42km (26 miles) north of León
Open: 10am-2pm and 4-7pm
mid-May to October.

PALENCIA (Province)
Aguilar de Campoo

Santa Maria la Real Monastery
Open: 8am-1pm and 3-7pm

summer, 9am-1pm and 3-6pm winter. Closed Sundays and holidays.

Frómista

San Martin Church
Open: 10am-2pm and 4-8pm. Closed Saturday afternoons and Sundays.

Baños de Cerrato

San Juan Bautista Basilica
Open: 9am-1pm and 4-8pm March to October. 9am-1pm and 4-6pm November to February.

Palencia

Cathedral Museum
Open: 10am-1pm and 4-6pm. Closed Sunday afternoons.

LA RIOJA (Province)
Nájera

Santa Maria la Real Monastery
Open: 9.30am-12.30pm and 4-7.30pm May to September, 10am-12.30pm and 4-6.30pm October to April.

San Millán de la Cogolla

Suso Monastery
Open: 10am-2pm and 4-8pm summer, 10am-2pm and 4-6pm winter.

Yuso Monastery
Open: 10.30am-12.30pm and 4.30-7pm summer, 10.30am-

12.30pm and 4-6pm winter. Closed Monday.

Santo Domingo de la Calzada

Cathedral
Open: 9am-2pm and 4-8.30pm.

SALAMANCA (Province)
Ciudad Rodrigo

Cathedral
Open: 9am-1pm and 4-8pm summer. 12noon-1pm and 4-7pm winter.

Salamanca

Las Dueñas Convent
Behind cathedral
Open: 10am-1pm and 4-7pm.

Old Cathedral
Open: 10am-2pm and 4-8pm summer. 9.30am-1pm and 3-6.30pm winter.

Salamanca Museum
Alvarez Abarca House
Open: 9.30am-2pm and 4-6pm July to September. 10am-1.30pm and 4-6pm on weekdays and 11am-2pm Sundays and holidays October to June. Closed Saturday afternoons and holidays.

University
Open: 9.30am-1.30pm and 4-7pm June to October, 9.30am-1.30pm and 4-6pm November to May. Closed Saturday, Sunday and holiday

afternoons and 1 January, 6
January, 24 June, 25 December
and on the first day of term.

SEGOVIA (Province)
Coca

Castle
50km (31 miles) north-west of
Segovia
Open: 11am-1pm and 3-5pm.
Closed mid-July to mid-August.

La Granja de San Ildefonso

Palace
Guided tours 10am-1pm and
3-6pm. Closed some holidays.
Gardens open 10am-7pm
summer. 10am-6pm winter.
Fountains play from 5.30pm
Thursdays, Saturdays, Sundays
and holidays mid-April to
mid-November.

Segovia

Alcázar
Open: 10am-2pm and 4-6pm
weekdays, 10am-6pm Saturdays
and Sundays. Closed 1 January,
6 January, 25 December.

Cathedral
Open: 9am-7pm May to
September, 10am-1pm and
3-6pm October to April. Closed
1 January, 6 January, Good
Friday and 25 December.

Daniel Zuloaga Museum
San Juan de los Cabelleros
Open: 10am-1pm and 3-6pm.

Closed Mondays.

Fine Arts Museum
Open: 10am-1pm and 3-6pm.
Closed Mondays.

Monasterio de El Parral
Open: 10am-1.30pm and 3-7pm
summer, 10am-1pm and 3-6pm
winter. 9am-12noon and 3-6pm
Sundays. Closed 1 January,
6 January, Good Friday and
25 December.

Vera Cruz Church
Open: 10am-1pm and 3-6pm.
Closed Mondays, 1 January, 6
January, 25 December and
November.

SORIA (Province)
El Burgo de Osma

Cathedral
Open: 9am-1pm and 4-7pm
summer, 10am-1pm and 3-5pm
winter. Treasures, enquire at 1
Plaza de la Cathedral.

Santa Maria de Huerta
Monastery
Open: 10am-1pm and 3.30-7pm
summer, 10am-1pm and
3.30-6.30pm winter. Closed
11am-12noon Sundays and
holidays.

Soria

Cathedral
Open: during services. If closed
enquire at the tourist office or
1 Calle Santa Mónica.

San Juan de Duero
Open: 10am-2pm and 4-7pm.
Closed Sunday, Monday and
holiday afternoons.

San Saturio Hermitage
Open: 10.30am-6.30pm.

Numantia Ruins
7km (4 miles) north-east
Open: 10am-2pm and 4-7pm.
Closed Sunday, Monday and
holiday afternoons.

VALLADOLID (Province)
Medina de Rioseco

Churches
Open: 11am-2.30pm and 4-7pm
weekdays, 11am-2.30pm
Sundays, holidays and in winter.

Tordesillas

Santa Clara Convent
Open: 9.30am-1pm and 3-6pm.
Closed sometimes Monday or
Tuesday and some holidays.

Valladolid

Archaeological Museum
Open: 10am-2pm and 4-7pm.
Closed Sunday and holiday
afternoons.

Cathedral
Open: 8am-2pm and 5.30-8pm
weekdays. 8am-2pm and 5-7pm
Sundays and holidays.

Cervantes Museum
Calle del Rastro

Open: 10am-6pm weekdays.
10am-2pm Sundays and
holidays. Closed Mondays.

Columbus Museum
Calle Colón
Open: 10am-1pm and 4-7pm
weekdays, 11am-1pm Sundays.
Closed Mondays.

Oriental Museum
Philippines Convent
Open: 10am-1pm and 4-7pm
weekdays. 10am-2pm Sundays
and holidays.

San Gregorio College
Cadenas de San Gregorio
Open: 10am-2pm and 4-7pm.
Closed Sunday and holiday
afternoons and Mondays.

Simancas Castle
11km (7 miles) south
Open: 8am-1.30pm July and
August, 9am-1.30pm and
4-7.30pm September to June.
Closed February and November
afternoons and second week in
September.

ZAMORA (Province)
Zamora

Cathedral Museum
Open: 11am-2pm and 4-8pm
summer, 10am-1pm winter.

Semana Santa Museum
Opposite Church of Santa Maria la
Nueva
Open: 10am-2pm and 4-8pm
summer, 10am-2pm and 4-7pm

winter. Closed Sundays and
holidays.

TOURIST INFORMATION CENTRES

ÁVILA (Province)
Ávila
Plaza Catedral
☎ 918 21 13 87

BURGOS (Province)
Burgos
Plaza Alonso Martinez
☎ 947 20 31 25

LEÓN (Province)
Astorga
Plaza de España
☎ 987 61 68 38

León
Plaza de Regia
☎ 987 23 70 82

Ponferrada
Gil y Carrasco
☎ 987 42 42 36

PALENCIA (Province)
Aguilar de Campoo
Plaza Mayor
☎ 988 12 20 24

Frómista
Paseo Central
(No telephone number)

Palencia
Mayor 105
☎ 988 72 00 68

LA RIOJA (Province)
Haro

Plaza Hermanos Florentino
Rodriguez
☎ 941 31 27 26

Logroño
Miguel Villanueva
☎ 941 25 77 11

SALAMANCA (Province)
Ciudad Rodrigo
Arco de Amayuelas
☎ 923 46 05 61

Salamanca
Gran Via 41
☎ 923 24 37 30 also Information
Booth Plaza Mayor % 923 21 83
42

SEGOVIA (Province)
Segovia
Plaza Mayor
☎ 911 41 16 02

SORIA (Province)
Soria
Plaza Ramón y Cajal
☎ 975 21 20 52

VALLADOLID (Province)
Medina de Rioseco
Ayuntamiento
Plaza del Generalisimo
☎ 983 70 08 25

Valladolid
Plaza de Zorrilla
☎ 983 35 18 01

ZAMORA (Province)
Zamora
Cortinas de San 5
☎ 988 53 64 70

4
Madrid

Madrid is probably the most controversial city in Spain. To some visitors it is an acquired taste, essentially lively and entertaining below the surface, while others can find practically nothing at all complimentary to say about it. This may be due in part to the fact that it was created by decree in the sixteenth century instead of developing automatically and gracefully into a national capital. It lacks the beauty of Paris, the antiquity of Rome and the poise of so many other outstanding European cities, while at the same time sharing all their disadvantages like ugly, sprawling suburbs and everlasting traffic jams. It is also amazingly insular, with a cynical disregard for foreigners and a haughty contempt for a good many of its own countrymen, at the same time providing them with countless hotels, restaurants, cafés and bars, museums of every description, magnificent art galleries sporting facilities and attractive parks.

Travelling to and from Madrid and round the city requires the minimum amount of effort. The international airport has regular fast and inexpensive buses linking it with the Plaza de Colón. The two main railway stations, Chamartin and Atocha, operate independently to the north and south of the country respectively but are connected by an underground train that stops at least twice along the way. Long distance coaches whisk their passengers off to places of interest in the surrounding regions with all the relevant details available from the coach stations and the tourist office. The Metro is fast, clean and inexpensive, but necessarily impersonal, whereas buses are better for sightseers trying to orientate themselves and pinpoint some of the more obvious landmarks. A good many of the buses converge on the Plaza de la Cibeles where there is a booth that provides all the necessary information. Taxis are plentiful and not too expensive provided they have a meter, but they charge extra for going out to the airport or to the railway stations and the fare should always be agreed in advance for journeys outside the city limits.

Historically Madrid had its beginnings in prehistoric times but it only really emerged when the Moors built a fortress on the site and called it *Mayrit*. This meant 'running waters' which was somewhat ironic because the Río Manzanares was useless when it came to navigation and everything had to be transported by mules before the railway took over from them in the mid-nineteenth century. Various kings had looked in from time to time, including Alfonso VI who turned the mosque into a church. The Catholic Monarchs stayed long enough to found a monastery and Charles V rebuilt the *alcázar*. However it was Philip II who chose it as the capital of Spain in 1561 for no apparent reason other than that it was located in the middle of the country. Building only started in earnest during the reign of Charles III in the late eighteenth century, with the addition of street lighting and a sewerage system, but by 1911 whole stretches were being knocked down again to make way for the Gran Via. The Civil War broke out just 25 years later, in the course of which the siege of Madrid, lasting for more than 2 years, did nothing for either the architecture or the atmosphere. At the end of 1939 life returned to normal but by then the demand for change and modernisation was in full swing and what was left of old Madrid largely disappeared to provide space for new buildings and ideas. Nevertheless there are still a few places where the past lingers on, mainly in the area between the Palacio Real and the Retiro park.

The old city includes both the magnificent Plaza Mayor and the far less spectacular Puerta del Sol. Its Sun Gate disappeared nearly 500 years ago, leaving behind an oddly shaped open space, bearing little resemblance to a square, which is the official centre of Spain. The Kilometre O in front of the police headquarters is the marker from which all the distances in the country are measured. With this in mind it is as good a place as any to start exploring the city.

The Calle Arenal runs straight as an arrow from the Puerta del Sol to the Opera House overlooking the small, well manicured gardens of the Plaza de Oriente. Here the focal point is a huge bronze statue of Philip IV on horseback, designed by Velázques and said by many people to be the finest piece of sculpture in the capital. The roads running down on either side of the gardens are lined with statues of Spanish monarchs who were intended to grace the façade of the Palacio Real (Royal Palace) just opposite, but they proved to be too heavy and now form a regal guard of honour instead. The palace stands on the site of the *alcázar* which was turned into a royal residence by Charles V and burned down in 1734. The present building was completed for Philip V and contains nearly 3,000 rooms, including sumptious state apartments, an extensive library, a pharmacy and a throne room decked out in crimson velvet. The palace was home to each succeeding monarch up to and including Alfonso XIII, but after he abdicated in 1931 it became more of a museum with suites set aside for visiting dignitaries and state rooms that are only used on very important occasions.

A guided tour of the palace can turn out to be something of a marathon but it is also a fascinating if rather indigestible experience. There are so many things to see and admire, from the grand staircase up to Charles IIIs apart-

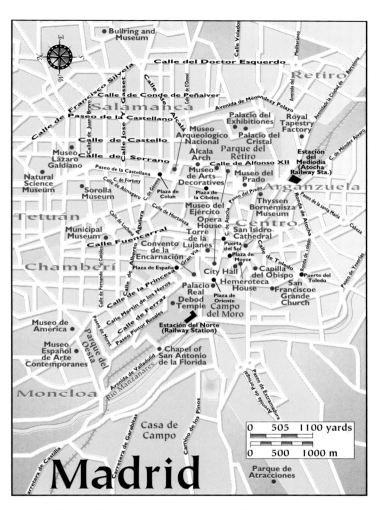

Madrid

ments with their Goya portraits of Charles IV and Queen Maria Luisa, to the magnificent Mirror Room, an enormous banqueting hall and the former Music Room full of clocks which have been added to at intervals since 1770. Queen Maria Cristina of Habsburg's apartments have been turned into a tapestry museum while those of Princess Isabel of Bourbon are devoted to paintings by famous artists as well as embroidery and displays of exquisite glass and porcelain. There are also collections of coins and medals covering more than four centuries, beautiful furniture and precious old musical instruments. In addition to all this, the Armoury facing on to the Plaza de la Armeria contains such things as weapons used by the Turks and the Moors, a suit for the royal greyhound and armour worn by Charles V which is more decorative than functional. The Carriage Museum (Museo de Carruajes Reales) situated in the grounds between the palace and the river, lost most of its vehicles in the fire of 1734. Nevertheless the fairly modern pavilion has several interesting exhibits, among them the nineteenth-century coronation coach that still bears the scars of the attempted assassination of Alfonso XIII and his bride Victoria Eugenia in 1906. Also on display are carriages that belonged to Charles IV and his wife Maria Luisa and an earlier litter used by the Emporer Charles V when he retired to the monastery at Yuste.

Adjoining the Plaza de Oriente, almost but not quite opposite the palace, the Convento de la Encarnación (Incarnacion Convent) was founded by Philip IIIs wife, Margaret of Austria, and received its very viewable collection of museum pieces from a succession of royal patrons. The pictures and sculptures date for the most part from the seventeenth century but they are rather overshadowed by well over a thousand caskets in the Reliquary Gallery. These contain all manner of relics, among them a phial believed to hold the dried blood of St Pantaleon which is said to liquify once a year, on 27 July. A block away, on Calle de Bailén, the Museo del

Pueblo Español is housed in an eighteenth-century mansion and is filled with costumes, jewellery and artifacts from all over the country.

Before venturing any further afield it is well worth visiting the little chapel of San Antonio de la Florida, close to the river behind the Estación de Norte. It was built in 1798 and decorated by Goya whose remains were transferred here from Bordeaux in 1888. The frescoes, completed in the space of 5 months, are superb, depicting St Anthony surrounded by a large crowd which had gathered to watch him performing miracles. Each face is a portrait from life, registering a different emotion, and even the angels immortalise some of the most beautiful women who were living in Madrid at the time.

A little further up river the carefully landscaped Parque del Oeste is marginally unusual because its centrepiece, the Debod Temple, was built in Egypt around 400BC. It was presented to Spain instead of being inundated by the Aswan Dam, shipped over block by block and reconstructed on the site of the Montaña barracks that came to grief during the Civil War. Beyond the park are two museums which have absolutely nothing in common with each other. The Museo de América, standing slightly aloof from the Calle Reyes Católicos, is only concerned with items brought back from the overseas territories that once belonged to Spain. The Aztecs and the Incas are well represented, highlights from Mexico and Peru, while the section devoted to crafts of all descriptions has a number of examples from the

Philippines thrown in for good measure. A block or so away, on the other side of the Avenida Puerta de Hierro, the Museo Español de Arte Contemporanes (Contemporary Spanish Art Museum) is devoted to twentieth-century paintings and sculptures. There are a great many of them but, apart from an occasional Miró or Picasso, nothing of any exceptional interest.

This section of Madrid is often referred to as the University City, regardless of the fact that the campus is completely dwarfed by the vast Casa de Campo, a leisure area par excellence. At one time it was heavily wooded but most of the trees were cut down to provide building materials and firewood, only to be replaced by Philip II who wanted somewhere convenient for hunting. These days there is a cable car up to the top from the Paseo del Pintor Rosales, one or two small roads and a variety of attractions round the perimeter. These include a boating lake, an amusement park and a large zoo as well as a race track and a selection of golf courses augmented by several other golf clubs on the outskirts of the city.

It is a tidy walk back down the Calle Princesa to the Plaza de España which is easily recognised by the lofty Torre de Madrid and the bronze figures of Don Quixote and Sancho Panza in the square. Slightly off to one side, in the Calle Ventura Rodriguez, the former home of the Marqués de Cerralbo has changed very little since his death and contains more than enough of interest to be numbered among the city's private museums. The paintings are especially noteworthy and include El Greco's *St Francis*, on view in the chapel, and a gallery hung with the works of such artists as Titian, Tintoretto, Van Dyke, Ribera and Zurbarán. There are also a number of tapestries, displays of porcelain and ceramics and a quantity of arms and armour as well as some nice pieces of furniture and objects d'art.

From the Plaza de España the Gran Via sheers its way through the city in a welter of highrise buildings, shops, offices and a handful of comfortable hotels. Just where it makes a wide-angle turn to the left at the Plaza de Callao the Postigo de San Martin leads more or less directly to the Descalzas Reales Convent. This was founded by Charles Vs daughter, Juana of Austria, as an offshoot of Santa Teresa's poor Carmelites, but whatever else it may have been it certainly was never poor. In addition to the building itself with its imposing staircase and highly decorative chapels it accumulated enough treasures to fill its own museum. The dormitory used originally by the nuns is hung with fine seventeenth-century tapestries, there are religious paintings and royal portraits, sculptures by Pedro de Mena, admirable furniture and an array of ornate caskets containing holy relics.

The area to the south could be described with complete accuracy as Old Madrid and the Plaza Mayor as its focal point. This is one of the loveliest squares in the country — large, impressive and historic but at the same time very much lived-in, as it

The Royal Palace gardens in Madrid city

Siesta is a time for relaxing

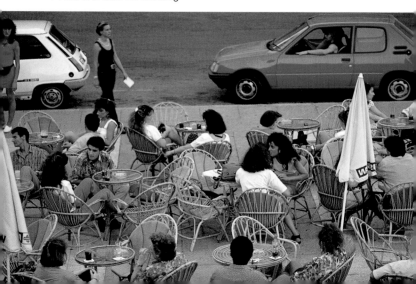

has been for centuries. The surrounding buildings date from 1620 and were completed in time for a tournament held in honour of England's Charles I before he succeeded to the throne. It was also the scene of *autos-de-fe*, when heritics were tried and burned to death, as well as bullfights and fiestas presided over by the king and members of his court from the Casa de la Panaderia, named after a bakery that occupied the site.

The Plaza Mayor is much less aggressive these days, more suited to concerts and festivals, the Sunday morning coin and stamp market, students strumming guitars and visitors sunning themselves at tables outside the various cafés and watching the world go by. Life is a good deal more hectic along the Calle Ribera de Curtidores which branches off to the left below the San Isidro Cathedral. It is a forbidding seventeenth-century church that once belonged to the Jesuits and now stands in for the unfinished Nuestra Señora de Almudaina which seems to be universally ignored. This area is the site of Madrid's much publicised flea market, known as El Rastro, that spills over into all the surrounding streets and alleys and does a roaring trade in everything from highly suspect Old Masters to unmitigated junk of every description. At one time it was possible to pick up antiques at bargain prices but the traders have grown wise to the ways of tourists and generally have a very good idea of the value of their merchandise.

Virtually cheek by jowl with El Rastro is the Puerta de Toledo market, a five-storey labyrinth of glass-fronted designer shops, galleries, bars and restaurants. Here it is possible to pick up a genuine antique for anything up to twenty million pesetas, Toledo work inlaid with gold and silver which originated in Damascus and has now all but died out in Spain, haute couture clothes, glass, ceramics, bronze and porcelain, or visit one of the special exhibitions where the articles are not for sale.

The whole of the surrounding area is a trifle rundown but nevertheless has a number of interesting old features. The most distant of these is San Francisco el Grande Church on the far side of the Puerta de Moros and in a direct line with the Palacio Real on the Calle Bailén. It is the largest church in the city, dates from the late eighteenth century and has both an impressive dome and a chapel decorated by Goya before he became famous. A short walk away, up the Carrera San Francisco, the Capilla del Obispo on the Plaza de la Paja is a Gothic chapel with an impressive altarpiece and a finely carved tomb belonging to a medieval archbishop of Plasencia. More or less round the corner the Church of San Pedro has one of the only two Mudejar towers left in Madrid but nothing else of any consequence.

From here it is only a short walk through the Plaza del Cordón to the historic Plaza de la Villa, surrounded by some of the oldest buildings in the capital. The Torre de los Lujanes, now considerably altered and updated, was where Francis I of France was held prisoner following his capture at the battle of Pavia in 1525. He was released after signing a treaty and promising to marry Charles Vs sister but once safely out of the clutches of the emperor he said the whole thing had been an unfortunate mistake and hostilities were resumed immediately. Next door, the Hemeroteca houses both an overflow from the city library and two Renaissance tombs behind its Gothic entrance. The City Hall opposite was the work of Gómez de Mora, who designed the Plaza Mayor, while the statue in the middle of the square is of Álvaro de Bazán, who made his name at the battle of Lepanto. The only other place of interest in the vicinity is the San Miguel Basilica on the Plaza Puerta Cerrada, an excellent example of Italian Baroque.

One of the most obvious things about the old quarter of Madrid is its plethora of *tasca*, or *tapas*, bars. The name comes from the saucer-sized portions of dozens of different types of food For Spaniards these bridge the gap between lunch and a traditionally late dinner but many tourists find that, having sampled a reasonable selection, they can forget about a restaurant altogether.

This would be a pity because Madrid has some of the finest restaurants in Europe and even more extremely good ones, making it virtually impossible to select one or two from among so many. However, historically speaking, one that comes to mind is the Jockey, founded by Clodoaldo Cortéz nearly half a century ago on the Calle Amador de los Rios. It soon became the exclusive haunt of bankers, politicians and important foreign visitors, went into a decline after the death of the owner but is now back on course under the watchful eye of his son Luis Eduardo Cortéz, himself a politician. Everyone seems to have heard of the considerably older Casa Botin in the Calle Cuchilleros near the Plaza Mayor. It was founded in 1725, was used as a model by several other establishments and is said to have been one of Hemingway's particular favourites. The Zalacain, Alvarez de Baena 4, is both exceptional and expensive while an up-and-coming place to watch is El Mentidero de la Villa on the Calle Santo Tomé.

Still to the south of the Gran Via, but east of the Puerta del Sol, there is not much to write home about before the Paseo del Prado. However, determined museum addicts might well enjoy a small collection in the Academia Real de la Historia (Royal Academy of History) on the Calle Heurtas containing a selection of antiquities, examples of medieval religious art and a few well chosen paintings. About two blocks away, the Casa Museo de Lope de Vegá (Lope de Vegás House) on the Calle Cervantes has been reconstructed to give some idea of what the house and garden looked like when the famous seventeenth-century dramatist was in residence. Cervantes lived on the same street, at the intersection with the Calle de León, and created a further exchange of names by being buried at the Trinitarias Convent in the Calle Lope de Vegá.

An impressive newcomer to the

Paseo del Prado is the Museo Thyssen-Bornemisza, housed in the early nineteenth-century Palacio de Villahermosa. It contains more than 800 paintings collected by Baron Heinrich Thyssen, most of them transferred from his 'Villa Favorita' home on the shores of Lake Lugano in Switzerland. The paintings occupy some fifty rooms and range from the thirteenth century to the present day. Old Masters of many nationalities are represented including such famous Italians as Carpaccio, Ghirlandaio and Veronese; Dutch painters of the calibre of Frans Hals, Hobbema and van Ruysdael; Germans like Holbein and Dürer; the French painter and engraver Fragonard and his fellow countryman Watteau and Spain's El Greco, Goya and Murillo. Visitors with a preference for nineteenth- and twentieth-century art can follow the trends set by the so-called 'Paris School', German expressionism, Russian avant-garde and well-known American artists. Among the host of famous names to look for are Manet, Renoir, Cezanne, Van Gogh, Toulouse-Lautrec, Dali and Picasso. Both the range and quality of the exhibits in this newly installed collection make it a perfect companion for the Museo del Prado opposite, which is generally acknowledged to be one of the truly great art galleries of the world.

The Prado itself occupies a large, neo-Classical building, designed by Vallanueva as a natural history museum but appropriated by Fernando VII in order to bring most of the royal art treasures together under one roof. Every crowned head from the Catholic Monarchs onwards had made a valuable contribution, patronising local artists, inviting foreign painters to the Spanish court, liberating an occasional masterpiece in the course of a campaign or dipping into the State coffers to pay an asking price. One example was Philip IV who bought several pictures in London when Charles Is collection was auctioned after his execution.

It is difficult to think of many artists who are not represented in the Prado, from the weird fantasies of Hieronymus Bosch — known in Spain as El Bosco — personified by his *Garden of Earthly Delights* —to the strictly factual portraits by Dürer, Botticelli's ethereal beauties, or Raphael's conception of the Holy Family. Rubens and Brueghel are out in force along with others of their countrymen such as Rembrandt and Van Dyke who settled in England as court painter to Charles I and is famous for his portraits. There are walls all but papered with Titians, including a splendid portrait of Charles V on horseback providing a striking contrast to the rather candy-floss attractions of his epic *La Gloria*. The canvases by Tintoretto, one of Titian's most famous pupils, are very viewable although for the most part they do not really come up to the standard of his finer works, particularly those in Venice.

Among a host of other artists to look out for are El Greco and Ribera, especially the latter's unpleasantly explicit *Martyrdom of St Bartholomeu*, offset by Murillo's beautiful madonnas and several pictures reflecting his early days as a street artist in Sevilla. This was before he was commissioned to supply nearly a dozen paintings for the cloister of a Franciscan convent. The most attractive representative of the French school is usually considered to be Watteau although there are some other delightful offerings. Examples of the work of British artists are decidedly thin on the ground because they scarcely figured in the royal collections, but this has been redressed to a certain extent by the acquisition of a handful of works by Lawrence, Reynolds and Gainsborough.

Pride of place at the Museo del Prado undoubtedly goes to Diego Velázquez, widely acclaimed as Spain's greatest master, although he was in fact the son of an impoverished Portuguese nobleman who practiced as a lawyer in Sevilla at the end of the sixteenth century. He took the name of his Andalucian mother, Jerónima Velázquez, while he was apprenticed to Francisco Pacheco. Later, in his book *El Arte de la Pintura*, Pacheco wrote that, after 5 years of teaching and education, he married the young Diego to his daughter, 'moved by his virtue, honour, excellent qualities and the hopefulness of his very great natural genius'.

Little is known of the artist's private life, either before or after his marriage, but his son-in-law, Juan Martinez del Mazo, was responsible for a delightful family scene in which Velázquez is shown in the background, absorbed in his painting of Philip IVs second wife, Mariana of Austria. As the official court painter Velázquez had his own apartments in the reconstructed *alcázar*, on the site of the present Palacio Real, and was the only person Philip would allow near him with a paint brush. The result is an amazing record of the king from the age of 18 until the artist's death in 1660. A tangible sign of royal esteem is perfectly obvious in *Las Meninas*, in many ways his greatest achievement, which has been given a room all to itself. It shows the Infanta Margarita and her ladies in waiting watching the artist at work on a portrait of her parents. Three years after it was completed in 1656 the king outraged several of his nobles by making Velázquez a knight of the exclusive Order of Santiago and is said to have personally added the red cross of the Order to his favourite's tunic in the painting so that there could be no mistake.

The Prado owns more than one third of all his known canvases including the *Adoration of the Magi*, painted when he was 20 and believed to show him as the youngest of the Three Kings, his father-in-law as the older, bearded one, his wife Juana as the Virgin and their first child as the Baby Jesus. Among others are *The Surrender of Breda*, known locally as *Las Lanzas*, *Los Borrachos* (*The Drunkards*) and *Las Hilanderas* (*The Spinners*). His famous *Water Seller* was stolen by Napoleon's brother Joseph Bonaparte during his short spell as king of Spain, was liberated by Wellington and included among his trophies in Apsely House, in London.

Francisco de Goya carried on more or less where Velázquez left off. He was the official painter at the court of Charles IV and either had little regard for his royal patron and the other members of the family or else saw no good reason to flatter them. Almost without exception they appear stupid, slovenly, vaguely evil or merely disagreeable. His other works are much more interesting. The cartoons he designed for a set of tapestries to be hung in the Escorial are enchanting and lighthearted while his *Maja Nude* and *Maja Clothed* speak for themselves. However he was deeply affected by the War of Succession which is all too obvious in his *Disasters of War* etchings and the so-called 'black paintings' that compliment them.

War had much the same effect on Picasso whose famous painting *Guernica* takes up a large proportion of the Casón del Buen Retiro, an annex to the Prado three blocks away near the entrance to the Retiro Park (same opening times as the Prado). It recalls the saturation bombing of this small Basque town by German aircraft supporting the Nationalists during the Civil War. When it was completed Picasso lent it to the Museum of Modern Art in New York to be returned to Spain whenever the country shook itself free of Franco's dictatorship. The museum honoured this undertaking in 1981 and the painting, together with a number of preliminary sketches, was given a permanent home in Philip IVs old ballroom which is virtually all that remains of a royal palace. The building also contains a number of nineteenth-century art works that are mildly interesting but in no way remarkable.

El Retiro is a delightful place, full of shady paths threaded between the old trees, well maintained hedges, statues, fountains and flowerbeds. It is possible to hire a canoe or a paddleboat for a spell on the lagoon presided over by an equestrian statue of Alfonso XII, hire a horsedrawn carriage near the entrance opposite the Calle Antonio Maura, a little to the north of the Prado, visit the Botanical Gardens or an exhibition in either the Palacio de Exhibiciones or the Palacio de Cristal or, perhaps, stumble across an impromptu puppet show.

A block or so to the south of El Retiro, on the far side of the Paseo Reina Cristina, the Real Fábrica de Tapices was founded in the mid-seventeenth century to provide Philip IV and well-heeled members of the nobility with beautiful tapestries to decorate their palaces and keep out the draughts. The best known of these are the ones designed by Goya for the Escorial, showing various facets of life in Madrid at the time and taken from about forty of his cartoons which are preserved in the Prado. There are copies of Goya's designs at the factory where master weavers still produce tapestries and carpets by the same methods that were used 200 years ago. Visitors are welcome to look round any weekday morning and, provided money is no object, order one to take home as a souvenir.

Anyone who would prefer to leave the park and the tapestry factory for another day and concentrate on museums instead, will find the Museo del Ejército (Military Museum) conveniently placed on the Calle Mendez Núñez between the Casón del Buen Retiro and the Calle

Antonio Maura. It is a strictly military establishment with upwards of 25,000 exhibits recalling many of the great battles of the past. Some of the arms and armour belonged to the Conquistadores. There is El Cid's sword, a piece of the cross Columbus took to the New World, flags and paintings as well as documents, letters and the army's assessment of the Civil War.

The Maritime Museum is only a block away, sharing a building with the Ministry of Defence on the Paseo del Prado. It also looks back to the Age of Discovery with a number of superb maps and charts including Juan de la Casa's *Mapa Mundi*, the first Spanish map to show part of the American coastline. Among the many fascinating exhibits are several model ships, built to scale and correct down to the last detail, as well as items of early navigational equipment. The Museo de Artes Decorativas (Decorative Arts Museum) is the third of this particular group, just down the Calle Montalban near the entrance to the park. It has a less specialised appeal, containing examples of decorative art from the fifteenth century to the present day. Apart from furniture, ceramics and glass, a reconstructed kitchen smothered in tiles and woodwork of various descriptions, there are any number of traditional and period costumes as well as jewellery and gold and silver articles.

The Paseo del Prado ends at the Plaza de la Cibeles, presided over by a statue of the Greek goddess of fertility riding in an open chariot drawn by lions. She and her fountain were already famous when one of the most extrovert post offices imaginable was built in the 1920s overlooking the square. It cannot quite make up its mind whether to look like a palace or a church with its imposing entrance, ornamental pinnacles, statues and balustrades. As a result it has been given an appropriate nickname, Nuestra Santa de Comunicaciones. The nearby Plaza de la Independencia was a fortified gateway on the road to the east but this was replaced by the triumphal Alcalá Arch to mark the entry of Charles III into the capital in the eighteenth century. Further along the Calle Alcalá is the Plaza de Toros, the site of the largest bullring in Spain. It has seating for more than 22,000 spectators and an extremely comprehensive bullfighting museum.

Anyone who is more interested in archaeology than bullfighting can follow either the Paseo de Recoletos up from the Plaza de la Cibeles or the Calle Serrano from the Plaza de la Independencia to the nearby Museo Arqueológico Nacional (Archaeological Museum). It is a most absorbing museum which pays a certain amount of attention to other Mediterranean countries such as Egypt and Greece but concentrates mainly on the Iberian peninsula. The place of honour among a vast display of antiquities goes to the famous Dama de Elche, the bust of a haughty Iberian beauty with a splendid headdress, discovered in the ruins of Alcudia, on the outskirts of Elche, in Alicante, nearly a hundred years ago. Other personalities from pre-history include the Dama de Baza and the Dama de Cerra de los Santos. Elsewhere there are displays of Bronze Age crafts and items showing the influence of visiting Phoenicians, Greeks and Carthaginians.

The Romans are represented largely by statues of various emperors, mosaics and working models from their armoury of catapults and cross-bows. The Visigoths in their turn contribute the Treasure of Gurrazar consisting, for the most part, of gold crosses and elaborately jewelled votive crowns. Moorish art helps to bridge the gap between Muslim Spain and the Renaissance when new ideas from Italy and France added a fresh dimension. Also included are examples of typically Spanish ceramics, glass and furniture, while an underground gallery near the entrance gate contains an excellent facsimile of the famous cave at Altamira with its pre-historic rock paintings. Meanwhile, on the far side of the Paseo de Recoletos, the Museo Colón is a waxworks museum full of people who have played a leading role in the history of Spain.

Further north, on the Calle Serrano, the Museo Lázaro Galdiano is an Aladdin's Cave of treasures, accumulated by the owner who died in 1948. His interests were extremely varied, covering everything from arms and armour to Renaissance jewellery, gorgeous fans and intricate embroideries. The collection of enamels traces the development of the art from Istanbul in the days before it changed its name from Byzantium to Constantinople, across Europe to Limoges in the sixteenth century. There are also Celtic relics, beautiful medieval gold and silver work and early clocks and watches as well as Moorish and Persian artifacts. The paintings are just as memorable, highlighting works by Spanish artists such as Goya, El Greco, Murillo, Ribera and Zurbarán. In addition to some Italian and Flemish canvases there are more examples of the British School than can be seen at the moment in the Prado. Among them are paintings by Gainsborough, Reynolds, Romney, Constable and Turner.

A block or so away are the Natural Science Museum, with departments of geology, mineralogy and zoology, and the Sorolla Museum, full of the painter's works displayed in the house where he used to live. It takes time and some additional walking to track down the Municipal Museum on the Calle Fuencarral, north of the Gran Via, but for anyone interested in the history of Madrid it is well worth the effort. Apart from a room-sized model of the capital as it was in the eighteenth century, several old prints and maps trace its various stages of development but draw a veil over the Civil War by simply ignoring it altogether. Other museums which might be of interest are the Museo Romántico (Romantic Museum), a stone's throw away on the Calle San Mateo, which concentrates on late nineteenth-century furniture and paintings; the Ethnology Museum on the Paseo Infanta Isabel, facing the south-west corner of the Retiro Park, whose contents come mainly from South America, the Philippines and the Canary Islands, and the National

Railway Museum housed, appropriately, in an old railway station on the Paseo de las Delicias further to the south.

It would be perfectly possible to spend a week in Madrid and book into a different luxury hotel every night, the most famous being undoubtedly the Ritz. There are even more to choose from in the first class bracket, all of them comfortable and well appointed but conforming to much the same pattern, with the selection getting wider but less predictable further down the list. There are representatives of well-known chains such as the Holiday Inn, Plaza Carlos Trias Beltrán 4 or the Novotel Madrid, Albacete 1. The Hotel Laibeny, Salud 3, is large and excellently sited between the Puerta del Sol and the Gran Via, within easy reach of the Metro, the shops and most of the main attractions of Old Madrid. The Hotel Suecia, Marqués de Casa Riera 4, between the Puerta del Sol and the Prado, is in the same bracket with similar advantages in addition to the well patronised Bellman restaurant. The Hotel Puerta de Toledo on the square of the same name is commercial, comparatively inexpensive and provides parking for the car. One of the best places to look for a fairly cheap hostel is in the vicinity of the Municipal Museum. As Madrid stays up until all hours there is plenty to do in the evening from classical plays and opera, flamenco shows designed mainly for tourists, jazz clubs and bars to gambling at the Casino de Madrid outside the city with a special bus service from the Plaza de España.

There are any number of places to visit within a short radius of Madrid including such famous cities as Toledo, Ávila and Segovia. Much closer and, perhaps, less well known, is **Alcalá de Henares**, 31km (19 miles) along the N11 on the way to Barcelona. It was an important city called *Complutum* in the days of the Romans and a formidable Arab stronghold known simply as *Al-Qalat*, or *Al-Kala*, meaning the fortress. After the Reconquest it came under the jurisdiction of the archbishops of Toledo and particularly Cardinal Cisneros who founded the Complutense University in 1498. This soon became one of the country's most important seats of learning and published Europe's first polyglot Bible in 1517 with parallel columns in Latin, Greek, Hebrew and Aramaic.

Just 30 years later Miguel de Cervantes Saavedra was born in a house thought to have been on the Calle Mayor, an event which caused no interest at the time, nor in fact for the next half century or so. He became a soldier, was wounded, captured by the Turks and spent 5 years as a slave in Algeria before being rescued. His first novel, *La Galatea* and a number of minor works hardly caused a ripple but in 1605 he published the first part of *Don Quixote* which was an immediate success. The second half appeared 10 years later but even this, along with many other publications, brought in comparatively little money before he died on 23 April 1616, the same day as Shakespeare.

There is an eye-catching statue of Cervantes, sword in hand, near the bandstand in Alcalá de Henares but no trace of the house where he was born. By way of compensation a new

Street markets are held around the city of Madrid

Dancing is part of traditional Spanish culture

building was put up in 1956 at Calle Mayor 48 which tries to create an appropriate atmosphere with an arcaded patio, wooden balconies supported by eight granite columns, period furniture and plenty of old manuscripts as well as copies of *Don Quixote*. More recently, during excavations at the Teatro Cervantes, workmen uncovered the remains of a Comedy Playhouse dating from 1601. Plans for a new department store were immediately scrapped and the job of restoration began.

The ancient university was transferred to Madrid in 1836, and most of the town's historic landmarks were left to take care of themselves before being further damaged or destroyed during the Civil War. However, determined efforts have been made to recreate as much of the town's original character as possible. The old university building with its sixteenth-century façade on the Plaza San Diego is now home to the Alcala University, one of Spain's main centres of North American Studies, arranged in company with the Washington Irving Centre in the capital, the Fullbright Commission and the Michigan State University. Other places of interest include the Magistral de los Santos Justo y Pastor church in the Plaza Santos Ninos where two child saints were murdered and the San Ildefonso chapel containing the decorative marble tomb of Cardinal Cisneros. There are no hotels of any particular merit but the sixteenth-century Hosteria del Estudiante on the university campus is a good place to sample typical Castilian dishes.

Due south of Alcalá de Henares, reached by any number of minor routes including the C300 through Arganda on the N111, the village of **Chinchón** has its own parador in a former seventeenth-century convent. It is very secluded with a small chapel, attractive tiles, painted furniture and a beautiful garden full of trees, shrubs and fountains in addition to a swimming pool. The village boasts its own large parish church on the Plaza Mayor which is more of a circle than a square and is used as a bullring during the season when the balconies of the surrounding houses are crowded with spectators. Below them the little bars do a roaring trade in the local anis, either sweet or dry, which is distilled in the old castle up on the hill. Some 300 years ago the Countess of Chinchón, whose husband was Viceroy of Peru, developed a fever while she was in South America and was cured by an Indian doctor using a local remedy obtained from the bark of a tree. The samples she brought back to Europe are known to us as quinine and in the eighteenth century the Swedish botanist, Carl Linneas, named the tree chinchona as a tribute to her.

From Chinchón a minor road strikes out across country to **Aranjuez,** a green oasis on the Castilian plain which has been popular with royalty since the Catholic Monarchs stayed there in a mansion owned by the Grand Master of the Knights of Santiago. Philip II went one better and had his own castle built but it caught fire in the eighteenth century, was rebuilt and promptly burned down again. The present building is an excellent reconstruction which bears a marked resemblance to the palace at La Granja. It is impressive from a distance and even more so inside where the state apartments have been left almost as they were a hundred years ago.

Everywhere the walls are hung with Brussels tapestries and the floors carpeted by manufacturers in Madrid where they were designed along Persian lines. The Porcelain Saloon is awash with coloured tiles complimented by carved and painted wooden doors, a marble floor and a large chandelier, while the king's smoking room was inspired by the Hall of the Two Sisters in the Alhambra at Granada. The throne room with its painted ceiling and crimson velvet draperies was where Napoleon forced Charles IV to sign his abdication in 1808. The Museum of the Royal Robes contains replicas of the court dress worn by sovereigns up to the time of Charles II, augmented by authentic examples from the nineteenth century and an array of impressive service uniforms.

The east front of the palace looks out on to formal gardens, separated by a canal from the Jardin de la Isla, designed at the time of Philip II on an artificial island created inside a sharp bend of the Río Tajo. The Prince's Garden, which also borders on the river, is considerably larger. It contains the so-called Casa del Labrador, or Labourer's Cottage, which does not even begin to describe the regal little building with its marble statues, magnificently embroidered silks, furniture, pictures and objects d'art.

The green malachite table and matching chair were a present from Tsar Alexander III but the Cabinete de Platino, whose walls are decorated with inlays of gold, platinum and bronze, is said to have been Charles IVs own idea. Finally the Casa de Marinos, or Sailors' House, near the river bank contains a selection of royal vessels that belonged to six different sovereigns. There is nowhere very up-market to stay in Aranjuez but this should not present any problems because it is only 47km (29 miles) from Madrid.

El Pardo, 13km (8 miles) north-west of the capital on the Río Manzanares, has a palace built by Philip III in the early seventeenth century to replace an earlier one that was burned down. It was occupied by General Franco for more than 30 years but is now open to the public with its seemingly endless array of tapestries, attractive furniture, chandeliers and valuable Sèvres porcelain. Other attractions include the Casita del Principe, a pavilion built in 1772 as a present from Charles IV for his wife Maria Luisa, the Quinta which once belonged to the Duke of Arcos and the Convento de Capuchinos whose church is known for its seventeenth-century paintings and a masterful polychrome figure of Christ Recumbent by Gregorio Fernández which is said to be his masterpiece.

North-west of Madrid and about 55km (34 miles) along the C505, is the monastery-palace of **El Escorial** which can only be described with superlatives. It is gigantic to the point of

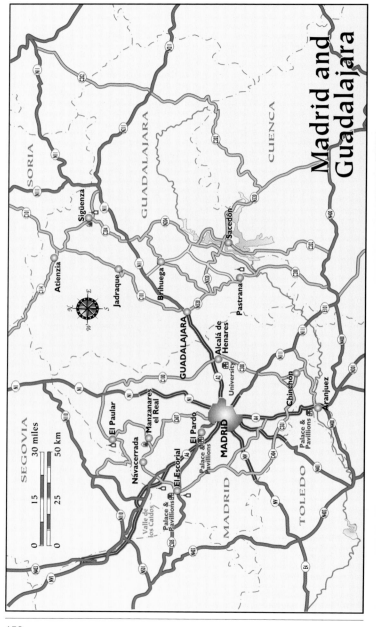

Madrid and Guadalajara

The monastery-palace of El Escorial

The overwhelming size of El Escorial is best appreciated close up

being overwhelming, built by Philip II between 1563 and 1584 in fulfilment of a vow made to St Lawrence and designed to rival the Temple of Solomon. To its admirers it is the eighth wonder of the world while other people agree with its Victorian detractor, Richard Ford, who found it 'as cold as the grey eyes and granite heart of its founder'. Factually it is 207m (679ft) long and 162m (531ft) high and contains a large domed basilica, 16 courtyards and as many cloisters, 86 staircases, 89 fountains and 24km (15 miles) of corridors.

The contents of El Escorial include a library unsurpassed except by the Vatican, something like 2,000 art treasures and the remains of twenty-three Spanish kings and queens, all neatly stored away in marble urns. Both Philip II and his father, Charles V, are buried in the vaults while the present king's grandmother, Victoria Eugenia, has been left to moulder in an adjoining chamber until she has decomposed sufficiently to fit into an urn. Legend has it that the Emperor Charles Vs body has remained intact and was found to be in an excellent state of preservation the last time it was inspected in the 1870s. There is even an empty tomb which Philip earmarked for his second wife, Mary Tudor, and was confident enough to decorate it with the English coat-of-arms. Lesser royalty are relegated to the corridors with an extremely elaborate confection for all the princes and princesses who died in childhood.

Above the mausoleum the basilica is cold and rather dark with a massive red marble, jasper and onyx retable inset with Italian paintings and surmounted by a golden crucifix which is, in fact, only gilded bronze. In Philip's time and for years afterwards the building was filled with precious treasures but almost without exception they were carried off by Napoleon's troops who overran the Escorial in 1808. The king's apartments, leading directly off the church, are unexpectedly restrained. It was here in a modest two-roomed suite that he ruled his empire, going through enormous piles of documents so thoroughly that, on occasions, he would order a model of himself to be wheeled out to acknowledge the crowds while he got on with his paperwork. The throne room, hung with sixteenth-century Brussel's tapestries, is where he received foreign ambassadors seated on what was once described as being 'hardly grander than a kitchen chair'. Also on view is the sedan chair in which he was carried when his gout turned to gangrene and he was unable to walk. The Bourbon apartments upstairs are more sumptuous despite the fact that his successors spent as little time as possible in them. Apart from the tapestries, some of which were made in the Royal Tapestry Factory in Madrid, there are two splendid frescoes in the Hall of Battles depicting Juan IIs victory over the Moors at Higuerela in 1431 and the defeat of the French at the battle of San Quentin.

The chapterhouses are filled with exceptional paintings by artists of the calibre of Velázquez, Titian, Tintoretto, Hieronymus Bosch, Ribera, Murillo and El Greco. Philip II commissioned El Greco to paint the *Martyrdom of St*

Maurice and the Theban Legionary and then disliked it so much that he refused to hang it anywhere, but nevertheless allowed him to complete a somewhat fanciful portrait entitled *The Vision of Philip II*. Other works to look out for are the Velázquez masterpiece *Joseph's Tunic*, Titian's *Last Supper* and a portrait of the king towards the end of his life by Pantoja de la Cruz hanging in the royal apartments. Meanwhile the architectural museum in the basement is filled with exhibits connected with the building of the monastery.

The library is housed in a long, splendidly decorated gallery and contains some 50,000 priceless printed volumes and about 4,000 manuscripts, some of the most valuable being kept in glass cases on the marble tables. Despite his religious fervour Philip preserved well over a hundred books that were banned outright by the Inquisition, refusing to burn them but making a minor concession by storing them out of the way on the topmost shelves. He also insisted that all the volumes should be arranged with their gilt-edged pages facing outwards, ostensibly to allow the air to circulate and so help to preserve them, a practice which still exists today.

A guided tour of the immense building lasts for something like 2 hours and even then only covers about one fifth of it. Behind the scenes it is a hive of industry with more facets than most visitors have any reason to suspect. For example, an unmarked door off the library leads to a reading room where scholars from many parts of the world have an opportunity to study treasures like the *Cantigas de Santa Maria*, a thirteenth-century collection of songs compiled by Alfonso the Wise, a German New Testament written in letters of solid gold, ancient atlases and illuminated manuscripts dealing with natural history. The Arabic collection is especially memorable, due in no small measure to a cargo of books destined for the Sultan of Morocco which was captured in 1611 and others that fell into the hands of the Inquisition after the reconquest of Granada.

Other sections of the Escorial are just as functional but far less romantic. The monks run a co-educational school for about 800 pupils which takes up a quarter of the building, in addition to which there are special classes in everything from art restoring to business management. Facilities are provided for concerts and conferences as well as tennis and basketball with the addition of an 18-hole golf course and an exclusive country club. Anyone who has time to explore the surrounding area will discover yew trees brought back from England by Philip after a short visit to his wife, Mary Tudor, and a jumble of rocks 7km (4 miles) away beyond the golf course known as Silla de Felipe II. It looks as though four seats have been hollowed out and Philip is said to have spent hours sitting in one of them, watching his monastery-palace take shape. There may or may not be any truth in the story but certainly the view is magnificent.

The Prince's Pavilion, situated

along the road to the station, was built in the eighteenth century for Charles IV while he was still Prince of Asturias. It is an elegant little palace with painted ceilings, silken draperies, some nice furniture, chandeliers, porcelain and a variety of clocks. Most of the best paintings have been rehoused in the Prado but there are still enough pictures left to fill vacant spaces on the walls. The Upper Pavilion or Casa de Arriba, 3km (2 miles) to the south-west on the road to Ávila, was originally a hunting lodge, decorated in the style of the period, where the present king, Juan Carlos, had a suite of apartments before his accession to the throne.

The most popular place to stay in San Lorenzo de El Escorial is the Victoria Palace on the Calle Juan de Toledo, which has both a swimming pool and a bingo hall. It is also possible to find a room with a bath at one of the smaller establishments, some of which have their own restaurants. Visitors with tents or caravans have a choice between the Caravaning El Escorial, officially a first-grade site, and the two-star La Herreiro, both of them open throughout the year. There are several other campsites on the outskirts of Madrid, two of these — the Madrid and the Osuna — offering accommodation.

Due north of El Escorial, along a minor road off the C600 just short of the *autopista*, is Franco's **Valle de los Caidos**, built in the 1950s. It is a vast basilica blasted out of the granite mountainside and surmounted by what is claimed to be the biggest cross in the world. This 'Valley of the Fallen' was designed as a memorial to the dead of both sides during the Civil War. A wrought iron screen incorporating metal statues of saints and soldiers guards the entrance to the nave which is longer than those of St Peter's in Rome or St Paul's in London and a good deal darker than either of them. A series of sixteenth-century Brussel's tapestries of the Apocalypse, statues of the Virgin and angels with swords alternate with small, dimly-lit chapels up to the altar with its wooden figure of Christ crucified against the trunk of a tree. To one side is a plain stone slab marking the grave of General Franco and on the other the funeral stone of José Antonio Primo de Rivera, the founder of the Falangist Party. The remains of 40,000 war dead have their own coffins in the crypt.

Not far from an outlandish souvenir stall a funicular runs up to the base of the cross where the plinth is embellished with statues of the Evangelists, gigantic figures symbolising the four cardinal virtues and an assortment of lions and eagles. The cross itself towers up another 125m (410ft). There is a magnificent view across the valley to the Monasterio El Valle de los Caidos whose Benedictine monks are responsible for looking after the basilica. Although it is not open to casual visitors the monastery combines a seminary and a centre for social studies and sets aside fifteen rooms for male guests only.

On the far side of the *autopista* the C600 climbs still further up into the Guadarramas to the small mountain towns of Cercedilla and **Navacerrada**. These double as holiday playgrounds during the summer and winter sports resorts. Navacerrada is particularly well equipped with a slalom, a cross-country course, several ski lifts and a selection of hotels including La Barranca, a comfortable establishment a short drive away in the Valle de la Barranca, that also provides tennis and a swimming pool. From Cercedilla both the road and a funicular give easy access to the Navacerrada Pass on the border between the provinces of Madrid and Segovia. From here the C604 follows the border along to Valcotos, which has some challenging ski runs of its own, and then makes for **El Paular** where Castile's first Carthusian monastery was founded in 1309. Part of the ancient building has been converted into the Hotel Santa Maria del Paular which is equipped for tennis and boasts a heated swimming pool. The monastery church adjoining a Gothic cloister has a superb fifteenth-century alabaster altarpiece whereas the Sag-rario Chapel is extravagantly Baroque.

Fractionally to the north, at Rascafria, which has nothing of interest to offer, the C604 deteriorates somewhat on its way past the Pinilla Dam to join the main road linking Aranda de Duero, in the province of Burgos, with Madrid. An alternative route back to the capital crosses a stretch of bare moorland, negotiates the Morcuera Pass and calls in at the village of Miraflores de la Sierra where there is a reasonable hotel. Its guests are often fishermen or rock climbers en route for the streams, ravines and jumbled mass of colourful rocks that are characteristic of the area. From here it is a fairly uncomplicated run to **Manzanares el Real**, with its fifteenth-century castle

and a modest campsite near the Santillana Dam, or straight on southwards towards Colmenar Viejo where the traditional heifer-run was reintroduced quite recently. Either way there is a left-hand turn on to the C607 which leads directly to Madrid.

Madrid is not too sophisticated to enjoy a good fiesta and observes the ceremonial Burial of the Sardine with due solemnity each year on Ash Wednesday. However the Festival of St Isidore is an even greater attraction lasting, as it does, for two weeks in the second half of May with celebrations of every sort and description. It is also an extremely good place to look for souvenirs. There are shops that specialise in fans, umbrellas, handmade gloves, mantillas and even the habits worn by nuns. Shoes are also a good buy and so are antiques, whether you are looking for the real thing or a variety advertised quite happily as 'genuine, made in our own factory'. El Arco de los Cuchilleros, in the Plaza Major, is probably the best place to see or buy an amazingly wide range of modern Spanish arts and crafts. There is something of everything from all over the country — ceramics and textiles, leather goods, jewellery, silverware and articles made from wood or glass, available to tourists free of tax. In addition, exhibitions are held at intervals in the gallery next door.

GUADALAJARA

Guadalajara is a province in its own right although in many respects it is little more than a satellite of Madrid with a turbulent past but the promise of better things in the future. This is largely because of the so-called Mar de Castilla, a string of artificial lakes on the Río Tagus created initially as part of the country's hydro-electric system. However, in due course the water will also be used to irrigate large tracts of land which at the moment are arid and rather uninteresting despite the fact that they have the strange fascination common to most wide open spaces. Already some of the immediate areas have been cultivated and provide the basis for a much needed holiday playground with facilities for a whole range of water sports and other forms of relaxation.

The city of **Guadalajara** has been in existence for well over 2,000 years in one form or another and reached its peak in the fourteenth and fifteenth centuries when it belonged to the influential Mendoza family. The Civil War of the 1930s put an end to all that. The town was fought over repeatedly during the long drawn out battles for Madrid and lost all its original characteristics in the process. Anything that survived, apart from the palace of the Dukes of Infantado, has disappeared under a welter of modern industry so unattractive that it has hardly bothered to provide acceptable accommodation for visitors passing through on the N11 to Madrid, 55km (34 miles) to the south-west. Travellers spending the night in the vicinity usually opt for the Hotel Pax on the main highway, which has a certain amount to recommend it, including facilities for tennis and swimming.

The palace of the Dukes of Infantado was built in the mid fifteenth century and was a splendidly ornate pile in its day, so much so that Philip II chose to be married there in 1559. It suffered, along with everything else, during the Civil War when bombs intended for the barracks flattened a large part of it. However, the impressive façade and the main courtyard escaped the worst of the damage and have been carefully restored. Other sections had to be rebuilt and it now provides a home for a fairly nondescript museum.

A somewhat unenterprising road, the N320, links Guadalajara with Sacedón, 59km (37 miles) to the south-east in the heart of the Mar de Castilla between the Entrepeñas reservoir and the Embalse de Buendia. At the same time there is a righthand fork after 18km (11 miles) which is longer, a bit more scenic and calls at **Pastrana**. This is a pleasing little village with a castle looking out on the main square and an elderly church where the Dukes of Pastrana are buried. Its prize possession is a set of four tapestries from Tournai depicting the exploits of Afonso V of Portugal in North Africa towards the end of the fifteenth century. From here there are three alternative routes to Sacedón followed by several cross-country options that lead eventually to the Zaragoza-Madrid highway.

Motorists who prefer to head east along the N11 with time to spare will find other places to interest them, but this does mean deviating from the main route on each occasion. A case in point is **Brihuega**, reached along the C201 from Torija. It is stepped up the hillside overlooking the Río Tajuña with narrow streets and the remains of its ancient walls smothered in ivy beside the Plaza Santa Maria. The town has one important battle to its credit, the small Church of San Felipe and an enviable reputation for bullrunning through streets during the Virgen de la Peña celebrations on 16 August.

On the opposite side of the highway, **Jadraque** is understandably proud of its domineering castle built by the Dukes of Osuna in the fifteenth century. From here there is a back way through to the C204 linking the main road with **Sigüenza** which suffered as an advance post for Nationalist Spain during the Civil War. The town has been adequately restored and still has its fortified cathedral, a clutch of small churches, a Diocesan Museum and a parador occupying the remains of a medieval castle.

It takes quite a while to look round the cathedral adjoining the Plaza Mayor with its battle-scarred tower and fine rose windows that somehow managed to preserve their ancient glass. Behind the somewhat sombre façade the nave, its roof supported by two rows of sturdy pillars, took the best part of 3 years to build. The cloister and the ambulatory were added shortly afterwards but the roof and the dome had to be replaced after the fighting ended. Two alabaster pulpits and a fine wrought-iron grille guard the entrance to the sanctuary where a number of tombs have been let into the walls, but the *piéce de résistance* is the Doncel Chapel on the right. This contains the sepulchre of Don Martin Vázquez de Arce, a page at the court of the Catholic Monarchs, who was killed during the fighting to liberate Granada from Moorish domination. The superb reclining figure of the young man, obviously amused by something in the book he is reading, was commissioned by Queen Isabel and is generally considered to be unique. His parents are also buried in the chapel, beyond which the annex is hung with medieval paintings. On the opposite side of the church the sacristy is memorable for its wood carving and extremely ornate ceiling, crowded with cherubs peeping out from a dense cloud consisting mainly of roses. Nearby the Santa Librada altar recalls the death of the saint and her eight sisters who are all supposed to have been born on the same day. Finally a decorative doorway leads through into the cloister, notable for its coloured marble and small chapel hung with Flemish tapestries.

A typical jigsaw of narrow streets converges on the square adjoining the cathedral, some of them lined with elderly mansions whose doorways are worth a passing glance. So is the Diocesan Museum and its collection of sacred art including paintings and sculptures by men of the calibre of Morales, El Greco and Zurbarán. The best view of the town and the wooded hillsides surrounding the valley is from the castle ramparts outside the Parador Nacional Castillo de Sigüenza. It is appropriately furnished with suits of armour, dark wood and local ceramics, has a small garden, parking space and is open throughout the year.

From Sigüenza the C114 strikes out in a north-westerly direction to **Atienza**, which also had serious problems during the Civil War but still retains its medieval atmosphere and the keep left over from an ancient castle. Two small churches have managed to survive, the most interesting being the Iglesia de la Trinadad that was a present from Philip II in recognition of services rendered during the earlier War of Succession. Roughly 4km (2 miles) short of Atienza the C101 branches off to the right for a cross-country trip to Almazán in Soria. On the other hand it is quicker and easier to leave Sigüenza by the C114 in the opposite direction to rejoin the highway where a number of alternative routes are on offer — namely into Soria, Zaragoza or Teruel or back through Guadalajara to Madrid, 129km (80 miles) away.

ADDITIONAL INFORMATION

PLACES OF INTEREST

GUADALAJARA (Province)
Pastrana

Church
Open: 10am-2pm and 4-7pm and 1-3pm Sundays and holidays April to November. 11am-3pm and 4-6pm, and 11am-1pm Sundays and holidays December to March.

Sigüenza

Cathedral
Open: 11am-2pm and 4-8pm summer, 11am-2pm and 4-6pm winter. If closed apply to the sacristan.

Museum
Open: 11.30am-2pm and 5-7.30pm late March to early January. Otherwise 11.30am-2pm and 4-6.30pm Sundays and holidays only.

MADRID (Province)
Alcalá de Henares

University
Open: 11am-1pm and 6-8pm summer, 11am-1pm and 4-6pm winter. Closed Sundays, holidays and during August.

Aranjuez

Palace and Pavilions
Open: 10am-1pm and 3.30-6.30pm April to mid-September, 10am-1pm and 3-6pm mid-September to March. Gardens open 10am to sunset. Closed 1 January, 1 and 30 May, 5 September and 25 December.

El Escorial

Church
Open: 9am-1pm and 3.30-6.30pm summer, 9am-1pm and 3-6 winter.
Palace and Pavilions

Open: 10am-1pm and 3.30-7pm summer,10am-1pm and 3-6pm October to April. Closed Mondays, 1 Jan, 1 May, 8 September and 25 December.

El Pardo

Capuchin Monastery
Closed 1.30-4.30pm.

Palace
Open: 10am-1pm and 4-7pm April to September. 10am-1pm and 3-6pm October to March. Closed Sunday and holiday afternoons, some holidays and during official visits.

Pavilions
Open: 10am-1pm and 4-7pm April to September, 10am-1pm and 3-6pm October to March. Closed Sunday and holiday afternoons and some holidays and official visits.

Valle de los Caidos
Open: 10am-7.30pm summer. 9am-6.30pm winter. Closed 1 and 6 January, 19 March, 1 May, 8 and 25 December afternoons, 17 July and 19 November all day.

Madrid (City)

Archaeological Museum
Paseo de Recoletas
Open: 9am-1.30pm. Closed Monday, 1 January, Thursday and Friday of Holy Week, 1 May and 25 December.

Arco de los Cuchilleros
Shop and Gallery.
Plaza Major

Open: weekdays 11am-8pm. Closed Sundays and holidays except in Holy Week and in December when it is open 11am-2.30pm.

Bullfighting Museum
At the bullring
Open: 9am-3pm. Closed Monday.

Cerralbo Museum
Calle Ventura Rodriguez
Open: 9am-2pm. Sometimes 4-7pm. Closed Tuesdays and August.

Contemporary Spanish Art Museum
Avenida Juan de Herrera
Open: 10am-6pm weekdays, 10am-3pm Sundays and holidays. Closed Mondays, 1 January, Good Friday, 1 May and 25 December.

Decorative Arts Museum
Calle Montalban
Open: 10am-5pm weekdays, 10am-2pm Sundays and holidays. Closed Monday, 1 January, Good Friday, 1 and 15 May, 1 and 9 November, 25 December.

Descalzas Reales Convent
Calle Arenal
Guided tours 10.30am-1.30pm and 4-6pm weekdays, 10.30am-12.45pm Friday and Saturday. Closed 1 January, 1 May and 25 December. Wednesday to Saturday in Holy Week.

Ethnology Museum
Paseo Infanta Isabel
Open: 10am-2pm and 4-7pm. Closed Mondays and Sunday and holiday afternoons.

Incarnacion Convent
Plaza de Oriente
Guided tours 10.30am-1.30pm and
4-6pm. Closed Sunday, holiday
and Wednesday to Saturday in
Holy Week afternoons and 27 July,
28 August and some holidays.

Lázaro Galdiano Museum
Calle Serrano
Open: 10am-2pm. Closed
Mondays, 1 January, Friday and
Saturday in Holy Week, 1 May,
25 December and throughout
August.

Lope de Vegás House
Calle Cervantes
Open: 11am-2pm. Closed
Mondays, mid-July to
mid-September and some holidays.

Maritime Museum
Paseo del Prado
Open: 10.30am-1.30pm. Closed
Mondays and throughout August.

Military Museum
Calle Mendez Núñez
Open: 10am-5pm weekdays,
10am-1.30pm Sundays. Closed
Mondays.

Municipal Museum
Calle Fuencarral
Open: 10am-2pm and 5-9pm
weekdays, 10am-2.30pm Sundays.
Closed Mondays and holidays.

Natural Science Museum
Plaza de San Juan de la Cruz
Open: 9am-2pm and 3-6pm
weekdays, 10am-2pm Sundays
and holidays.

Museo del Prado
Paseo del Prado
Open: 10am-4.45pm Tuesday,
Thursday, Friday and Saturday,
3-8.45pm Wednesday,
10am-11.45am Sunday. Closed
Monday, 25 December and some
holidays.

Romantic Museum
Calle San Mateo
Open: 10am-6pm weekdays,
10am-2pm Sundays and holidays.
Closed Mondays and throughout
August.

Royal Academy of History
Calle Heurtas
Unspecified hours
☎ 239 82 63

Royal Palace
Plaza de Oriente
Guided tours 10am-12.45pm and
4-5.45pm weekdays, summer,
10am-12.45pm and 3.30-5.15pm
winter October to April
10am-1.30pm Sundays and holidays. Closed 1 January, 1 May, 24
June, 25 December, 24 and 31
December afternoons and State
Occasions.

Royal Tapestry Factory
Calle Fuenterrabia
Open: 9.30am-12noon. Closed
Saturdays, Sundays, holidays and
throughout August.

San Francisco el Grande Church
Open: 11am-1pm and 4-7pm.
Closed Sunday, Monday and
holidays.

Sorolla Museum
Calle Martinez Campos

Open: 10am-2pm. Closed
Mondays, 1 January, Thursday and
Friday of Holy Week, 1 May, 1
November, 25 December and
throughout August.

Waxworks Museum
Plaza de Colón
Open: 10.30am-2pm and 4-9pm.

Zoo
Open: 10am to sunset.

TRAVELLING IN MADRID

Bus
The bus timetable is from 6am until
midnight. At night there is a skeleton
service which leaves the Plaza de
Cibeles and the Puerta del Sol every
half hour from midnight until 2am
and from 2am-6am every hour. In
the Plaza de Cibeles there is an information kiosk belonging to the
Empresa Municipal de Transportes
(Transport Company), and up to 20
more at different points in Madrid for
the sale of the *bonobus* (reduced
bus tickets).
For information ☎ 401 99 00.

Underground (Metro)
The Metro runs from 6am-1.30am.
There is a tourist card which enables
you to use the Metro for 3 or 5 days
consecutively as often as you wish.
For information ☎ 435 22 66.

Taxi
For your information the list of prices
and supplements is on display in a
visible place. Radio telephone taxi ☎
247 82 00. Radiotaxi ☎ 404 90 00.
Teletaxi ☎ 445 90 08.

ORA
There is a parking control in the central areas of the city known as ORA,
which means paying a charge for
every half hour, up to a permitted
maximum of 2 hours.

TOURIST INFORMATION CENTRES

Alcalá de Henares
Callejón de Santa Maria
☎ 91 889 26 94

Aranjuez
Plaza Santiago Rusiñol
☎ 91 891 04 27

El Escorial
Floridablanca
☎ 91 890 15 54

Guadalajara
Plaza Mayor
☎ 911 22 06 98

Madrid
Torre de Madrid
Plaza España
☎ 91 241 23 25
Open: 9am-7pm weekdays,
9.30am-1.30pm Saturday. Also at
the airport and Chamartin Station.

FACTS FOR VISITORS

ACCOMMODATION

Northern and Central Spain have more than enough accommodation to cater for every taste and pocket. The categories range from luxurious establishments to rooms in private houses.

Paradores

There are about eighty of these comfortable, well-equipped state-run hotels, some thirty of them in the northern half of the country, less than one day's drive apart. Many are in converted castles, palaces, convents or monastries and furnished accordingly, augmented by modern buildings to complete the chain. They are open throughout the year, have their own restaurants and are required to meet a fairly high standard.

Hotels (H)

Hotels are given star ratings from one to five, and are classified according to their service and amenities, not to price. The five-star category is predictably elegant and expensive whereas the one-star variety may be perfectly acceptable but on the sparse side.

Hotel Residencias (HR)

The main difference between these and the ordinary hotels is that they do not have a restaurant.

Hostales (Hs)

These are more modest establishments, sometimes taking up only part of a larger building, graded from one to three stars, the best of them being roughly comparable to a one-star hotel.

Pensiones (P)

Pensiones are also given one to three star ratings and may request their guests to pay either full or half-board prices.

Hostales Residencias (HsR)

These differ from their hotel counterparts mainly because they do not supply any food, sometimes not even a continental breakfast, and only rate one to three stars.

Unlisted types of accommodation include *fondas* (F) which may be cheaper than a one-star *hostale*, the comparable *casa de huespedes* (CH), *habitaciones* which are merely rooms and *casas particulares* that are simply private homes with rooms to let.

Youth Hostels and Campsites

The youth hostels are not very plentiful or particularly attractive. They are often closed out of season and may well be more expensive than a one-star hostale or a fonda. On the other hand there are plenty of campsites, graded from three to one-star, most of the latter having plenty of amenities whereas the former can be fairly basic.

These are not particularly attractive, often closed out of season and maybe more expensive than a one-star *hostale* or a *fonda*. Campsites are graded downwards from one to three, with the grade three variety only providing the basic amenities.

All the different types of listed accommodation are identified by blue plaques outside with the relevant letters and the number of stars. Prices in every case must be posted up in the lobby and in the relevant rooms so it is easy to see what you are getting before signing in. Heating is installed in most establishments with a better than one-star hostale rating, extra blankets are usually obtainable but anyone who needs a soft pillow would be well advised to take their own. In the unlikely event of an unresolved argument with the management it is only necessary to ask for the complaints book, the *libro de reclamaciones*. As this has to be shown to the authorities immediately the request is usually sufficient to solve the problem except in the case of a serious disagreement.

The prices shown cover the cost of a double room; a single occupant will pay about 60 per cent of the price whereas if an extra bed is provided the cost will be about 35 per cent extra. Breakfast is nearly always additional unless otherwise stated and 6 per cent TVA, or VAT, will be added to the bill. Guests who have to watch their *pesetas* should remember this and pay for drinks and snacks rather than having them charged to the number of their room.

HOTELS

ALBERCA
Las Batuecas H**
Carretera Las Batuecas.
☎ 923 41 51 88
Fax: 923 41 50 55

ALFARO
Palacios H**
Carretera de Zaragoza.
☎ 941 18 01 00
Fax: 941 18 22 36

ALMAZAN
Antonio H*
Avenida de Soria.
☎ 975 30 07 11

ARANDA DE DUERO
Tres Condes H***
Avenida de Castilla 66.
☎ 947 50 24 00
Fax: 947 50 24 04

ARANJUEZ
Isabel II H***
Infantas 15.
☎ 91 891 09 45
Fax: 91 891 52 44

ASTORGA
Gaudi HR***
Eduardo de Castro 6.
☎ 987 61 56 54
Fax: 987 61 50 40

Motel de Pradorrey ***
Carretera NV1.
☎ 987 61 57 29
Fax: 987 61 92 20

ÁVILA
Palacio de Valderrabanos H**
Plaza de la Catédral.
☎ 920 21 10 23
Fax: 920 25 16 91

Parador Raimundo de Borgoña ***
Marquéz de Canales y Chozas.
☎ 920 21 13 40
Fax: 920 22 61 66

Don Carmelo HR**
Don Carmelo 30.
☎ 920 22 80 50

BARCO DE AVILA
Manila H***
Carretera Plasencia.
☎ 920 34 08 44
Fax: 920 34 12 91

BAYONA
Parador Conde de Gondomar ****
Monterreal.
☎ 986 35 50 00
Fax: 986 35 50 76

Tres Carabelas HR**
Ventura Misa 72.
☎ 986 35 54 41

BÉJAR
Colón H***
Colón 42.
☎ 923 40 06 50
Fax: 923 40 06 50

BENAVENTE
Parador Rey Fernando II de Léon ****
Paseo Ramón y Cajal.
☎ 980 63 03 00
Fax: 980 63 03 03

Arenas H*
Carretera NV1.
☎ 980 63 03 34

BURGOS DE OSMA
Virrey Palafox.
Restaurant with rooms.
Universidad 7.
☎ 975 34 02 22

BURGOS
Landra Palace H****
On road to Madrid.
☎ 947 20 63 43
Fax: 947 26 46 76

Condestable H***
Vitoria 8.
☎ 947 26 71 25
Fax: 947 20 46 45

Rice H***
Reyes Católicos 30.
☎ 947 22 23 00
Fax: 947 22 35 50

CALAHORIA
Parador Marco Fabio Quintiliano ***
Era Alta.
☎ 941 13 03 58
Fax: 941 13 51 39

Chef Nino H**
Padre Lucas.
☎ 941 13 20 29
Fax: 941 13 35 16

CAMBADOS
Parador El Albariño ***
Paseo Cervantes.
☎ 986 54 22 50
Fax: 986 54 20 68

CANGAS DE **O**NSIS
Ventura H**
Avenida de Covadonga.
☎ 98 584 82 01
Fax: 98 584 02 01

Acebos II, Los H**
Carretera de Covadonga,
☎ 98 594 00 22
Fax: 98 584 91 53

CASTRO-**U**RDIALES
Miremar H***
Avenida de la Playa.
☎ 942 86 02 04
Fax: 942 87 09 42

CELANOVA
Betanzos H*
Celso Emilio Ferreiro 7.
☎ 988 45 10 11

CERVERA DE **P**ISUERGA
Parador Fuentes Carrionas ***
Carretera de Ruesga.
☎ 979 87 00 75
Fax: 979 87 01 05

CHINCHÓN
Parador de Chinchón ****
Avenida Generalisimo.
☎ 91 894 08 36
Fax: 91 894 09 08

Nuevo Chinchón H**
Carretera de Titulcia.
☎ 91 894 05 44
Fax: 91 893 51 28

CUIDAD **R**ODRIGO
Parador Enrique II ***
Plaza del Castillo.
☎ 923 46 01 50
Fax: 923 46 04 04

Conde Rodrigo H***
Plaza San Salvador.
☎ 923 46 14 08
Fax: 923 46 14 08

COMILLAS
Casal del Castro H***
San Jerónimo.
☎ 942 72 00 36

El Capricho de Gaudi Restaurant
Barrio de Sobrellano.
☎ 942 72 03 65

CORCUBIÓN
Hórreo, El H***
Santa Isabel.
☎ 981 74 55 00
Fax: 981 74 55 63

COVADONGA
Pelayo H***
☎ 98 584 60 61

COVARRUBIAS
Arianza H***
Plaza Major.
☎ 947 40 30 25
Fax: 947 40 63 59

CORUÑA, **L**A
Finisterre H****
Paseo del Parrote.
☎ 981 20 54 00
Fax: 981 20 84 62

Raizor HR***
Avenida Barrie de la Maza.
☎ 981 25 34 00
Fax: 981 25 34 04

Espinama
Parador Rio Deva ***
☎ 942 73 66 51
Fax: 942 73 02 12

Ferrol, El
Parador de El Ferrol ***
Plaza Eduardo Pondal.
☎ 981 35 67 20
Fax: 981 35 67 21

Almirante HR***
Maria 2.
☎ 981 32 56 90
Fax: 981 32 53 11

Gijón
Parador El Molino Viejo ****
Parque Isabel la Católica.
☎ 98 537 05 11
Fax: 98 537 02 33

Begõna H***
Carretera de la Costa 44.
☎ 98 514 72 11
Fax: 98 539 82 22

Grove, O
Gran Hotel de la Toja *****
Isla de la Toja.
☎ 986 73 00 25
Fax: 986 73 12 01

Bosque Mar H***
Reborado el Grove.
☎ 986 73 10 55
Fax: 986 73 05 12

Molusco, El H**
Puente La Toja.
☎ 986 73 07 61
Fax: 986 73 29 84

Guadalajara
Husa Pax H***
Carretera NII.
☎ 949 22 18 00
Fax: 949 22 69 55

Infante H**
San Juan de Dios 14.
☎ 949 22 35 55
Fax: 949 22 35 98

Haro
Augustinos, Los HR****
San Agustin 2.
☎ 941 31 13 08
Fax: 941 30 31 48

Iturrimurri H***
Carretera N232.
☎ 941 31 12 13
Fax: 941 31 17 21

Laredo
Ancia, El H***
González Gallego 10.
☎ 942 60 55 00
Fax: 942 61 16 02

Miramar H***
Alto de Laredo.
☎ 942 61 03 67
Fax: 942 61 16 92

León
San Marcos H*****
Plaza San Marcos.
☎ 987 23 73 00
Fax: 987 23 34 58

Riosol HR***
Avenida de Palencia 3.
☎ 987 21 68 50
Fax: 987 21 69 97

Independencia Restaurant
Independencia 4.
☎ 987 25 47 52

LOGROÑO
Murrieta H***
Marquéz de Murrieta 1.
☎ 941 22 41 50
Fax: 941 22 32 13

Isasa HR*
Doctores Castroviejo 13.
☎ 941 25 65 99

Merced, La Restaurant
Marquéz de San Nicolás 109.
☎ 941 22 11 66

LUGO
Gran Hotel Lugo ****
Avenida Ramón Ferreiro 21.
☎ 982 24 41 52
Fax: 982 24 16 60

Méndez Nuñez HR**
Reina 1.
☎ 982 23 07 11

MADRID
Ritz Madrid H*****
Plaza de la Lealtad 5.
☎ 91 521 28 57
Fax: 91 532 87 76

Palace H****
Plaza de las Cortés.
☎ 91 429 75 51
Fax: 91 429 82 66

Melia Madrid H****
Princesa 27.
☎ 91 541 82 00
Fax: 91 541 19 88

Alondras Sol, Las H***
José Abascal 8.
☎ 91 447 40 00
Fax: 91 593 88 00

Convención HR***
O'Donnell 53.
☎ 91 574 68 00
Fax: 91 574 56 01

Tryp Washington HR***
Gran Via 72.
☎ 91 541 72 27
Fax: 91 547 51 99

Condes, Los H**
Los Lebreros 7.
☎ 91 521 54 55
Fax: 91 521 78 82

Aristos HR***
Avenida de Pio XII, 34.
☎ 91 345 04 50
Fax: 91 345 10 23

MEDINACELI
Nico H**
Carretera N11 (3.5km)
☎ 975 32 60 11

MUROS
Muradana, La H**
Avenida de la Marina.
☎ 981 82 67 00

NAVACERRADA
Arcipreste de Hita H****
Carretera Madrid-León.
☎ 91 856 01 25

Barranca, La H***
Valle de la Barranca.
☎ 91 856 00 00
Fax: 91 856 03 52

NAVARREDONDA DE GREDOS
Parador de Gredos ***
☎ 920 34 80 48
Fax: 920 34 82 05

ORENSE
San Martin HR***
Curros Enriques 1.
☎ 988 23 56 90
Fax: 988 23 65 85

Sila H**
Avenida de la Habana 61.
☎ 988 23 63 11

OVIEDO
Reconquista, De la H*****
Gil de Jaz 16.
☎ 98 524 11 00
Fax: 98 524 11 66

Gruta, La H***
Alto de Buenavista.
☎ 98 523 24 50
Fax: 98 525 31 41

Casa Fermin Restaurant
San Francisco 8.
☎ 98 521 64 52

Trascorrales Restaurant
Plaza de Trascorrales 19.
☎ 98 522 24 41

PADRÓN
Escala 11 H***
Pazos-Padrón.
☎ 981 81 13 12
Fax: 981 81 15 50

PALENCIA
Rey Sancho de Castilla HR***
Avenida Ponce de León.
☎ 979 72 53 00
Fax: 979 71 03 34

Monclus H**
Menéndez Pelayo 3.
☎ 979 74 43 00

PEDRAZA DE LA SIERRA
Posada de Don Mariano HR**
Mayor 14.
☎ 921 50 98 86

Hosteria Pintor Zuloaga Restaurant
☎ 921 50 98 35

PONTEVEDRA
Temple, Del HR****
Avenida Portugal.
☎ 987 41 00 58
Fax: 987 41 35 25

Madrid H**
Avenida de la Puebla 44.
☎ 987 41 15 50
Fax: 987 41 18 61

PONFERRADA
Galacia Palace H****
Avenida de Vigo.
☎ 986 86 44 11
Fax: 986 86 10 26

Parador Casa del Barón ***
Plaza de Maceda.
☎ 986 85 58 00
Fax: 986 85 21 95

PUEBLA DE SANABRIA
Parador de Puebla de Sanabria ***
Carretera Zamora.
☎ 980 62 00 01
Fax: 980 62 03 51

RIBADEO
Parador de Ribadeo ***
☎ 982 11 08 25
Fax: 982 11 03 46

Eo H**
Avenida de Asturias.
☎ 982 11 07 50

RIBADESELLE
Gran Hotel del Sella ****
La Playa.
☎ 98 586 01 50
Fax: 98 585 78 22

Marina H**
Gran Via 36.
☎ 98 586 00 50
Fax: 98 586 01 57

SADA
Sada Palace HR***
☎ 981 62 34 06
Fax: 981 62 38 06

SALAMANCA
Parador de Salamanca ****
Teso de la Feria.
☎ 923 26 87 00
Fax: 923 21 54 38

Gran Hotel HR****
Poeta Iglesias 5.
☎ 923 21 35 00
Fax: 923 21 35 01

Condal HR**
Santa Eulalia.
☎ 932 21 84 00

Chez Victor Restaurant
Espoz y Mina 26.
☎ 923 21 31 23

SAN **L**ORENZO DE **E**L **E**SCORIAL
Victoria Palace H****
Juan de Toledo 4.
☎ 91 890 15 11
Fax: 91 890 12 48

Miranda Suizo, El H**
Floridablanca 18.
☎ 91 890 47 11
Fax: 91 890 43 58

SANTANDER
Real H*****
Paseo de Pérez Galdós 28.
☎ 942 27 25 50
Fax: 942 27 45 73

Ciuded de Santander H***
Menéndez del Pelayo 13.
☎ 942 22 79 65
Fax: 942 21 73 03

Molino, El Restaurant
Carretera N611.
☎ 942 57 40 52

SANTIAGO DE **C**OMPOSTELA
Reyes Católicos H*****
Plaza de España.
☎ 981 58 22 00
Fax: 981 56 30 94

Peregrino H****
Avenida Rosalia de Castro.
☎ 981 52 18 50
Fax: 981 52 17 77

Gelmirez HR***
General Franco 92.
☎ 981 56 11 00
Fax: 981 56 32 69

SANTILLANA DEL MAR
Parador Gil Blas ***
Plaza Ramón Pelayo 11.
☎ 942 81 80 00
Fax: 942 81 83 91

Altamira H***
Canton 1.
☎ 942 81 80 25
Fax: 942 41 01 36

SANTO DOMINGO DE LA CALZADA
Parador de Santo Domingo de la Calzada ****
Plaza del Santo.
☎ 941 34 03 00
Fax: 941 34 03 25

Corregidor H***
Zumalacárregui 14.
☎ 941 34 21 28
Fax: 941 34 21 15

SANTO DOMINGO DE SILOS
Tres Coronas H***
Plaza Major.
☎ 947 38 07 27

Arco de San Juan H**
Pradera de San Juan.
☎ 947 38 07 94

SEGOVIA
Parador de Segovia ****
☎ 921 44 37 37
Fax: 921 43 73 62

Acueducto H***
Avenida del Padre Claret 10.
☎ 921 42 48 00
Fax: 921 42 84 46

SIGÜENZA
Parador Castillo de Sigüenza ****
☎ 949 39 01 00
Fax: 949 39 16 34

Doncel, El Hs**
General Mola 1.
☎ 949 39 00 01
Fax: 949 39 00 80

SORIA
Parador Antonio Machado ***
Parque del Castillo.
☎ 975 21 34 45
Fax: 975 21 28 49

Alfonso VIII H**
Alfonso VIII 10.
☎ 975 22 62 00
Fax: 975 21 36 65

TORDESILLAS
Parador de Tordesillas ***
Carretera N620.
☎ 983 77 00 51
Fax: 983 77 10 13

Juan Manuel Hs**
Carretera Burgos/Portugal.
☎ 983 77 09 51
Fax: 983 77 00 16

TUY
Parador de Tuy ***
Avenida de Portugal.
☎ 986 60 03 09
Fax: 986 60 21 63

Colón Tuy HR***
Colón 11.
☎ 986 60 02 23
Fax: 986 60 03 27

VALLADOLID
Olid Meliá H****
Plaza de San Miguel.
☎ 983 35 72 00
Fax: 983 33 68 28

Meliá Parque H***
Garcia Morato 17.
☎ 983 22 00 00
Fax: 983 47 50 29

VERIN
Parador de Monterrey ***
☎ 988 41 00 75
Fax: 988 41 20 17

VIGO
Bahia de Vigo H****
Avendia Cánovas del Castillo 5.
☎ 986 22 67 00
Fax: 986 43 74 87

Gran Hotel Samil ***
Playa Samil 15.
☎ 986 20 52 11
Fax: 986 23 14 19

Puesto Pilato Alcabra Restaurant
Avenido Atlántida 98.
☎ 986 29 79 75

VILLAFRANCA DEL BEIRZO
Parador de Villafranca del Beirzo ***
Avenida Calvo Sotelo.
☎ 987 54 01 75
Fax: 987 54 00 10

San Francisco HR*
Plaza Generalisimo 6.
☎ 987 54 04 65

VILLALBA
Parador Condes de Villalba ***
Valeriano Valdesuso.
☎ 982 51 00 11
Fax: 982 51 00 90

Vilamartin H***
Avenida Tierra Llana.
☎ 982 51 12 15
Fax: 982 51 11 57

ZAMORA
Parador Condes de Alba y Aliste ****
Plaza Viriato.
☎ 980 51 44 97
Fax: 980 53 00 63

Sayagues, El H***
Plaza Puentica 2.
☎ 980 52 55 11
Fax: 980 51 34 51

CLIMATE

The climate in Northern and Central Spain is far from uniform, changing quite dramatically from one area to another. The interior is extremely hot in summer and bitterly cold in winter, whereas the coastal regions are more temperate. The arid plains of the meseta range in temperature from well below zero with heavy snow up in the mountains to an unpleasant 37°C (100°F) or more in July and August. On the other hand the north-western regions may have frost occasionally but seldom experience anything above 27°C (80°F). There is no truth in Bernard Shaw's contention that 'the rains in Spain fall mainly in the plains'. To the contrary, they are confined very largely to the provinces bordering on the Bay of Biscay and the Atlantic, but may often be not much more than a heavy drizzle interrupted by bursts of sunshine. The best months for

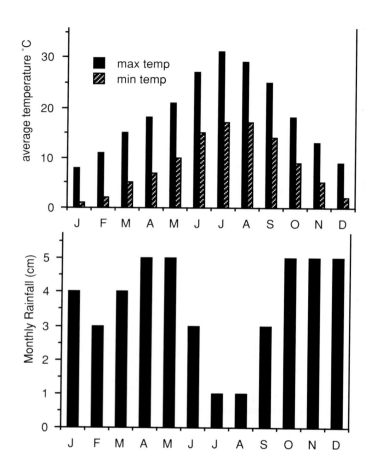

touring any of these areas are in the spring and autumn, especially in Galicia where the early wild flowers and the changing colours later in the year are memorable.

CURRENCY AND CREDIT CARDS

The Spanish currency is the *peseta* and the coins in use are 1, 5, 10, 25, 50, 100 *ptas*, augmented by 1,000,

2,000, 5,000 and 10,000 denomination notes. In street markets and out-of-the-way places the prices may be given in *duros*, which is a 5 *peseta* piece, or *notas*, indicating 100 *pesetas*.

Any amount of foreign currency may be taken into Spain but only limited amounts of pesetas or foreign currency taken out again unless it can be proved that the excess was imported initially. As the exact amounts concerned may vary it is wise to get expert advice if quite large sums are involved. Most banks will change money and cash travellers cheques and Euro-cheques, giving a better rate than the average hotel.

One or more of the major credit cards are usually accepted by the larger hotels and restaurants, especially in cities and established tourist resorts, but even if the relevant logo is displayed in the window or at the reception desk it does no harm to confirm this in advance. Some garages in the cities and on the main highways also take credit cards but very few others are prepared to accept them, nor will the majority of supermarkets. Banks displaying the logo concerned will usually pay out a reasonable sum against a credit card provided it is backed up by some form of identification.

CUSTOMS REGULATIONS

Customs regulations in Spain are similar to those in force elsewhere in the EU. Comprehensive lists of duty free articles and personal possessions which can be taken in by holiday makers for their own use can be obtained from local travel agents at home. Visitors planning to take in anything out of the ordinary should make sure of the position before setting out.

FACILITIES FOR THE DISABLED

Comparatively few provisions are made for disabled visitors so anyone in need of special facilities or attention would be well advised to make enquiries before leaving, particularly in relation to hotel accommodation.

DRESS

The type and variety of clothes required for a visit to Northern and Central Spain are very similar to those included in any other holiday wardrobe — a blending of personal preference and common sense. The kind of formal or semi-formal outfits called for in Madrid are unnecessary almost anywhere else where the emphasis is on casual wear. However, care should be taken not to give offence when visiting churches, convents and monasteries although it is no longer necessary for women to wear stockings or cover their heads. Flat shoes are essential for exploring old ruins or antiquated cobbled streets and it is as well to have something warm to put on if the evening turns chilly and a waterproof or umbrella can be very useful, especially in Galicia.

ELECTRICITY

The usual voltage is 220 AC but American visitors will need a converter and British holidaymakers should provide themselves with an adaptor or a Continental two-pin plug. However there are some places off the beaten track which have totally unexpected electricity supplies, such as 150 AC, so anyone exploring in sparsely populated areas would find a battery-driven radio and razor extremely useful.

EMBASSIES

U K
Spanish Embassy
24 Belgrave Square
London SW1X 8OA
☎ 235 5555

Canada
350 Sparks St
Suite 802 Ottawa
☎ 2372193

HEALTH CARE

British visitors should obtain an E111 form before leaving home which entitles them to free medical treatment in other countries of the EU. However there are some tiresome formalities involved in Spain so it is wise to have additional health insurance, which is essential for everybody else. All the usual services are available and chemists in the larger towns, known as *farmacias* and identified by a green cross, can deal with most minor ailments and suggest the best place to go for any additional assistance. Several familiar types of medication are on sale in the larger pharmacies but a few basic preparations to deal with such things as minor cuts, insect bites, sunburn or a mild attack of diarrhoea would not come amiss.

LANGUAGE

Although Castilian is the official language of Spain many people favour a dialect, especially in Galicia where, in some respects, it bears a marked resemblance to Portuguese. It is difficult to find anyone in the outlying areas who speaks either English or French, and even in Madrid it is not always easy to make oneself understood. A dictionary and a phrase book are useful and even a modest attempt at a little basic Spanish is polite and much appreciated.

VOCABULARY

General

Yes	*Sí*
No	*No*
I don't know	*No sé*
I don't understand	*No comprendo*
Can you help me?	*Puede usted ayudarme*
Please	*Por Favor*
Thank you	*Gracias*
It is nothing	*De nada*
It doesn't matter	*No importa*
All right	*Está bien*
Excuse me	*Perdóneme*
Hello	*Olá*
Good morning	*Buenos dias*
Good afternoon	*Buenas tardes*
Good evening	*Buenas noches*
Goodbye	*Adios*
What?	*Qué?*
Who?	*Quien?*
Where?	*Dónde?*
When?	*Cuando?*
Why?	*Por qué?*
How?	*Cómo?*
How much?	*Cuánto?*
How many?	*Cuántas?*
I am lost	*Me he perdido*
I am hungry	*Tengo hambre*
I am thirsty	*Tengo sed*
I am ill	*No siento bien*

Hot	*Caliente*
Cold	*Frío*
Large	*Grande*
Small	*Pequeño*
Fast	*Rápido*
Slow	*Despacio*
Closed	*Cerrado*
Monday	*Lunes*
Tuesday	*Martes*
Wednesday	*Miércoles*
Thursday	*Jueves*
Friday	*Viernes*
Saturday	*Sábado*
Sunday	*Domingo*
Day	*Día*
Week	*Semana*
Month	*Mes*
Today	*Hoy*
Tomorrow	*Mañana*
Yesterday	*Ayer*
Now	*Ahora*
Soon	*Pronto*
Later	*Despues*

Places

Bank	*Banco*
Post Office	*Correos*
Hospital	*Hospital*
Museum	*Museo*
Church	*Iglesia*
Pharmacy	*Farmacía*
Tobacconist	*El Estanco*
Telephone	*Teléfono*

Travel

Airport	*Aeropuerto*
Bus	*Autobús*
Coach	*Autocar*
Station	*Estación*
Train	*Tren*
Automobile	*Coche*
Boat	*Barca*
Ticket	*Billete*
Seat	*Asiento*
Customs	*Aduana*

Toilet	*Servicios*

Food and Drink

Breakfast	*Desayuno*
Lunch	*Comida*
Dinner	*Cena*
Sandwich	*Bocadillo*
Bread	*Pan*
Butter	*Mantequilla*
Salt	*Sal*
Pepper	*Pimentón*
Sauce	*Salsa*
Rice	*Arroz*
Potatoes	*Patatas*
Cabbage	*Col. Repollo*
Salad	*Ensalada*
Green Peas	*Guisantes*
Soup	*Sopa*
Eggs	*Huevos*
Omelette	*Tortilla*
Fish	*Pescados*
Prawns	*Gambas*
Lobster	*Langosta*
Sole	*Lenguado*
Plaice	*Platija*
Turbot	*Rodaballo*
Salmon	*Salmon*
Sardines	*Sardinas*
Meat	*Carne*
Pork	*Cerdo*
Ham	*Jamon*
Sausage	*Chorizo*
Chops	*Chuletas*
Lamb	*Cordero*
Fillet	*Filete*
Tongue	*Lengua*
Chicken	*Pollo*
Turkey	*Pavo*
Beef	*Ternera*
Fruit	*Fruta*
Apple	*Manzana*
Orange	*Naranja*
Banana	*Plátano*
Grapes	*Uvas*
Cherries	*Cerezas*

Cheese	Queso
Mineral water	Agua Mineral
Beer	Cerveza
Coffee	Café
Tea	Té
Milk	Leche
Wine	Vino

On the Road

Give Way	Ceda el Paso
Slow	Despacio
Diversion	Desvio
No Entry	Paso Prohibido
Dangerous Bend	Curva Peligrosa
One Way Street	Direccion Unica
Road Works	Obras
Danger	Peligro
No Parking	Prohibido Aparcar
Drive on the right	Llevar la Derecha
Drive on the left	Llevar la Izquierda
Garage	Garage
Fuel (Petrol)	Gasolina
Unleaded	Sin Plomo

MAPS

Nobody should attempt to explore the backwoods of Northern and Central Spain without a comprehensive map of the area concerned and it is just as well to have a more general map available if you plan to deviate very far from the major roads and highways. The *Michelin 1/400 000* series can be bought almost everywhere, the *Mapa de Communica-ciones* is excellent, and the tourist offices can usually supply more detailed maps of their respective areas as well as town plans.

MEASUREMENTS

The metric system is used in Spain.

1kg (1,000g)	=	2.2lb
1 litre	=	1¾ pints
4.5 litres	=	1 gallon
8km	=	5 miles

OPENING HOURS

Banks

Generally speaking banks in Spain are open 6 days a week — 9am-2pm on weekdays and 9am-12.30pm or 1pm on Saturdays. Smaller out-of-town branches may close earlier on Saturdays or decide not to open at all.

Post Offices

The majority of post offices close for lunch which may be from about 1.30 to 4.30pm or 5pm. Stamps can be bought from most tobacconists and some paper shops. The mail boxes are bright yellow and quite frequently are few and far between. It is easy to confuse a post office (*correos*) with a *caja postal* which is a post office savings bank.

Shops

Most supermarkets stay open all day but other shops usually open 9am-1pm and again from 4.30pm or 5 to 7.30pm or 8pm. Open-air markets start packing up for the day at about 12.30pm.

Museums

Apart from important museums in the larger towns and cities individual opening and closing times vary quite considerably, especially from one year to the next but sometimes from day to day. However it is fairly safe to assume that they close for a long lunch at about 12.30pm, stay open fractionally longer in the evenings during the summer than in winter and are usually closed on Mondays.

Churches
Most churches are a law unto themselves. The majority close for lunch but some stay open all day; others welcome visitors except during services while one or two take the opposite view. Little country churches are usually kept locked, in which case it is necessary to find the sacristan or caretaker who is seldom far away and who will produce a key, except at lunchtime, and act as guide for a modest donation to the church funds. Ecclesiastical buildings with their own museums or treasuries often have set opening and closing times and charge an entrance fee.

PASSPORTS

A valid passport is the only document necessary for entry into Spain for the citizens of more than fifty different countries including Britain, Canada and the USA. A holiday is assumed to last for up to 3 months but extensions are available for tourists who are planning to stay a little longer. However, anyone travelling from a country with an epidemic such as cholera will undoubtedly need a certificate of vaccination.

PUBLIC HOLIDAYS

Spain has around twelve official public holidays a year, augmented by any number of local feast days when everything in the area closes for the celebrations. In addition, if an official holiday falls on a Tuesday or a Thursday it is automatically assumed that the intervening Monday or Friday will be regarded as a holiday as well. Banks and post offices are closed on public holidays but certain shops, especially in the established tourist areas, may decide to stay open. The main national holidays are:-

New Year's Day
Epiphany — 6 January
Maundy Thursday — the Thursday before Easter
Good Friday
May Day — 1 May
Corpus Christi — late May or early June
St James's Day — 25 July
Ascension — 15 August
All Saints Day — 1 November
Constitution Day — 6 December
Immaculate Conception — 8 December
Christmas Day

RELIGION

Spain is essentially a Catholic country and a large percentage of the population take their religion very seriously. Important church occasions are marked by solemn processions which can be extremely spectacular, in addition to which there are any number of pilgrimages and saints days which may well include traditional celebrations.

RESTAURANTS AND BARS

Mealtimes in Spain differ from those in many other countries. Breakfast generally consists of nothing more than a roll and a cup of coffee. Lunch is quite substantial and is served from about 1-3pm while dinner seldom starts before 9pm and continues until midnight, or later in Madrid. One exception is Galicia where dinner is usually available at about 8pm but some tourist resorts are starting to vary their times to accommodate foreign visitors.

The gap between lunch and dinner is bridged by *tapas* bars where a whole variety of dishes of the hors d'oeuvre type are served with the drinks. It is possible to sample a *porcion*, or small helping, of any that look appetising and return for a second helping or a *racion*, a larger quantity, if you are still hungry. There are also cafeterias where coloured photographs of *platos combinados* or combination plates, such as hamburgers and chips solve the language problem. Except in the case of international type restaurants it is better to choose a busy place than an empty one and sample the local dishes. The *menú del dia* or menu of the day, usually consists of three courses and is almost invariably better value for money than à la carte. The bill of fare is always displayed outside the door so it is easy to see in advance what is on offer and how much it will cost.

SPORTS

Facilities are available for all the usual holiday sports and pastimes such as tennis and swimming, boating and windsurfing with some water skiing. There are quite a number of golf courses, especially in the Madrid area, a few riding stables and plenty of opportunities for climbing and walking, the most interesting being in remote mountain regions like the Sierra de Urbión in Soria and the Picos de Europa. Apart from the Pyrénées winter sports are restricted mainly to the Guadarrama mountains north-west of Madrid where there are ski lifts and several runs, a few of which are quite demanding.

Fishermen have a wide choice, from salmon and trout to bass, shad, mullet, carp and barbel. However it is essential to have a licence which can be obtained from the Provincial Headquarters of the National Institute for the Conservation of Nature (ICONA). Applications should include the name, postal address and passport number of the person concerned and a cheque for the relevant amount in *pesetas*. A useful brochure *Fishing. Spain* is available from tourist offices and gives information about such things as the permitted size of the catch, the minimum dimensions for various species, open and closed seasons and the address of the nearest ICONA office..

Facilities are available for hunting and shooting on some national reserves, common lands and private properties, but only under licence. There are regulations governing the temporary importation of firearms into Spain and each individual must be covered by the appropriate insurance. The brochure *Hunting. Spain* gives useful information such as the names of recognised companies who organise hunts, open and closed seasons and protected game and is available from tourist offices. Other details are obtainable from the Provincial Headquarters of ICONA in the area concerned.

TELEPHONES

Direct calls can be made from all the provincial capitals, large towns and established tourist resorts. For international calls dial 07 and wait for a higher tone. Then, for the UK dial 44 followed by the STD number, remembering to drop the 0 at the beginning. The national code for Canada and the USA is 1 instead of 44. The central telephone offices *(telefonica)*in the larger towns have metered booths where you talk first and pay afterwards plus a percentage added for the service but this is still less than the surcharge imposed by most hotels.

TIPPING

Hotels and restaurants automatically include the equivalent of VAT in their bills and most of them also add a service charge. However it is as well to confirm this, especially in out-of-the-way places, and it is customary to leave a small tip anyway unless the food or the service has been unsatisfactory. Anyone who provides a personal service, such as cloakroom attendants, guides, porters and usherettes expect a gratuity and so do taxi drivers when the amount should be about 10 per cent to 12 per cent of the fare.

TOILET FACILITIES

Apart from the facilities provided in bus and railway stations there are very few public conveniences in Spain. However every bar, restaurant and hotel has its own *los servicios* which one may use on request even if they have no intention of buying anything. There is no charge in most cases but in out-of-the-way places it might be as well to take toilet paper.

TOURIST INFORMATION CENTRES

UK
Spanish National Tourist Office
57/58 St James Street
London SW1A 1LD
☎ 44 17 499 0901

USA
Spanish National Tourist Office
665 Fifth Avenue
New York
NY 10017
☎ 1212 759 8822

Canada
Spanish National Tourist Office
60 Bloor Street West
Suite 201
Toronto
Ontario M4W 3B8
☎ 1416 961 3131

TRAVEL

By Air
There are regular international flights to Madrid and Santiago de Compostela from both Britain and the USA i It is as well to enquire about fly-drive holidays and any discounts that may be available. Charter flights are less expensive but are often more restricting where times are concerned.

Most internal flights go to Madrid with airports at Burgos, La Coruña, Logroño in La Rioja, Oviedo in Asturias, Salamanca, Santander, Santiago de Compostela, Valladolid and Vigo.

By Train

Train journeys from Britain involve changing in Paris and again at Hendaye on the French frontier. Some reductions are available, especially for people under 26 or over 65 who are planning to use the internal services, although this does not include the many narrow-gauge railways.

Spain has at least a dozen different types of trains from the luxury TEE (Trans Europe Express), the TALGO and TER which are fast and comfortable, and the more complicated RENFE services down to the little local varieties which are rather unpredictable. The 'Transcanta-brica' provides a luxury 7-day excursion through north-western Spain with stops for the night and at places of interest along the coast from León to El Ferrol. Tickets should be bought in advance to avoid any last minute confusion.

By Coach, Bus or Taxi

Long distance coach services operate to and from London several times a week and take slightly longer than the trains but do not charge quite so much.

Internal coach services are both comfortable and efficient, are generally air conditioned and may have some of the additional advantages usually associated with conducted tours. In addition there are a vast number of buses that shuttle backwards and forwards round their own provinces, and are frequently the only link with outlying villages.

Public transport is available in the larger towns and cities but, with the exception of Madrid, the distances between local places of interest are so short that it is often easier to walk. Taxis are plentiful and inexpensive but for long journeys an overall price should be agreed in advance.

By Car

Visitors travelling with their own cars who want to avoid the long drive down through France can use either the Brittany Ferries, the P&O European Ferries or the motorail service to Madrid and other cities like La Coruña and Santander. On the other hand, motorists who look on the journey as part of their holiday have a choice between the various Channel Ferries, Hoverspeed and the Channel Tunnel. Thereafter the most popular routes are down the French coast to Hen-daye or across the Pyrénées to Pamplona, with a number of less frequented options where the frontier posts are only open at certain hours and may close altogether in the winter. There are plenty of car hire companies for travellers arriving by other means, and occasionally mopeds and bicycles for hire.

Spain has an excellent network of *autopistas*, some of which are subject to tolls, as well as major highways linking all the main centres. In addition there are any number of secondary roads, which may sometimes be in need of repair, and a spider-web of minor lanes and byways that call for care and attention in some cases while others are only suitable for jeeps.

The Highway Code applies in Spain in exactly the same way as it does in other European countries. However, drivers using their own cars should consult one of the motoring organisations before leaving home because there are certain rules and regulations which must be observed. These include essential documents such as a Bail Bond and a Green Card as well as adequate insurance cover and an International Driving Licence or an official translation of their United Kingdom licences. Various accessories must be carried such as a spare set of light bulbs, a red triangle and a First Aid kit. Children under 10 should always travel on the back seat and hitchhiking is frowned on but not forbidden. Motor cyclists must wear crash helmets and observe the Highway Code, 18 is the minimum age for taking any vehicle over 75cc out on the roads, no-one under sixteen is allowed to drive at all, but this does not apply to cyclists who, nevertheless, must observe all the appropriate rules.

Drive on the right hand side of the road in Spain. Traffic approaching from the right at roundabouts has priority except where there are official signs to the contrary, such as on a designated major route where the traffic automatically has the right of way. The Real Automovile Club de España operates a 24 hour breakdown service and anyone in trouble can contact their headquarters in Madrid ☎ 91 441 2222. The Central Traffic Department also operates a round-the-clock service on the major highways where there are emergency telephones for motorists in need of assistance which can be summoned by simply requesting *auxillio en carretera*.

Fuel is quite widely available in Northern and Central Spain, except in the more remote areas where it would be foolish to go exploring without a reasonably full tank. Unleaded petrol (*sin plomo*) is becoming more easily obtainable, especially on the major highways and in the larger towns and cities. Parking can be quite a problem, even in towns where there are both meters and special designated areas set aside for motorists so a hotel which provides a garage or private parking for its guests is well worth considering.

By Sea

There are only two direct sea links between Britain and Spain — the Plymouth-Santander and the Portsmouth-Santander services operated by Brittany Ferries and the P&O European Ferries service between Portsmouth and Bilbao. Both have regular sailings every week throughout the summer but the numbers are reduced in mid-winter. The crossing takes from 24 to 36 hours, with air-conditioned cabins available as well as individual berths and some Pullman seats. Passengers can travel either with or without their cars, motorcycles, mopeds or bicycles. In addition to the ordinary travel arrangements both companies organise Short Break Holidays or BreakAway Holidays for people whose time is limited. Details of the former can be obtained from Brittany Ferries, Millbay Docks, Plymouth PL1 3EW, ☎ 01752 22 13 21 and the latter from the Continental Ferry Port, Mile End, Portsmouth PO2 8QW, ☎ 01705 82 76 77. In Spain information is available from the Estación Maritima, in Santander, ☎ 942 21 45 00. For Brittany Ferries and Cosme Echevar-rieta 1, 48009 Bilbao, ☎ 94 423 44 77, in the case of P&O European Ferries.

Index